RESURRECTION JOURNEY

JESUS' 40-DAY JOURNEY FROM RESURRECTION TO ASCENSION

DR. SHAN ALEXANDER

*To Rajender Dichpally
with all the best for
your help
Please read and enjoy*

Shanth

10-1-2013

Shan Publishing House
Atlanta, Georgia

Published by:
Shan Publishing House
1946 Carrington Court
Stone Mountain, GA 30087-1446 USA
www.ResurrectionJourney.com
email: resurrectionjourney@gmail.com
email: shanpublishinghouse@gmail.com

Requests for information should be addressed to the above.

Book design and composition by
Shan Alexander and Nancy Addison

Printed in USA by Atlanta Book Printing, Atlanta, GA
(www.atlantabookprinting.com)

ISBN: 978-0-9829006-8-0

Dedication

This book is dedicated to all Christians who believe in Jesus Christ resurrection, and accepts him as their Lord and Savior

To my dear children - for their patience, advice, company, and the many nourishing hearty meals

Acknowledgement

The author wants to sincerely thank Nancy Addison for the competent editing of this complicated manuscript in a timely fashion, and for input on Biblical facts during the editing.

Disclaimer

All names and characters except those taken from the Bible are fictitious and any resemblance to real persons, living or dead, is purely coincidental.

Table of Contents

Introduction

The resurrection of Jesus is one of the most important events in Christianity. But have you ever wondered about what Jesus did and where He went during the 40 days between His resurrection and His ascension? Have you wondered what happened to the people whose lives were touched and changed by Jesus in His three year ministry? What if we could travel with Jesus during the 40 days of His resurrection journey to meet for a second time with those people that He had healed, forgiven, and taught? What if we could see how He had changed their lives?

I have long been captivated by this period in our Lord's ministry, starting from His death on the cross, His rising from the dead on the third day and then continuing all the way to His ascension. I meditated and deliberated on the subject for 33 years. Finally our Lord showed me what I was seeking and opened the door for me, true to His teaching:

> Ask, and it will be given you. Seek, and you will find. Knock, and it will be opened for you. For everyone who asks receives. He who seeks finds. To him who knocks it will be opened. Matt 7:7-8

Our Lord opened my imagination and soul to travel with Him during the 40 days of His resurrection journey. The more I contemplated, the more He guided me, pouring out His knowledge and leading me in a breathtaking, incredible journey with Him.

As Jesus guided me through this last part of His life on earth, He inspired me to write this account of His journey. I wrote *Resurrection Journey* to share this vision of where Jesus might have traveled and whom he might have visited during His last 40 days on earth. I wrote *Resurrection Journey* to share this vision of what might have happened to the people whose lives He had touched. Finally, I wrote *Resurrection Journey* to show His compassion continuing beyond His death on the cross and resurrection, and to inspire us on our own journey with Jesus.

1

The gospels do not tell the whole story about His resurrection journey.

There are many verses in the New Testament which clearly tell us that there were more places He visited, after His resurrection, than just the ones mentioned. The Apostle John reveals this to us at the end of his gospel writings:

This is the disciple who testifies about these things, and wrote these things. We know that his witness is true. There are also many other things which Jesus did, which if they would all be written, I suppose that even the world itself would not have room for the books that would be written. John 21:24-25

Four accounts of Jesus being seen alive at different places during the 40 days after His resurrection.

Besides the apostle John telling us that Jesus did more than what was written in the gospels, the following verses of the New Testament are also testimony to the 40 day journey of the resurrected Jesus. Here are four of the accounts that Jesus was alive and active 40 days after rising from the dead, and that He travelled throughout the countryside:

1. The resurrected Jesus was seen by many according to Luke:

To these He also showed himself alive after He suffered, by many proofs, appearing to them over a period of forty days, and speaking about God's Kingdom. Being assembled together with them, He commanded them, "Do not depart from Jerusalem, but wait for the promise of the Father, which you heard from Me." Acts 1:3-4

2. Luke also tells us that the resurrected Jesus is not only seen by many, but that He also sat with people and ate and drank with them:

God raised Him up the third day, and gave Him to be revealed, not to all the people, but to witnesses who were chosen before by God, to us, who ate and drank with Him after He rose from the dead. Acts 10:40-41

3. For many days after His resurrection Jesus saw people from Galilee to Jerusalem. Some even followed Him to Jerusalem:

. . . and He was seen for many days by those who came up with Him from Galilee to Jerusalem, who are His witnesses to the people. Acts 13:31

4.   Paul's account of those who saw Jesus after His resurrection:

. . . that He was buried, that He was raised on the third day according to the Scriptures, and that He appeared to Cephas (Peter), then to the twelve. Then He appeared to over five hundred brothers at once, most of whom remain until now, but some have also fallen asleep. Then He appeared to James, then to all the apostles, and last of all, as to the child born at the wrong time, He appeared to me also. 1 Corinthians 15:4-8

The gospels say what happened on five of the 40 days after His resurrection, but they are silent on what happened on the remaining 35 days, which is where my own meditations begin. His resurrection ministry was much more active and widespread than the few accounts we read in the Bible. *Resurrection Journey* presents what His ministry might have been like during the 40 days between His resurrection and His ascension. It is my belief that these 500 people whom Paul describes are people Jesus encountered or visited during His 150 mile journey from Jerusalem to Galilee and back to the Mount of Olives during those 40 days.

These are the people who were healed by Jesus, forgiven by Jesus; taught by Jesus, and simply loved by Jesus. This was His last opportunity to see them again, with human eyes, before He ascended into heaven. This was His last occasion to hear their voices with human ears, to touch them with human hands.

And this is now our opportunity to journey with Him. This is our chance to see what might have happened to those people, to see how their lives might have been changed forever.

I have chosen to use a fictional guide, a present day preacher named Jeremiah, to take us to a place where we can see everything as it might have been. The Apostle Peter is with him, also, to help explain the context of what we are seeing.

I have been blessed by my journey with Jesus during this time. It is my hope that this book becomes a blessing for you.

3

The Beginning of the Journey: Jeremiah's Heavenly Encounter

Easter Sunday was the Reverend Jeremiah's favorite day of the year. The children in his congregation would probably vote for Christmas, but it was Easter's promise of turning grief to joy, of turning death to life, of beginning all things new that had always captured his heart.

As he walked to the pulpit to give the sermon he looked around the church. It was full – the ushers had brought in folding chairs so that everyone could be seated. Everything about this Easter service had seemed especially beautiful, and Jeremiah was grateful to be a part of it. He had not felt well at all that morning, but he was hoping it was just the exhaustion he normally felt at the end of Holy Week. 'I am not old enough to feel this tired,' he thought, then remembered his graying beard, and smiled at his own vanity. He took a deep breath, and began:

"Open your Bibles with me," he said, "as we look today at the passages recounting the resurrection of our Lord Jesus."

"You see, it was on this day – almost two thousand years ago – our dear Lord was raised from the dead. It has been said that it was on this day that His ministry changed forever – and changed us in the process." The Reverend paused to catch his breath, and then continued, "But what actually happened during the resurrection, before the ascension? We have a few facts, but most of what happened is shrouded in mystery."

The Reverend Jeremiah paused for another breath. His chest felt a little tight, but he continued, "Today I would like to take you through the events as we know them, and urge you to invite the resurrected Jesus into your hearts and homes. In the next few weeks we will be exploring the possibilities of what Jesus might have been doing before His ascension. We will be using what some call the sanctified imagination – an imagination inspired by the Holy Spirit – to really bring alive this part of His ministry, His last 40 days on earth."

5

As he finished speaking, suddenly Jeremiah started to shake. His words trailed off as his legs began to give way. He grabbed the pulpit for dear life – his knuckles white as he gripped the wood. Suddenly with a loud thud he dropped to the floor – his outstretched hand landing exactly at the foot of the cross standing by the pulpit.

The congregation was in shock. What had happened to their beloved pastor? His wife rushed to him from her place at the end of the first pew, calling for their doctor who had been sitting not far away. But he had already jumped from his seat, and was running to begin administering first aid.

Jeremiah thought, I must be dying. He could hear his wife calling his name. He was lying on his back, and the doctor was telling him to take a deep breath. The doctor started pressing the center of his chest in an effort to revive him. He could hear the associate pastor take control of the congregation, telling them to pray for their beloved pastor and asking the choir to sing softly to calm everyone.

He could feel his body, but could not speak. His consciousness was fading away – he could feel himself becoming lighter and lighter. He could no longer feel the doctor pressing on his chest. Suddenly Jeremiah felt himself ejected through a dark tunnel and then lifted from his body. A shining light surrounded him. He looked down to see his body lying by the pulpit, the doctor still working on him, and his wife kneeling by his side. He noticed the worried look on the physician's face, but to his surprise, Jeremiah felt no worry at all. He felt calm, without any feeling of pain. He felt oddly at peace.

Jeremiah felt himself moving up toward the ceiling. He took one last look at his motionless body, the Easter lilies massed at the front of the church, and the congregation with their heads bent in prayer. Then he drifted through the walls of the church and into the bright sky.

Suddenly something changed. A light appeared in the sky, dim at first, then growing brighter and brighter. He could still see everything around him: the church, the parking lot, and the neighborhood, but the light shone brightly amid all that with an irresistible intensity.

It was more than just a light: along with the brightness were feelings of such love and acceptance that Jeremiah instinctively turned away from everything he had known on earth and moved toward the light. Slowly at first, then faster and faster he moved, the light becoming brighter and brighter. Somehow he knew Jesus was in the center of that light, calling to him.

Suddenly, the light became so intense it seemed to fill Jeremiah's very soul. Then, just as suddenly, it vanished, and Jeremiah found himself standing in a beautiful city. He looked down, and, sure enough, the street was paved with stones of a golden color.

Before Jeremiah could notice anything else, he saw someone who could only be an angel walking toward him. There were no wings that Jeremiah could see, but the regal bearing, the speed at which the angel approached, and the serene confidence on the angel's face said it all.

"Greetings, Jeremiah! I am your guardian angel, Gabriel. I have watched over you during your life on Earth, and am here now to take you to a very special place."

"Am I dead?" Jeremiah asked. "If this is heaven, where are my parents?"

"Yes, Jeremiah, this is heaven, but you are not yet a permanent resident. You are here for a short time only, and for a specific purpose. I promise you, when your time on earth is completed and you return to us, you will be with your parents and all your loved ones." The angel gestured toward a distant hilltop and Jeremiah could see his parents, grandparents, and even some of his old professors from college, all waving to him. Somehow they looked younger than he remembered.

Gabriel continued, "They have heard about your special assignment, and are very excited about it. But they cannot speak with you now. The next time you see them you will be here forever – but now is not that time. Follow me." The angel turned and walked down the street. The hilltop and all his loved ones disappeared in a mist, and Jeremiah stood a moment, staring at where everyone had been.

Suddenly he realized Gabriel had moved on, and he ran to catch up with the angel. He was amazed at the beauty of his surroundings.

Everywhere he looked, he saw joyous people, wearing everything from blue jeans to garments much like royal robes. They were within the walls of the Heavenly City, and around him, Jeremiah saw many different kind of buildings – some were large mansions, others looked like houses of worship, and there were a few whose purpose he couldn't begin to guess. Many of the pillars of the buildings were massive, and rose all the way to the heavenly sky, whose end could not be seen. It was in front of one of these impressive buildings that Gabriel stopped.

"This is the House of Memory", the angel said. "If you were a permanent resident you would visit here first, and see all the events of your life." Jeremiah looked startled.

"Is that where we are judged?" he asked.

Gabriel laughed. "Surely you remember your own preaching," said the angel. "Believe in the Lord Jesus Christ and you will be saved. Yes, you will be judged, but Jesus has already taken any punishment you might have received when He died on the cross for your sins." Gratitude welled up in Jeremiah's heart, and he couldn't speak for a moment. Gabriel smiled at him, reading his emotion. "Come, Jeremiah; on to the Hall of the Apostles."

The sights and sounds as they walked filled Jeremiah with wonder. They passed artists and musicians. Some were painting – glorious scenes – a few of which Jeremiah recognized as scenes from the ministry of Jesus: teaching on a mountain side, feeding thousands of people, calming the sea, raising Lazarus from the dead, the triumphal entry into Jerusalem on Sunday, and many other stories about the Lord. Jeremiah said, "My favorite painting is the scene of the Last Supper by Leonardo da Vinci."

Gabriel smiled and pointed to one of the painters. "Jeremiah, there he is! But of course he does more than paint. Here also we call him a Renaissance man. And do you see Michelangelo over there?" Jeremiah followed Gabriel's pointing finger and saw someone putting the final touches on a sculpture of the ascension. Jeremiah was too awe-struck to speak, and Gabriel let him watch for a moment before they continued on their way.

Soon a large dome supported by twelve massive crystal columns came into view. Into each of these columns was carved the life-sized figure of a man. Each man's name was carved below him at the base of the column, on something that looked like a large piece of rectangular marble. As they drew nearer to the building, Jeremiah could read the names. The three that faced the golden road were Peter, James, and John. In the center of the hall, directly under the dome, was a statue of a beautiful woman. 'This must be the Hall of the Apostles,' he thought, 'but who is that woman?' Then he noticed the inscription at her feet: Mary of Magdala.

Jeremiah turned to Gabriel, who said, "We consider her the apostle to the apostles."

Curiously, Gabriel did not walk straight into the Hall, but continued around the structure and allowed Jeremiah to read each name and look at each apostle's carved form before moving on. Jeremiah was taken aback at the 12th column, which was carved with the names of Judas and Matthias. "Gabriel! I thought Judas was no longer one of the Twelve!"

Gabriel paused and seemed to ponder the question. "That is not for me to answer, Jeremiah, but for one who knew him in life. You are here to learn, and that answer is a small part of the teachings that are before you." The angel smiled at Jeremiah, who was amazed that a smile could convey such love.

"Jeremiah, here is where I will leave you, as a student to learn. Your teaching companion awaits you at the first column. When your lessons are through, he will escort you back to earth. Learn well, Jeremiah – not many have such an opportunity as you have. Use well the time our Lord has given." With that, Gabriel turned and disappeared. Jeremiah was left alone.

Suddenly, Jeremiah began to feel nervous. He remembered that the first column was the column of the Apostle Peter. Peter! The one they called the big fisherman. He was the one with the temper; the one who denied Jesus three times; the only disciple to recognize Jesus as the Messiah; the one who raised that little girl from the dead. Peter - the rock on which Jesus had built His church.

'I'm not sure I'm ready to meet Peter,' he thought, but then remembered that they had sent for him. They had chosen him to learn something, and all he had to do was learn what they were going to teach. 'I can learn,' he thought, as he began walking forward, past the column labeled Judas and Matthias, to the first column he and Gabriel had looked at. No one had been there before, he remembered, but as he passed the last column he saw a man appearing to emerge from the column labeled Peter.

As Jeremiah looked toward the man standing at the column his courage wilted. Suddenly he remembered this was more than just a man, this was an apostle. Smiling, the apostle left the base of the column and began to approach Jeremiah.

"Welcome, Jeremiah," he said. "Our Lord has brought you here today to learn. Are you willing to accept the teaching we will give you?"

"I am," said Jeremiah. "I will learn everything you have to teach me. And from what Gabriel told me, I know you must be Peter. But may I ask why I am here? What am I here to learn?

Peter grinned, a twinkle in his eye. "Do you remember the sermon you were preaching right before you arrived here? Your love for Easter and the resurrection is honored among us. And your curiosity about what happened between the resurrection and the ascension is also counted in your favor."

At Jeremiah look of astonishment, Peter almost laughed. "This is the reason you are here, Jeremiah. Our Lord has directed me to reveal to you the true story about what happened during the 40 days between His resurrection and ascension. I will be showing you not only what actually happened, but also why everything happened as it did."

He motioned to a crystal bench near the Hall. "Let's sit down a moment. I know you are not tired – and you will be neither tired nor hungry nor thirsty while you are here – but sometimes it is good to sit while we talk."

"I'm not sure I understand what you are saying," said Jeremiah, grateful for the chance to sit and regain his composure. "Heaven is rewarding my curiosity about the 40 days of the resurrection?"

"We have been peeking at your notes." Jeremiah's look of amazement changed to shock, but Peter went on: "We liked where you were going with that sanctified imagination, but wouldn't it be even better if you had some inside knowledge? Our Lord Jesus Christ has directed me to show you what really happened during those 40 days."

Jeremiah's face lit up. "You mean I'm going to be able to see Jesus and everything He did? How is this possible?"

Peter laughed. "Remember, we're in heaven now, where all things are possible. The events will appear like holographic images, which our Lord has arranged especially for you. We will be able to see everything that happened, and I will be there to give you any additional explanation you might need." He rose from the bench. "Are you ready?"

Jeremiah leapt to his feet and almost shouted, "I am ready! When do we start?"

Peter smiled at his enthusiasm as he led him to a different part of Heaven. Jeremiah was torn between his desire to see everything along their way in this beautiful Holy City, and his desire to hurry up so his education on the resurrected life of Jesus could begin. His gaze darted back and forth, from the children happily at play in a meadow to the circle of musicians jamming on a medley of tunes. He recognized a praise song, then something by Beethoven, then something completely unfamiliar – all played with such joy that Jeremiah realized he would never hear music the same way again.

They approached a white building with an arched doorway. Jeremiah followed Peter, his eyes slowly adjusting to the lower level of light. It was empty except for two crystal chairs in the center of the room. Their footsteps sounded loud on the stone floor.

"We can call this the House of Images," Peter motioned Jeremiah to sit. "It will seem as if we are present, but remember these are images from long ago. And please just let me know if you'd like to pause the story and ask me something."

Jeremiah nodded, unable to speak. "We will begin on day 1 of the resurrection, Easter Sunday, at the place you call the Garden Tomb," said Peter, and Jeremiah gasped as the building around them seemed to shift and transform into a garden with the city of Jerusalem in the background..

Day 1: Sunday

Day 1: Sunday: Resurrection day – Jesus visits 21 followers - first Mary Magdalene, then Peter, a group of women, two on the way to Emmaus, and eleven disciples that evening - Thomas absent, Judas present and forgiven.

Jeremiah recognized this garden instantly. "I know this place from my trip to the Holy Land when I was in Seminary. It's the garden where they believe Jesus' tomb might have been." The garden was beautiful in the dim light of early morning, with meandering pathways amid the flowering plants. Jeremiah could feel the soft breeze on his face, and turned to Peter in surprise. "I thought we'd just be watching something like a movie! But I can feel the wind and smell the flowers!"

Peter smiled gently and nodded. "These images will engage all your senses, not just your eyes and ears. And, speaking of ears, everyone will be speaking in their own language, which most of the time will be Aramaic, but you will be able to understand, as if they were speaking in your American English." Jeremiah nodded to show he was listening, but his attention was fixed on an opening in one of the rock walls, with a large stone nearby.

Peter seemed to understand: "Go ahead, Jeremiah, you can walk around and even look inside. It is the empty tomb of Jesus." Jeremiah ran to the opening, but stopped abruptly at the entrance. Everything looked so real. The rock felt cool and slightly rough to his touch. He knelt, looking within at the folded cloth and rolled up linen. Spices that Jeremiah remembered Nicodemus had provided were scattered over the floor, giving a sweet scent of myrrh and aloes. He knelt there a moment, breathing the spice-scented air. Hesitantly he touched the cloth, and then turned as he heard steps outside on the path of crushed rocks.

Two women were walking up the path in his direction. They carried bundles of cloth and small boxes. Jeremiah thought they must be Mary Magdalene and Mary, the mother of James, and that

13

they carried sweet spices for the body of Jesus. They were heading straight for the tomb, and Jeremiah quickly moved away from the entrance. He held his breath, realizing he was about to see something that was one of his favorite parts of the Easter story.

As the two women neared the tomb, they stopped, realizing the stone had been rolled away. They looked around for the guards they had been expecting, but saw no one. Jeremiah had never felt invisible before, and he wasn't sure he liked it. But at least he didn't have to explain himself to the women.

The younger one turned to her companion. "I was hoping the guards would help us with the stone, but I see that has been done for us." She took a deep breath -- perhaps to steel herself for what she was about to do -- walked slowly to the doorway, and bent to go inside. Her scream, amplified by the small tomb, seemed to echo in the hills around them. She stumbled out of the tomb, tears streaming down her face. "Mary, He's gone! They've taken Him somewhere!"

Her companion rushed to the opening to look for herself. "What could have happened? Did the guards take Him? But the linen cloths that wrapped His body are still here. If someone took Him, wouldn't they just have taken Him as He was?" They stared at each other, unsure of what to do next, then Mary Magdalene spoke.

"We must search for him." Through her tears, her voice was strong and sure. "Perhaps we can find someone to tell us what happened." The women separated and started searching the garden. Near one of the sheds Mary Magdalene saw a man standing silently. Jeremiah's heart raced as he realized he must be looking at the risen Jesus. But she didn't seem to recognize Him. Mary Magdalene looked around for her companion, but she was out of earshot. Hesitantly she approached the man. Jeremiah remembered that she thought this man was a gardener.

"Why are you crying," asked Jesus. "Who are you looking for?"

"Sir," she said, "have you seen the one who was laid in this tomb? Have you taken Him away somewhere?"

Jesus looked straight into her eyes, and said, "Mary."

She stared at Him; almost silently breathing the word "Master" and Jeremiah thought the realization creeping over her face was like a second sunrise. She reached out as if to hug Him close to her, but He stopped her with an outstretched hand.

14

"You must not touch me, for I am not yet ascended to My Father." Jeremiah could see the wound on His hand, and realized His side must still be affected as well. There were bloody marks around His forehead from the crown of thorns, and His hair was matted with blood. But Jesus had more to say. "Go and tell Peter and the disciples that I ascend to my Father and your Father, to my God and to your God. Tell them to meet me in Galilee."

The sound of their voices must have alerted the other woman, as she came running up just as Jesus turned away from Mary.

He walked toward the western part of the garden, and disappeared amid the trees. Before anything else could happen Jeremiah raised his hand for Peter to stop the images.

Jeremiah was clearly shaken. "I thought the resurrection made His body like new, maybe even better. I thought that was why no one recognized Him."

"Something like a new and improved body?" Peter thought for a minute, searching for a way to make the explanation understandable. "When Jesus raised Lazarus from the dead, whatever had troubled the body of Lazarus was healed. His body had been made whole. But that was something completely different. The body of Lazarus had been healed of all sickness. The body of Jesus still had the wounds of His crucifixion."

Peter noted Jeremiah's dismay, and knew there was some confusion that needed clearing up. "Remember when Jesus invited Thomas to put his hand in His side? If He had been healed that would not have been possible. His wounds had to be there as proof. The disciples had to know that He was the resurrected Jesus. The resurrection of Jesus refers to His spirit returning and giving life back to His body, but that body was still wounded from the thorns, the nails of the cross, and the spear that had pierced His side. He was resurrected, but not yet ascended. This was His last chance to be human. It was painful, you can see that. But isn't pain involved in being human? It was never His way to seek His own comfort."

Jeremiah was silent for a long time. His gaze was on Mary, staring after Jesus as He walked away, but his mind was reeling from this new information. Finally he spoke. "So, if Jesus didn't look different from having a new resurrection body, why didn't anyone recognize Him?"

"Basically," said Peter, choosing his words carefully, "He's just spent three days in a tomb after having been whipped, nailed to a cross, stuck by a spear – and don't forget the crown of thorns. He chose to retain the wounds as proof of who He is, and to experience His final days on earth as a human." He nearly smiled at Jeremiah's astonishment, but continued on. "Over the next few days, His wounds get better as He is being cared for by the women He visits, but right now He is suffering as any human would."

Jeremiah slowly nodded, and Peter let the images continue.

Mary Magdalene watched Jesus go and then turned to her companion. "I have just seen the Master! We must tell them! He's alive!" They hurried away, and Jeremiah gasped as the scene shifted, focusing on the two women as they walked swiftly through the streets of Jerusalem. They stopped at a small house and knocked on the door. Jeremiah couldn't hear the whispered conversation, but the door was soon opened and the women rushed in.

Jeremiah blinked as the images shifted to place him in the room. It was dark and a little warm after the cool fresh air in the garden. A single smoky lamp revealed a table and a couple of stools. The women who had let them in gestured to the big, rough looking fellow sitting on a pallet in the corner, his head buried in his hands. The women ran to him, and Jeremiah realized this must be Simon Peter, still miserable after his denial of Jesus.

"Simon," began Mary Magdalene. Jeremiah remembered that Jesus had said his new name was Peter, the Rock, but evidently no one was thinking of him as a Rock now. "We have seen the Master! He is alive!"

Simon Peter looked, if anything, even more miserable than before. "Do you taunt me?" he cried. "Is it not enough I denied Him three times?" His shoulder shook as if holding back sobs.

The two women knelt on the floor before him and Mary Magdalene gently touched his hand. "Simon, He was there. He told us to tell you and the disciples." At his lack of response, she said, "He called you Peter. He told us to tell Peter and the disciples."

At that, Simon Peter raised his face, caught between disbelief and hope. "He called me Peter?" At a noise from an inner room he turned to see a young man standing in the doorway. "John!" said

Simon Peter. They say the Master is alive, that they have seen Him and talked with Him!"

"I didn't recognize Him at first," Mary Magdalene broke in. "But the wounds in His hands and feet, and the marks and blood on His head – when He talked about rising on the third day, I didn't know what was supposed to happen, but I did not expect anything like this."

At the mention of wounds, Simon Peter's face looked even more pained, but John stepped forward, his face expressionless, as if afraid to give hope even a foothold. "We must go and see." He moved for the door, barely glancing to see if anyone else followed. Simon Peter jumped up and ran after him out into the street. The women rose to their feet and turned to those who had let them in.

"Is it safe to go?" one of them asked.

Mary Magdalene nodded. "The guards have all left. It is still early – we didn't see any soldiers on the streets."

"We'll all go," said one of the other women, urging them before her, the images shifting to follow them into the street outside. As she turned to fasten the door, Jeremiah realized he was looking at one of the women followers of Jesus who had cared for the disciples and had opened her home to them when needed.

The women sped back to the tomb, but the images shifted to show Simon Peter and John running far ahead. John easily ran ahead of Simon Peter, reached the tomb, and looked in. Simon Peter ran up, breathing a little heavily, and bent to enter the tomb. Jeremiah saw him reach out and touch both the linen that was folded so neatly near the foot of the niche, and a long cloth rolled by itself, at the head of the niche.

He came out, and both disciples looked around. "If the guards had taken Him, they would not have removed that linen." John said, as if by hard thought he could reason it all out.

"He is definitely not here." Simon Peter strode back and forth, an animal in an invisible cage. "But we must try to find Him."

John nodded. "We'll separate. I don't see any guards about, and we can look until we hear the soldiers coming. It's still not safe for us to be out during the day."

Simon Peter looked relieved at some form of action. "I'll go this way," he said, turning west, "and I'll meet you back at the house."

The two men separated and Jeremiah held his hand up for Peter to pause the images.

"Peter," he asked, "why was it so difficult to believe that Jesus had risen? Didn't He say that He would? When Mary Magdalene told you, how could you not believe her? She was radiant!"

Peter paused, sadness creeping into his eyes. "None of us believed her – frankly, she looked a little crazy to me, but of course I wasn't in the best condition myself for judging craziness. But she insisted that she had seen Jesus and that He told us to meet Him in Galilee. We were all so devastated -- too devastated to even hope that what she said was true."

His voice faltered, recalling the grief and confusion of those days so long ago. "I could not rest that whole time thinking about what had happened to Jesus. I kept thinking about His claims to rise on the third day. Did that really mean what I hoped it meant? And if He did rise," he said, his voice a whisper, "what would He think of me? I denied Him three times – and He knew I was going to! He told me, and I didn't believe it until it happened!"

Jeremiah was struck by the depths of emotion. All this had happened nearly 2,000 years ago, but the memory was obviously one of deep pain.

Peter slowly regained his composure. "I remember being so upset that He didn't appear to me first – but Mary was there, putting aside her grief to care for His body. I only went to the tomb after she said she had seen Him. Most of the time, we stayed indoors, not daring to go outside for fear of the Temple guards. Mary was the true apostle that day." He paused another moment, and said, "Are you ready to see more?"

At Jeremiah's nod the images again swirled about them. This time they saw Simon Peter rushing around the garden. As he made his way back to the trees, he suddenly stopped, staring at a bent figure in white sitting on a low bench. At Simon Peter's approach He raised His head, and Jeremiah again saw the misery on Simon Peter's face as he took in the wounds and matted hair of his Master.

Simon Peter stood silent a moment, then slowly moved toward Jesus. He seemed both reluctantly and irresistibly drawn, but all at once he flung himself at His feet. "Master," he began and then a flood of tears overcame him.

Jesus looked down at Simon Peter, and Jeremiah had never before seen such love. "Peter." His voice was gentle, but Simon Peter was weeping a storm of tears. Jeremiah was getting a little misty-eyed himself. "Peter," Jesus said, "You know who I am. Why do you weep?"

Simon shook his head. "You called me your Rock, but I have been less than shifting sand."

Jesus was silent a moment, then spoke: "The prophets foretold the suffering and the desertion – if I had chosen to avoid or change anything, how could the rest of it unfold? Even your denials were part of what had to happen for Me to die and return and prepare you all for the next part of your ministry."

Simon Peter's weeping had stopped, but his voice was still shaking. "But Master, am I still a part of Your ministry?" He dared not look into the face of the One he loved and yet had denied.

"I forgive you," said Jesus, placing His hands on Simon Peter's bent head. "I forgave the Temple priests who ordered My arrest, I forgave Judas who led the team of temple guards, and I forgave Pilate who condoned My crucifixion. I forgave those soldiers who nailed Me to the cross and speared Me.

Simon Peter slowly raised his face. The look of love and forgiveness on Jesus' face was something Jeremiah would never forget, but Jesus was speaking again: "You are My Rock. You are Peter. And when you and the other disciples are gathered I will give you the power to be the Rock that I have named you. You will all be empowered for the ministry that I will show you."

Simon Peter sat up, his eyes never leaving Jesus' face.

Jesus spoke again. "I have forgiven you, Peter. Now it is your turn to forgive. When the time comes, you will know it." He sat back as if weary. "Now go back to the other disciples. Tell them you have seen Me, and to meet Me in Galilee."

Simon Peter rose to obey, taking one last look at Jesus before walking quickly back toward the tomb. Jeremiah saw him find John; the two of them hurried away. Jesus stood, looking after them with a loving smile. Suddenly footsteps sounded on the crushed rock path and the women who had followed the two disciples came into view. They were clinging together as if for support, but were looking around as they walked.

When they saw Jesus they all looked at Mary Magdalene, who nodded. For a moment, they stood, then Jesus said, "Peace be with you," and the women threw themselves at the ground before His feet. They clasped His feet and worshipped him, tears streaming down their faces. "Do not be afraid," said Jesus, "go and tell My brothers to go to Galilee; there they will see Me." Jesus remained standing while the women rose, gazed at Him one more time in silent adoration, and then started down the path to town.

Suddenly the images shifted again and Jeremiah realized they were now on a road leading out of Jerusalem. It was hot and dusty, and in the scraggly shade of a small tree a man was resting. It took Jeremiah a minute to realize this was Jesus. A couple was walking toward Him, from the direction of town. Jeremiah was startled as Peter leaned over to explain. "The man is Cleopas and the woman with him is his wife. They are headed to Emmaus, which is about seven miles west of Jerusalem. It normally takes only a little over two hours to walk, but it will take Jesus three hours to walk this distance because of His wounds. His body is still in shock, and you can see that each step is an effort for Him."

Peter gestured to Jesus, who was getting to His feet, preparing to join the travelers. "Jesus walked here after He saw the women, and has been resting here ever since. He had to regain His strength for the walk ahead of Him. They won't recognize Him, not only because of His appearance, but also because of their grief. Remember what your Scripture says about what they were doing?"

Jeremiah seemed on firmer ground. "Luke 24:14-33 says as they were journeying to Emmaus they talked together of all these things which had happened. But Peter, why did Jesus go to Emmaus? Why did He have to go anywhere? Couldn't He just have stayed in Jerusalem and appear as having been raised from the dead?"

"It is around 2:00," said Peter, "and by now the guards have received orders from Caiaphas to find Jesus or anyone who has been seen with Him. They are searching all the places He has stayed at recently, and they are spreading the story that His followers broke into the tomb and took Him away while the guards slept. Jesus knew He had to be somewhere other than Jerusalem until His meeting with the disciples that evening, and so He is headed west, toward Emmaus. Remember, the rest of us stayed indoors out of sight of the temple guards most of the day in Jerusalem."

Jeremiah turned back to watch the couple walking slowly down the road. Cleopas said, "Tell me again, exactly what your friends said to you."

His wife looked as if she was tired of not being believed. "Mary Magdalene told me she had seen Jesus. That she had talked to Him, and He had called her Mary – and that she had not recognized Him at first." Her voice lowered. "She said that He looked just as bad as He did when they were wrapping Him in the linen to lay His body in the tomb -- maybe even worse. But that He was definitely alive!" She turned suddenly to her husband, "And we both saw Simon on our way out of town. He also said he had seen Jesus, alive, and that they were all to meet this evening and we were welcome to join them."

Cleopas looked even more skeptical. "Simon looked like a madman himself. I don't think he's eaten or slept since Thursday night. How do we know he really saw what he thought he saw?" As they neared the tree with Jesus standing under it, he said, "Maybe this fellow knows something. Although, he looks as mad as anyone else we've seen today."

Before his wife could rally with a sharp retort to her husband's skepticism, the stranger said, "What are you talking about?" Noticing the woman's tear-streaked face, He added, "And why are you so sad?"

Cleopas seemed taken aback. He stopped to face the stranger. "Haven't you just been in Jerusalem? Haven't you heard what has been going on the past few days?"

Jesus said, "What has been going on?" in such an innocent tone that Cleopas was appeased. Jeremiah realized Jesus looked a lot like someone who might have been beaten up and unconscious during the last few days.

"It was all about Jesus of Nazareth," began Cleopas. He gestured to his wife and they all began walking, the stranger making an effort to keep up with them. "He was a prophet whose words and deeds were obviously from God. But the chief priests and our rulers had Him brought to trial on false accusations of blasphemy and claiming to be king. He was condemned to death – crucified." He shuddered and drew his wife a little closer. "We believed that He was our promised Messiah, who would redeem Israel. But this is the third day from His death, and we have heard some strange things." He looked to his wife, and she took up the tale.

"I heard it first from some of my friends. They had gone to the tomb early to finish the anointing of the body of Jesus, but when they got there, the body was gone!" She took a moment to compose herself, remembering the astonishment and confusion of everything that had happened only this morning. "My friends said they had seen Jesus, and that He was alive! We all rushed to the tomb, but He was not there. We had to return to Emmaus today, but as we were leaving we saw Simon, who told us that he had seen the risen Jesus! But by this time . . ."

"We just didn't know what to think." Cleopas finished her sentence. "So much had happened . . . we wanted to believe them, but I'm just not sure we could have borne the grief if what they said wasn't true."

Jeremiah held his breath, knowing that was coming next. He strained to hear every word Jesus said, wondering as he did why none of the gospels mentioned His voice, so calm and strong, even in His extreme weariness.

Jesus slowly began, "Ah, foolish ones, how is it that you do not see the prophecies of old before your very eyes? Wasn't it foretold that the Messiah was to have suffered those things, and then enter into His glory?" He ignored their bristling response, and went on to point out the specific scriptures that referred to Him and His ministry, beginning at Moses and the prophets.

Jeremiah was entranced, and the couple, after their reaction to His first words, seemed equally drawn to His words and voice, although it was clear that they still did not recognize Him. The journey was a long one, as they matched their strides to His, and as they entered Emmaus, they pleaded with Him to stay. "It is close to evening," they said, "and you at least need to eat something. Please, you must be as tired as we are."

They welcomed Him into their home, giving Him water to wash His face, hands and feet. Jesus and Cleopas sat to eat, as his wife served them a hastily prepared dinner of flatbread, dates, olives, dried fish and cheese. Jeremiah saw Jesus take the bread, speak a soft blessing, break it and give the pieces to Cleopas and his wife. At this familiar act, Cleopas leapt to his feet. "Jesus! Master!"

Jesus briefly bowed His head in response, but said nothing as He slowly ate His meal. The couple stared at Him, unable to speak. As He rose to leave they cried, "Wait!" but He walked out of the house and headed back down the road to Jerusalem. "It was Him! It was," repeated Cleopas, tears running down his cheeks. "How did we not recognize Him?"

His wife clutched the bread He had given her. "Why didn't we see it before? When He was telling us about the prophecies – I've never felt so alive. I had only felt that way when Jesus was near."

Cleopas nodded in agreement. "How quickly can we start back to Jerusalem? We must tell the disciples! Didn't Simon say they were meeting at that upper room at the edge of the city?"

The images shifted again, and Jeremiah saw the meeting place in Jerusalem. Night had fallen, and the room was dimly lit with a few small lamps casting strange shadows on the walls and ceiling. Women were clearing the remains of a meal as some men sat around the table. Jeremiah realized these were the disciples, and guessed that the older woman was Mary, the mother of Jesus. He recognized some of the other women from the morning at the tomb. 'I could use some nametags,' he thought, and seemed to hear an echo of Peter's laughter in his mind.

Jeremiah looked around the table, silently counting. There were nine men, but before he could ask Peter who was missing the door was pushed open and two men entered the room. It took Jeremiah a moment to recognize Simon Peter. He looked so much better than he had this morning – clean, with freshly combed hair and a clear, purposeful look in his eyes. Behind him walked another man, who kept his eyes fixed on the floor. Simon Peter kept glancing back to see if the man was still following him, and when they had entered the room, Simon shut the door and took his place at the head of the table. The other man just stood there, as if uncertain what to do. At their entry, all the other men in the room had fallen silent. The women had retired to an alcove, out of the way of whatever was going to happen.

Simon Peter was the first to speak. "We are met here in the name of our risen Master, Jesus the Messiah." He stopped, seemed to make up his mind, and gestured to the man who had entered with him. "Judas, please sit down." Judas found the nearest chair and sat, the others moving a little away from him.

Jeremiah held up his hand for Peter to stop the images. He felt shocked to his core. What was Judas doing here? Wasn't he supposed to have hanged himself? He felt incapable of speech, but Peter only touched his arm. "Watch carefully now," he said, and the images continued.

Simon Peter stood at the table and turned to the other men, as if taking roll. "Where is Thomas?" he asked.

Some of them shrugged, others looking around as if in a daze, not sure who was here or who was missing. One of them spoke up. "We told him about the meeting, but evidently the guards had gotten to him first. He said he was too scared to come tonight, and the rumors of resurrection are tales." His tone was a little dismissive. Jeremiah thought of the sin of pride and knew the young man was headed for a little humbling somewhere down the line, but that wasn't the main issue now.

"I have spoken with most of you already," began Simon Peter. "You know that our Master rose from His tomb, and appeared to Mary Magdalene early this morning." All heads turned to look at Mary, whose face still held an inner glow and calm. Peter continued: "John and I went to the tomb, and I saw the Master myself. He did not look well – not like Lazarus after he was raised from the dead. Our Master still has the wounds He was buried with. But He is alive!" He stopped after this last sentence, too emotional to say anything more.

After a moment of silence, a couple of the disciples started asking John what it looked like, in the tomb, and there was a lively discussion for a few minutes. The women started to take this opportunity to leave, but suddenly there was a knock on the door, some muttered words, and Cleopas and his wife burst into the room.

"We have seen the Master!" Cleopas almost shouted. "He has risen, just as He said – and He told us all the prophecies that had been fulfilled as we walked to Emmaus."

His wife ran over and hugged Mary Magdalene. "It was true, everything you said!" She turned to Simon Peter at the table, her face a mixture of grief and joy. "Please forgive us for not believing you right away when you said you had seen the Master."

Simon Peter clasped her hand, reaching over to Cleopas as well. "Forgiveness is what we are all about this evening." They stood a moment in peace, and then the women hurried out as Cleopas found a seat at the table. Their entry had stopped the discussion, and they all looked at Simon Peter again.

Jeremiah saw the emotions that must have been warring within Simon Peter reflected in his face. Whatever he was about to do, Jeremiah could see he was both reluctant and resolved to do it. Finally Simon Peter turned back to the men at the table.

"Friends," he said, drawing every eye to him, his voice controlled and even. "Do you remember what the Master taught us about forgiveness?" He paused, obviously waiting for some response. "Remember when I asked Him how many times should I forgive my brother if he sins against me repeatedly? Should I forgive him seven times? Ha! I thought I was being generous."

One of the men answered him, "He said, not only seven, but seventy times seven."

Simon Peter nodded. "And we have come to realize that when He used those words, He meant a limitless number -- forever. There would be no end to the number of times of forgiving. What else did He say?"

Slowly, the other disciples spoke. Again, Jeremiah wished vainly for name tags, but was caught up in the responses. He sensed the men remembered words that they were somehow reluctant to speak.

"For if you forgive men their sins, your heavenly Father will also forgive you; but if you do not forgive men their sins, neither will your Father forgive yours."

"Judge not, and you shall not be judged. Condemn not, and you shall not be condemned. Forgive, and you shall be forgiven."

Simon Peter nodded again. "And what did He say on the cross?"

John said, "Father, forgive them; for they do not know what they are doing. I was there at the cross when He said that."

Jeremiah began to have a suspicion about where this was going – but he knew this conversation was in no Bible he had ever read.

"Our Master forgave me," said Simon Peter, his voice very quiet. "He forgave me for denying Him three times. When I saw Him today, all I could do was fall to the ground and weep. I couldn't speak, couldn't even ask for forgiveness. He forgave me, and reminded me that I was Peter, His Rock." He grinned suddenly, and Jeremiah saw a glimpse of the man he would someday become. "I felt more like a patch of sand than a rock at that point, but He said to gather the disciples and meet Him in Galilee."

Simon Peter paused, "And He said something else about forgiveness, too." He looked at the man sitting at the edge of the group and said, "Judas." Everyone turned as the man rose from his place at the table and walked around to stand before Simon Peter, keeping his head bowed and his eyes on the floor.

"You don't have to ask for forgiveness to receive it," said Simon Peter, looking more like Peter the Rock every moment. "And forgiveness does not mean condoning someone's actions. You did what you thought was right for our nation, even when it meant revealing our camp site and which man was our Master to the Temple guards."

The men stirred restlessly and Jeremiah wondered how close they were to becoming a mob. The emotions on their faces ranged from hurt to anger, with most a mixture of both. But Simon Peter went on: "Even this act was foretold by the prophets, as part of a larger plan for our Master's death to lead to His resurrection and glory."

Suddenly Judas dropped to his knees beside Simon Peter, his hands grasping the table for support, his face hidden in his arms. Simon Peter laid his big hands on Judas' head. "By the commandment of our Master, the Lord Jesus, and as He has forgiven me, I now forgive you." Judas took a deep, rasping breath; as if he hadn't dared to breathe the entire time he had been in that room.

James jumped up from the table, his chair crashing to the floor. "Simon, what are you doing?"

Another disciple was instantly on his feet, leaning over the table and shaking his fist. "James is right! You can't let him get away with that! If Judas hadn't brought the Temple guards to Jesus, He wouldn't have been put on trial, or beaten, or put to death. He'd still be with us today, leading us to victory over the Romans."

Jeremiah felt the other disciples' angry stirrings. Simon Peter sighed, and without moving from Judas' side, turned to face the two men. His voice was deceptively calm. "Have you boneheads listened to nothing that our Master has said?" The men, along with the rest of the disciples, stared in disbelief.

Simon Peter shook his head. With his act of forgiveness, he looked even more like the Peter sitting beside Jeremiah. "You begin on the right path, and then you overturn your cart. Our Master taught for three years about the Kingdom of God being near or within us. He never spoke of leading us to victory over the Romans. Our victory is over ourselves: our own will, our own temptations, our own moods. Our victory is being obedient to God and loving our neighbor as ourselves. Our victory is forgiving our enemies."

James and the other disciple stepped back a pace. Every word they heard rang true – they could remember Jesus' original words, and see the meaning that had been hidden in them.

Simon Peter saw they understood him, and went on. "Yes, if Judas had not betrayed Jesus He would not have died, and He would not have been resurrected, and the new life that begins today would never have begun." He had everyone's attention now. "Our Master has shown us a new way of living. This is just the beginning of new life, for us and for everyone else who believes with us. It begins with the resurrection of our Lord Jesus and the forgiveness of sins. It begins today. If all this was necessary for His resurrection, for our new life, then we must accept this as part of God's plan."

John spoke slowly, as if remembering a painful scene: "I remember that Thursday night that we were all at supper together: the Master told Judas 'to do what he does, quickly.' I had not thought anything about it at the time, but now I see He must have meant for Judas to go and get the Temple guards to arrest Him quickly."

The men slowly sat down. The other disciples looked expectantly at Simon Peter, who seemed to realize he had to lead them in the next step. If the men couldn't forgive Judas, how could they preach forgiving their enemies? The new life had to start now. "Come here," he said, indicating the space around Judas.

One by one, the men slowly rose and silently circled the kneeling Judas. As they waited for their next command, Jeremiah thought he felt Peter shift on his chair before the images and murmur something about sheep. But Simon Peter was talking: "Put your hands on Judas, and pronounce your forgiveness."

As they hesitated, he encouraged them. "This is an act of will, of obedience by faith as taught by our Master, the Messiah. It has nothing to do with your feelings toward Judas. Your emotions will change, but your obedience to God will not change. Remember His commandment of forgiveness, His commandments to love the Lord your God with all your heart and with all your soul, and to love your neighbor as yourself, and His commandment to love your enemies. Our Lord is God, and whether you think of Judas as your neighbor or your enemy, your obedience to God requires you to forgive Judas." No one moved, and Peter shook his head. "Why are you so slow to obey our Master?"

One by one, the other disciples put out their hands, touching the head, shoulders, or arms of Judas. James was the last. One by one they pronounced the words: "I forgive you." When they had finished, the room was perfectly silent. Jeremiah could now see Judas' face, wet with tears. Then Jeremiah heard the voice that had so entranced him along the way to Emmaus.

"Peace be with you," said Jesus.

Pandemonium. Several of the men jumped backwards, with stuttering phrases of "What the" and "Master! But I" Others fell to the floor as if stricken with terror. What spirit was this?

Jeremiah just stared, as if he could never see enough of that face. The dried blood had been cleaned from His face and hair, and His clean clothes gave Him an almost acceptable appearance. No one would mistake Him for someone who had been beaten up in a fight now.

Simon Peter also stared at Jesus, and at His brief nod of approval stood even straighter, a new look of understanding and command on his face. Jeremiah knew that this was the turning point, when Simon finally became Peter, the Rock.

As the disciples' reactions subsided, Jesus spoke again, "Why are you troubled? What are you thinking?" At their silence, He smiled, extending His hands. "No, I'm not a ghost, or a spirit. Look at my hands and feet – I've washed them, but you can still see the wounds from the nails. A ghost does not have flesh and bones as you see I have." Jeremiah saw some of the men looking intently at His hands and face, others at His feet, but no one said anything.

Jesus sighed. "Do you have anything to eat?" He sat at the table, and they hurried to bring Him a piece of fish and part of a honeycomb. Jeremiah realized He must have been very hungry by that time – after three days in the tomb, His first meal was at the house in Emmaus, and that was several hours ago. As He ate, Jesus talked, reminding them of everything He had said during His time with them, showing how the prophecies had been fulfilled in what He had done. "This is what I told you while I was still with you. Everything must be fulfilled that is written about Me in the Law of Moses, the Prophets and the Psalms. This is what is written: The Messiah will suffer and rise from the dead on the third day." He turned to look at Simon Peter.

"Did you listen to Peter as he talked to you about new life and forgiveness?" Jeremiah caught the look on Simon Peter's face as he realized that Jesus had heard him, followed by the knowledge of what He had called him. Priceless, thought Jeremiah, but quickly turned back to what Jesus was saying. "We have fulfilled the prophecies: I have suffered and I have risen from the dead on the third day. Now it is your turn to preach repentance, and remission of sins, in My name, among all nations, beginning here in Jerusalem. You are all witnesses of these things."

Even James was speechless, realizing how daunting a task lay before them. Seeing their rising dismay, He continued: "But you are not to begin yet. You will not be alone in this – I will send the promise of My Father to you."

It was a minute or two before Jeremiah realized that Jesus had left the room. Everyone seemed to be in a sort of daze. There was no official end to the meeting – the men drifted away in groups of two or three to their homes or to where they were staying with friends.

As the images faded Jeremiah turned to Peter. "I realize some of this is new to you," he said, "and there is much for you to take in."

Jeremiah nodded weakly. He didn't feel physically tired, but there was so much to think about. His head almost felt dizzy from everything he had seen. He turned as a young woman stepped into the room.

"We have prepared a place for you to meditate," she said. "Would you please come with me?" She held out her hand, and Peter nodded for him to go.

"I will be back for you when you are ready to continue," he said. "Remember when Mary pondered things in her heart? It would be well for you to do likewise."

Jeremiah rose and followed the young woman outside. He was shocked at the daylight. The images had been so real to him that he halfway expected to exit the building into a narrow alley in old Jerusalem under the night sky, but maybe it was always daylight here. He followed the woman through the city and out into the countryside. They walked down a hill, to a valley with a meadow that seemed vaguely familiar. He saw a stream flowing into a lake, and near the lake an open air tent gave shade to a number of bright cushions on a beautiful rug. The familiarity of it all tugged at his brain.

The young woman spoke. "When you first heard the 23rd Psalm you imagined something very like this." She waved her hand, indicating everything from the mountain-ringed valley to the fringed rug. "In my Father's house there are many mansions, and we thought you would feel most at home here." She smiled and repeated the words that Jeremiah loved:

"The Lord is my Shepherd; I shall not want.

He makes me lie down in green pastures.

He leads me beside still waters.

He restores my soul.

He guides me in the paths of righteousness for His name's sake.

Even though I walk through the valley of the shadow of death,

I will fear no evil, for You are with me.

Your rod and your staff, they comfort me.

You prepare a table before me in the presence of my enemies.

You anoint my head with oil; my cup runs over.

Surely goodness and mercy shall follow me all the days of my life

And I will dwell in the house of the Lord forever."

Jeremiah stared around him, completely speechless. Butterflies and birds dotted the meadow, and the stream ran noisily into the still deep waters of the lake. Suddenly overcome with the depth of caring, the overwhelming generosity, and the intensity of the day's teaching, Jeremiah sank to his knees on the grass, gratitude lighting his face.

The young woman smiled gently. "It really is more comfortable on the cushions," she said. "Take whatever time you need for your meditations and to refresh yourself. Peter will come for you when you are ready." She moved away, and Jeremiah jumped to his feet, entered the pavilion and kneeled on one of the cushions.

As he bent his head to review the day's teachings, he suddenly realized he hadn't jumped – actually jumped -- to his feet in years. Old age had made any kind of jumping a thing of the past, but there seemed to be no old age here. Tears of joy splashed his face, but soon he returned to his lesson. The stream seemed to carry his thoughts back to the beginning of the day. 'We began in the garden,' he thought, and sank into his meditations.

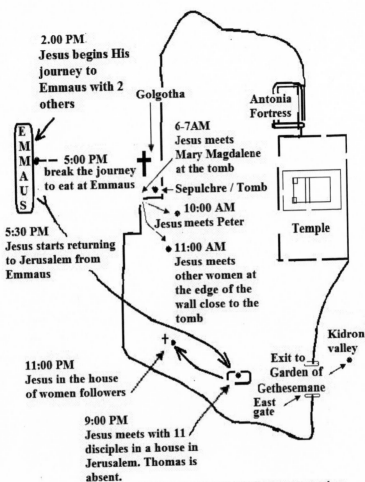

Sightings and movements of Jesus after resurrection
Day 1: Sunday from 6:00 AM to 11:00 PM

Day 2: Monday

Day 2: Monday: Angels born as women to care for Jesus before and after the resurrection – they are ascending and descending from heaven - image of body pierced by spear – women care for Jesus after His 40 days fasting/temptation

Jeremiah was just getting to his feet when he saw Peter approaching. "Peter," he began, "I have pondered and meditated, but I still have more questions about yesterday. Could we talk on our way back to the House of Images?"

"Of course," Peter replied, leading the way back toward the city.

Jeremiah's voice was eager. "I keep thinking about Jesus, and how He looked, and where He spent the night, and --"

Peter stopped him. "Let's take on one thing at a time. What is your first question?"

Jeremiah considered. "When we saw Jesus on the way to Emmaus, He looked dreadful. He looked a little better after He washed up in their house, but when He arrived where the disciples were meeting, they all recognized Him; even though at first they thought He was a spirit or a ghost. He looked so much better at the meeting than He had earlier. How did that happen?"

"Do you remember the women mentioned in the gospels?" At Jeremiah's nod Peter went on. "You know the names of many of them, but I assure you, there were many more. These were the women that cared for us as we traveled around following Jesus those three years. Some went ahead scouting for places to stay and to meet people who would provide food for us. Some went along with us to prepare our meals, tend to our clothes, and help with crowds."

Jeremiah seemed intrigued, so Peter continued. "Some of them, as you remember from the Gospel of Luke, were ones that had been cured of evil spirits or diseases. Many of them gave of their own money or from their own households to provide for us. You know some of their names: Mary Magdalene, Joanna the wife of Cuza, Susannah, and Salome." Jeremiah nodded, remembering the verses. "Without their help, we would not have had clean clothes, food, or even a place to sleep. Some of these women came to the crucifixion. They came to give His body the proper rites, and were actually the last to see Him laid in the tomb after Joseph of Arimathea and Nicodemus laid the body there." Jeremiah was trying to remember that verse when Peter quietly prompted, "The women, who had come with Him out of Galilee, followed after, and saw the tomb, and how His body was placed. They returned, and prepared spices and ointments. On the Sabbath they rested according to the commandment. Luke 23:55-56."

Peter continued, "Their caring did not end with the death of Jesus – you have already seen some of the women who came to the tomb that Sunday morning, and of course Mary Magdalene, who saw Him first."

"I remember they had bundles with them – I thought they must be the spices they needed," said Jeremiah. "They were going to finish the burial rites. But instead they found Jesus alive! I'll never forget the look on Mary's face when she recognized Jesus!"

He stopped, and then began again, more slowly. "But why didn't He want her to touch Him? I could see the wound still fresh on His hand, but it was so clear that she wanted, even needed, to touch Him and to hold Him in her arms. Some people think it was because He wanted them to realize He was always near them, even when He was not there physically, but I'm not sure."

"That might be part of it," said Peter, "but you might not realize the extent of His injuries and how that affected Him during those 40 days. The wounds in His hands and feet began to heal almost at once, after the nails were pulled from the cross. After a few days He could walk as well as ever. But His chest, where the spear pierced His side, was another matter." He paused, and Jeremiah was surprised to see they were already at the House of Images. He had been so focused on the conversation that he didn't even realize they had entered the city.

"Look," said Peter, settling himself in one of the crystal chairs. "We can see more than just the past here. See how the spear pierced His side and entered the chest cavity where the heart is?"

Suddenly the image of a body, pierced by a spear, appeared before Jeremiah. As in one of those crime shows on television, the skin and muscles disappeared to reveal the head of the spear in the chest cavity. Blood and water spewed from the entry wound. Jeremiah wondered why he didn't feel queasy, but then remembered that in Heaven, people probably didn't feel queasy.

Peter pointed to the area around the heart. "Here's where the most serious injury was. What you now call sepsis was setting in, and Jesus knew that if He had let Mary Magdalene hug Him that it would have made it even worse by contamination. He had to live out His remaining time on earth. His ministry to the disciples and other followers was not yet over. Yes, He was in pain, but that was not the point. Not letting Mary hug Him was necessary to keep Himself alive as long as He needed to be to complete His mission. He had to avoid coming into contact with external material - you would call that infection due to contamination."

"I had never considered any of this from a medical perspective," Jeremiah said. "None of my professors in Seminary ever talked about anything like this. Their teachings were all about the spiritual meanings behind everything."

"And that is as it should be," agreed Peter. "They have not had the medical training they would need to realize this. But now this is part of the story you can tell your congregation."

"And if they don't believe me?"

"Many of the prophets were not believed," said Peter. "But that is not your concern. You cannot do anything about their belief or unbelief. Your task is merely to tell the story as you see it here."

Jeremiah suddenly realized his concern about not being believed was a form of pride, of caring too much about the opinions of others. He breathed a silent prayer for forgiveness, and returned to his questions.

"All these women," he began. "Didn't they have other responsibilities? In that culture, I understood that women were always under the protection of men, and always caring for and serving them. How is it that so many were free to travel with Jesus and the disciples?"

"That is an excellent question, Jeremiah, and the answer will also explain what Jesus was doing on His second day of resurrection." The image of a mountain wilderness appeared. Jeremiah could see a man lying in the shade of a scrubby tree, with a group of women approaching him. Jeremiah suddenly knew the man was Jesus, but He appeared much younger here, and extremely thin.

"This is Jesus before He started His ministry. He has just spent 40 days in the wilderness, fasting. He has been tempted by Satan, and is exhausted, hungry, and dehydrated."

Jeremiah watched the women approach Jesus, uncover their baskets, and let Him drink from a skin of water. They fed Him slowly, with bread, dates, cheese, and olives. Suddenly Jeremiah remembered the scriptures.

"I thought angels ministered to Jesus! But these are clearly the same group of women that I have seen in these images before – the same ones who were holding onto His feet, the same ones who were serving the disciples that first evening."

"Yes," said Peter, "and these were the same ones who helped us in our three year ministry, who found places for us to sleep, who found food for us and mended our clothes. They do not appear as angels here, Jeremiah, because angels are spiritual beings, without bodies that need food and drink." Peter smiled at Jeremiah's look of surprise. "When you see angels mentioned in the Bible, Jeremiah, what are they usually doing?"

"They are announcing the birth of Jesus, or they are appearing to Mary and Joseph, or . . ." his voice trailed off as he remembered these angels popping in and out of clear air – something no physical body could do.

"These women," said Peter, "had been angels, but had chosen to be born as women in order to care for Jesus and His followers on earth. They are not ordinary people. After their physical death their spiritual bodies returned to heaven so they could be angels again."

Peter paused a moment for Jeremiah to take that in, and then continued. "It was not easy to be a woman in this culture. They had no rights, no legal recourse if they were mistreated by their husbands, and they were entirely dependent on men for their economic survival. If they did not marry, they were under the care of their parents, or later, their brothers or other kin."

"Like Mary and Martha lived with Lazarus," remembered Jeremiah.

"Yes, exactly!" said Pater. "Can you imagine giving up life in heaven, always in the presence of God our Father, always aware of His love and care, to live as women in old Jerusalem? It was a rough life, but they tell me they felt honored to be of service to our Lord and His mission."

The images still showed the younger Jesus lying on the mountain after His temptations. He had eaten, and now the women were bundling some rags and blankets together for a makeshift bed in the open air of the wilderness. Jeremiah could see their love and caring in the way they gently eased His body onto the blanket. Then the images shifted again.

Jeremiah saw these same women, this time in a small room. Morning light from a small opening in the wall lit a pallet where the resurrected Jesus lay. The women were moving about, washing and bandaging His wounds. One of them emerged from a back room, bringing a tray of food. No one spoke – everyone seemed to know what to do without any conversation.

Peter spoke again: "Jesus was our Lord, who gave His life for us, but He could not have survived the 40 days of His resurrection without the care giving system of the women who provided the food, water, and clothing, and attended to His wounds. This care giving might appear subtle, but it was no less dangerous than the work that Jesus was doing then, or that we were all doing later. These were silent heroes, or heroines, providing protection and much needed care for Jesus, at the risk of their own safety or even their lives. This was an act of altruism and dedication to His ministry."

"So these women who are risking their lives to care for Jesus, were once angels?" asked Jeremiah.

"That is correct," said Peter, "But since we are looking at images from the past, it is also true that they are angels now. Do you remember me telling you that when they died, their spirits rose to heaven and they resumed their lives as angels?" Jeremiah nodded. "Do you remember the young woman who led you to the pavilion last night? Do you recognize her there, putting the food on the table?"

Jeremiah peered intently at the image. "Yes! She looks a bit different, but I can tell it is the same person."

"All the angels who became women to care for Jesus developed quite a ministry of hospitality," said Peter. They found that they really enjoyed finding creative ways to serve and minister to people. Did you enjoy the meditation spot she arranged for you? It was her idea to try to make you as comfortable as possible in a familiar setting." He laughed. "I would probably just have let you stay here in one of these chairs. Hospitality is not my gift."

Jeremiah laughed along with Peter, and then turned back to the images of the women caring for Jesus. "So, these are the angels who became women to care for Jesus and His followers. Does Jesus stay here and rest all day on the second day of the resurrection? He looks so tired."

"Yes, Jeremiah, that is all He did. That first day was exhausting, and He needed to rest and prepare Himself for the next few days before His journey to Galilee. One of the women had opened her home to us whenever we were in Jerusalem, and He stayed there." Peter looked at Jeremiah. "Have you finished your questions? Are you ready for the next day?"

Jeremiah sat for a moment. "Yes, those were all the questions I had -- or at least have for now." He grinned. "I believe I am ready for the next day."

"Good," said Peter. "We'll begin."

Day 3: Tuesday

Day 3: Tuesday: Jesus visits Bethlehem – Jeremiah sees the birth of Jesus, and the arrival of the Wise Men over a year later – Jesus at the Inn

"This is Tuesday, the third day of our Lord's resurrection," said Peter, "As you saw, Jeremiah, He rested all day yesterday. Today He begins His journey through the countryside. He left before sunrise."

The images began, and Jeremiah saw a dilapidated shelter with mud walls and a roof thatched with grass. Some animals were nosing about a manger, which appeared as old as the shelter. There was a definite barnyard smell. Jesus approached and sat on a nearby stone wall.

"What is He doing?" whispered Jeremiah, forgetting for a moment that these were just images, and not wanting to disturb Jesus.

"You know where He is, don't you? This is Bethlehem, where He was born. And don't forget that King David was also born here. That is why Joseph had to come here for the census – David was his ancestor. Would you like to see that night?" At Jeremiah's nod, the images shifted and Jeremiah saw that same shed and manger, but both looked much newer and in better repair.

Night was beginning to fall, and a couple that could only be Joseph and Mary slowly made their way to the shelter, which was clearly in use as a stable. There had been no room in the inn they had seen on their way, but they had to find shelter of some sort, quickly. Joseph had raised a tent when they had camped in the evenings, but there was no time for that now. Mary was clearly in pain, and Jeremiah realized she was in labor; they had reached the stable just in time. Joseph quickly tied their donkey to the rail and prepared a bed of hay with a blanket on it. Mercifully, the images shifted so that Jeremiah was spared the actual birthing scene.

"Mary would skin me alive if I showed that part," laughed Peter. The images showed Joseph cleaning the baby with some kind of cloth and then giving Him to Mary, who accepted Him with open arms. After a while she wrapped the baby Jesus in sheets of white cloth, while Joseph filled the manger with fresh hay and carefully arranged a clean sheet of linen to cover it. Then Mary kneeled at the manger and carefully placed Jesus on His first bed – a manger lined with hay and a linen sheet.

The images shifted back to the present day, with Jesus sitting on the stone wall, looking at the place of His birth.

Jeremiah was silent for a moment. "All this happened, right here!"

"Yes," said Peter, "It was all as you have just seen. I do not know how much Jesus can really remember of that time – we all know He is both human and divine, but we have not spoken of what He remembers of His infancy. But He knows He has 40 days left on earth. If you knew you had only 40 days left on earth, what would you do?"

Jeremiah thought for a moment. "I suppose I would go back and visit everyone I loved and every place that was meaningful to me."

Peter nodded. "That is exactly what He is doing. Bethlehem was not only where He was born, but also His first home.

"His first home? But I thought they went to Egypt."

"They did, Jeremiah, but that was when He was about a year and a half or two years old. That was when the Wise Men came to them with gifts of gold, frankincense, and myrrh from the Far East. Those gifts helped them here in Bethlehem as they prepared for their sudden journey, along the way, and later when they settled in Egypt."

"I know there are different traditions about the Wise Men," said Jeremiah. I've seen many Nativity scenes with the wise men there, despite the scriptures about Herod ordering the death of all Hebrew male children in that area two years and younger. I had always thought that if He was only a baby when Herod heard about Him from the Wise Men, Herod would only have killed the babies, not the others as well."

"Well done," said Peter. "The only ones who visited Him on that night were the shepherds. There were three of them: two brothers, and the teenage son of one of the brothers." Jeremiah was thinking about the shepherds when he saw Jesus rise from the stone wall and continue toward the center of town. He paused before a very small house, gazing as if trying to fix it in His memory.

"This was where He lived while He was a baby and a toddler," said Peter. "His memories might not be entirely clear about that time. This was the house Joseph found for them. It was here where He was circumcised on the eighth day of His birth, by the local rabbi, and it was from here that they journeyed to the Temple in Jerusalem after Mary's 40 day purification time was complete, for Jesus to be presented at the Temple there."

Jeremiah said, "I remember reading in Luke's Gospel that Simeon, the old man who knew he would see the Messiah before he died, saw them in the Temple and blessed them, and said to Mary, 'Behold, this child is set for the fall and rising again of many in Israel.' There was also the prophetess named Anna who served God with fasting and prayers, and spoke of Him to all those who 'looked for redemption in Jerusalem.' - Luke 2:38"

Peter said, "From Jerusalem they returned here, and this was His first real home. Of course, after the Wise Men came, they found they needed to move out of town rather quickly."

"I am trying to imagine what it was like for the Wise Men, to travel so far and see a young boy instead of a baby."

"Indeed, think about the toddlers in your church. What would they do when strange men came to them with beautiful presents?"

Jeremiah laughed. "They would start by hiding in their mother's arms, but then come out and grab at the presents. And if there was any part that could be put in their mouths, they would try that, as well."

"All that, and more," said Peter. "Can you imagine the stir they made in town, these three men in foreign robes, riding camels? On a trip of that length, they also had their servants, tents, and all the belongings they needed to camp every night. It was quite an event, and the fact that Joseph and his family were last seen walking on the road toward Egypt the next week, never to be seen again, was scarcely worth mentioning. Their departure made for a little talk around the town well, but those rich foreigners provided the locals with gossip for many weeks."

Day 3: Tuesday

Jeremiah laughed as the images shifted to show the Bethlehem of old, with the Wise Men in their splendid robes and their ill-mannered camels. The Wise Men demanded food for their journey, supplies to mend their tents and clothing, and a place for them to camp and water their animals. Each of these transactions seemed to involve much bartering and posturing, and at one point Jeremiah began to wonder how much of this was just the Middle Eastern way of doing things, and how much was a planned distraction to help the Holy Family to make a quiet getaway.

Peter laughed with him. "It was not easy for Joseph and Mary to make that journey of 330 miles to Egypt with a toddler. That age is, as you know, a noisy one. They needed help to get far enough away that no one would come after them, and the Wise Men proved very helpful."

The images shifted again to show Jesus walking toward an old inn near the edge of town. He seemed to be arranging to spend the night there.

"Is that the inn that had no room for them?" asked Jeremiah in a hushed tone. Peter nodded.

The images showed Jesus resting in the common room of the inn. The elderly innkeeper came out of a back room, offering a tray of bread, cheese, dates, figs, and grapes. He sat a pitcher and a cup on the table, and then, seeing that his guest was in no mood for conversation, returned to the back room. The town seemed very quiet after the images of old.

"Jesus just eats and spends the night here," said Peter. "This is the end of the third day of the resurrection. Are you ready for more?"

"Yes, Peter. This part of the journey is not as intense as that first day was. So much happened on that first day, so much to think about! This part is much easier to grasp."

Peter sat back and the images of the following day began to form.

Day 4: Wednesday

Day 4: Wednesday: Jesus visits the shepherds near Bethlehem – site of David's grazing field - settlement of Kerioth – parents of Judas

"This is Wednesday, the fourth day of the resurrection, said Peter.

The images showed Jesus leaving the inn after breakfast and traveling southeast of the city, the sun casting a long shadow behind Him. Soon He was in a pasture where sheep were grazing under the watchful eyes of shepherds, who looked surprised that someone was walking toward them from town.

Peter explained their surprised looks: "Remember that the townsfolk avoided shepherds as much as possible. In those days, shepherds had the very lowest standing in the community. In a small community such as this, no one in town would risk their own reputation by speaking with shepherds. Usually their only visitors were rabbis who wanted to buy a sheep to offer at the Temple."

Jeremiah saw Jesus approach the shepherds, and the eldest one rose to greet Him. "Shalom," the shepherd began, but then stopped abruptly and stared intently into the face of Jesus. In a sudden flash of recognition, he knelt and cried, "Messiah!" Jesus smiled and touched his shoulder, indicating for him to rise. The other shepherds backed away, mystified by this behavior. Jeremiah was a little mystified, himself.

Peter stopped the images to explain that this shepherd was one of the ones who saw the angels and went to the manger to worship the baby Jesus.

"But how did he recognize Jesus now?" asked Jeremiah. "He didn't at first – his greeting was a respectful one to a stranger of a higher rank. But suddenly he knew it was Jesus!"

"Once an angel reveals Jesus to you," said Peter, "you will always know Him." He let that sink in a little, and then the images resumed.

Day 4: Wednesday

"We had heard about what was happening in Jerusalem," the shepherd was explaining, "but they kept us so busy getting the sheep ready for the Temple offerings that we couldn't get away to see for ourselves." He paused, remembering. "Thanks to the blessed angels, I was one of the first to see You and worship You that night 33 years ago. I heard that You were crucified, but here You are speaking with me. And You look wounded. Can You tell us what happened? Could we bind Your wounds with some healing liniment?" The old shepherd seemed genuinely alarmed at Jesus' wounds, anxious to be of help.

Jesus calmed his anxiety with a touch, saying: "Many thanks, good Joshua (and the look of shock on the elderly shepherd's face as he realized Jesus knew his name was almost comical) but I do not need any special treatment. These wounds will heal like any wound on any other human. I am here today as a man, and suffering is all just a part of that."

Joshua took a moment as if trying to accept something he didn't really understand, and then glanced over at the other men, motioning the younger one over. "This is my son, Jonathan," he said. Jonathan bowed before Jesus, and Jeremiah saw that same light of recognition in Jonathan's eyes. Joshua was clearly proud of his son. "He was just a teenager when he was out in the fields with us that night when the angels visited us and gave the message, but now look what a fine man he has grown into. His wife is also a good woman, and they welcomed me into their home after my own wife died three years ago."

Jesus acknowledged the son with a smile, and Joshua rushed on, as if this experience had awakened a flood of memories. "That night of Your birth long ago was one I never forgot. Why, it was on that night that my father regained his lost vision. He had been practically blind, but when we returned from visiting the manger he could see as well as ever. We did not understand."

He paused for breath, and then said, "We have heard that in the last three years Jesus has healed the sick, made the lame walk and the deaf hear, made the blind see and even raised the dead. We now believe that You as a baby somehow healed my father's eyes after we visited You. We all noticed that ever since that night of seeing the angels and worshipping the baby Jesus, that our flocks of sheep

44

have increased many times. They give such good wool and milk. They are healthier than any other flock, so they are sought by the Temple priests for their offerings and sacrifices at the altar."

Again Joshua paused, as if gathering his courage. "Please come and share our noon meal. Our prosperity is due to You. Please let us thank You in this small way."

Jesus looked touched, but declined the offer. "Joshua, you and your family were the first ones to visit Me after My birth. You were chosen and blessed to visit the Son of God on earth because of your pure heart." The shepherds looked both grateful and confused: grateful to be chosen, but not understanding completely why they had been.

Jesus continued, "Today I want to reveal to you that the land you are grazing your sheep on is the same ground where David, the second great king of Israel, the youngest of the eight sons of Jesse, walked and where he grazed his family herd before he was anointed king. I am from the seed of David as prophesied, and the angel appeared to you to announce My birth at the same field in which My ancestors walked and herded."

He held out His hands, and instinctively the shepherds bowed their heads. "Peace be with you, and with your family" said Jesus, and walked slowly away. Long after He had gone, the shepherds stood silently, each seeming lost in his own thoughts.

Jeremiah was lost in his own thoughts, as well, and Peter paused the images. "So many ripples from that first birth," said Jeremiah thoughtfully. "So many things happened that were not recorded in the gospels."

"The gospels, as with any of the ancient writings, were not meant as the final word on what happened, but as a starting point to explore the relationship between God and Man. The gospels speak of the essentials, but Jeremiah, even in your own world, a biography written about a famous man doesn't list day by day, hour by hour, everything that he did. No one would want to either buy or read such a book. Only the essentials, the things that gave that life meaning, are recorded. And your biographers are sometimes in just as much disagreement about details as the writers of the gospels were."

Jeremiah had to laugh at this. "I know, we can't even agree on what happened three days ago, let alone two thousand years ago." He looked up. "What else did Jesus do that day?"

"He is walking to the settlement of Kerioth, the boyhood home of Judas," said Peter.

"Judas!" cried Peter. "Why would Jesus visit the home of Judas?" He leaned forward, anxious not to miss any of the action.

Jesus paused in front of a house. An older couple were in the side yard, tending to the sheep fodder. The man looked briefly at Him, then at his wife. "Lucia, have we seen this man somewhere before?"

"I'm not sure," said Lucia, glancing over at the stranger. "You travelled to Jerusalem on the Sabbath day last week looking for our son. If He looks familiar that is where you might have seen Him."

Simon looked a little uncomfortable. "I told you that I did not find Judas, but I did not tell you the whole story of my journey."

"Simon, what do you mean? What story?"

"You remember that I went because we heard rumors that Jesus of Nazareth was there, and we thought we might be able to speak with Judas while they were in town, so close. But when I arrived there, I saw a large group of Romans, Temple priests, and their followers leading a man condemned to death by crucifixion. The man was bleeding, as if He had already suffered a beating. I thought I recognized Him, and the people in the crowd told me that He was Jesus of Nazareth, labeled as the King of the Jews."

Lucia grabbed her husband's arm. "Simon! Jesus of Nazareth, the man our son was following?"

Simon nodded. "Yes, but I did not see any of His followers, either with Him or in the crowd. The Romans were making Him carry His own cross. I have no idea why everyone would have turned on Him so quickly – it was just last week that He had ridden into the city in triumph, with everyone shouting Hosanna. The crowd seemed divided, some saying He was a troublemaker, others saying He was a healer and the Messiah."

Lucia's voice showed her concern. "Why did you not tell me all this when you came back?

Simon sighed. "I didn't tell you any of this because I was too upset about not finding our son. It had been such a long time since we had seen Judas – I was sure since he was going to be so near that I would get a chance to see him and urge him to come home, at least for a visit." He looked upset. "What I really wanted to ask him was how long was he going to wander around the countryside with that little group? I am sure he thought Jesus of Nazareth would be the liberator of our nation, but he's been following Him over two years, with no results. When was he going to come home and help out at the farm? Most of the young girls in the village have married by now."

"Perhaps it was well that you did not find him," said Lucia. "When did your words ever change his mind? But what happened to Jesus?"

Simon looked pained. "By the time I realized what was going on, I was caught up in the crowd, and was carried along with them to that hill west of the city. He fell on the way and someone carried the cross for Him. They crucified Him, but I did not stay to the end. I had no desire to see Jesus die. I looked at the people watching, to see if Judas was there. I saw two women and a young man at the foot of the cross, but not our son. He was nowhere to be found in the crowd. I walked back into the city looking for Judas, but I could not find him."

"You were two days later getting back than I expected," said Lucia.

"There was such a commotion going on the day after the Sabbath that I stayed till Sunday. Temple guards and Romans were rushing around everywhere, searching and questioning people. There was a rumor that Jesus had been raised from the dead on Sunday morning, but many did not believe it. I also heard that the Temple guards were saying that Jesus' body was stolen from the tomb by His disciples. I thought about our son at that news. I never did find Judas. You remember how tired I was when I came back."

"You have been having an adventure!" Lucia's concern was evident, but she had not forgotten the stranger at their gate. But have you remembered who that man at our front gate might be? The only person you've been speaking of was Jesus, but He was crucified. How could this man be Jesus? Unless those rumors that He rose from the dead are true. You saw Him on Friday," said Lucia. "Does this man look like Jesus?"

47

"I am not positive, but He does look like Him. His injuries appear to be the same ones – scratches on the forehead from the crown of thorns, and nail marks on His feet and hands. And He looks as weak as someone in that condition would be expected to look."

"Would you go and ask Him to come in and accept our hospitality?" But even as Lucia asked the question they turned to find an empty road – Jesus had walked on. "Simon! I know there was someone there! But He's gone! Could He have been Jesus? Raised from the dead? Do you think He might really be the liberator Judas sought? You remember that Zealot fervor he had? He always reminded me of your great-grandparents of Medione."

The images faded and Jeremiah looked at Peter. "Why did Jesus come here? And since He was here, why didn't He go in to visit them?"

"Did you notice that Simon had not told his wife about his experience in Jerusalem until Jesus walked up? It was important for that story to be told. They knew Judas had left to follow Jesus, and they both needed to know what had happened in Jerusalem that day. Also," Peter added, "Jesus was there to give them a silent blessing and show His grace to the parents. They have aged quite a bit in the few years that Judas has been gone. Since Judas would not return to care for them in their old age, Jesus gave them a blessing so their remaining years would be healthy and peaceful."

"So the mother of Judas is named Lucia! I am sure I never read that," said Jeremiah.

"Just another thing to bring back to your congregation," said Peter. "I think you are beginning to see how Judas became part of the ministry of Jesus, and how his actions were necessary to fulfill the prophecies about our Lord" He gave Jeremiah an encouraging smile. "I know this is a lot for you to take in. Are you ready for the next day's journey? Jesus is trying to go to every place that has meaning for Him before His ascension."

"I am ready," said Jeremiah, and the images shifted.

Day 5: Thursday

Day 5: Thursday: Jesus revives the withered fig tree on the way to Bethany – He stays overnight at the house of Lazarus, Martha, and Mary - Lazarus recounts his rising from death– Jeremiah sees the monument to the 12 Tribes of Israel in heaven

"It is the fifth day, Thursday, on our Lord's journey. Where is He going, Peter? It looks as if He is traveling in a northeast direction from Bethlehem and Kerioth. Is He going to Jerusalem?"

"He is just passing through the outskirts of Jerusalem right now," said Peter. "He is on His way to Bethany, about nine miles away."

They watched as Jesus stopped next to a withered tree in the Kidron valley on the way to Bethany. A few birds perched on the dried-out limbs, looking for fruit but finding nothing to eat. Jesus held out His hands and Jeremiah heard Him say, "In the name of My Father in heaven, I command you to return to life."

"Is that the fig tree that Jesus cursed when He was on His way to Jerusalem?" asked Jeremiah. He stared at the tree. "Is it my imagination or is that tree looking better? Are those green leaves coming out?"

"Yes, that was the fig tree that was not bearing fruit when Jesus and His disciples traveled from Bethany to Jerusalem twelve days ago on a Monday morning. Jesus was hungry, and needed to eat, but the tree had no figs. So Jesus cursed the tree, and it instantly withered. I can still remember how shocked we all were. We were so accustomed to His blessings that sometimes we forgot that He could be as angry as any other man.

"There are so many books written about the divine nature and the human nature of Jesus," said Jeremiah. "Bible scholars have been debating this subject for hundreds of years. I suppose that when He cursed the fig tree He was acting from His human nature, and when He blessed it He was acting from His divine nature."

"That sounds reasonable, Jeremiah, and I will add one more thing. As the kingdom of God is within us, as we give our lives to Jesus, we also have His divine nature working in us to help us with our human nature. We can be angry, as our human nature will be, but we do not have to act on that anger, which seldom helps any situation. The divine nature of Jesus working in us helps us choose which emotions to act on and which to just experience for ourselves."

Jeremiah nodded, already thinking how he could work that into a sermon. But the tree, which was slowly coming back to life, was so fascinating that he couldn't lose himself in future sermons for long. The green leaves unfurled and small flower buds appeared and then opened up. Suddenly Jeremiah realized he was looking at young figs ripening before his eyes. As the first one became ripe, Jesus picked it and began to eat. The birds which had been startled into flying a short distance away returned and started pecking at the figs. Butterflies circled the tree, and then swirled around Jesus, as if delighted by His very presence.

"There is one more lesson about the fig tree, Jeremiah. Do you remember what our Lord said long ago, when I told Him the fig tree which He cursed had withered away? He told me, 'Have faith in God' -- can you see what He was trying to tell me?"

Jeremiah was still in awe of the tree coming back to life. "I am still so amazed at this – I can't imagine what that might be."

"The other lesson is that when we commit a sin, our Lord is not going to curse us forever to wither away. We can be redeemed and come back with our Lord's grace, just as it happened to the fig tree." Peter stopped to give Jeremiah a chance to take it all in.

"I just can't get over witnessing a miracle like this." Jeremiah was transfixed by the images before him.

Peter laughed, "Now you know how we felt! Do you see now how our Lord had the power to dry up the fig tree when there was no fruit and He also has the power to bring it back ten days later? It is all about faith. Our Lord wanted His disciples and followers to have faith in Him as the Son of God. Remember what He said about the mustard seed, that if you have faith, even if the faith is as small as a mustard seed, if you command a mountain to move, it will move; nothing will be impossible to you."

Jeremiah thought about the connection. "We teach that if you have faith you can do these things, and I see that our Lord has the power to do both. One time I counted how many times our Lord used the word Faith in the Gospels. The word Faith is mentioned 29 times. The word Forgive is mentioned 24 times. I thought that meant both faith and forgiveness were necessary parts of our lives."

"You are right," said Peter. "And isn't it easier now to remember, as you are looking at this fig tree, about faith, forgiveness and the grace of God?"

"My congregation will love that story of the fig tree!" Jeremiah noticed the images changing before him. Jesus had left the fig tree and was moving toward a small village. "Where is He going now, Peter?"

"This is Bethany, where Lazarus, Mary and Martha live. We camped there for five days, the last week of our ministry with Jesus."

Jeremiah saw Jesus stop before a large home. A man and two women hurried out to greet Him, their shrieks of surprise and delight loud in that drowsy residential street. Jesus was urging them back into the house. The scene shifted to follow them into the inner courtyard. The women were inviting Jesus to sit on their best chair. Lazarus drew up a stool, one of the women snuggled up by Jesus' feet, and the other bustled off toward an inner room.

"Nothing ever changes," observed Jeremiah, and Peter laughed. Jesus was laughing, as well, and Jeremiah was suddenly worried that he had missed something.

"I think He was just making the same observation," said Peter. Lazarus was explaining to Jesus, "I know it appears as if nothing has changed since the last time you were here eight days ago, but wait until after our meal. They switch places after dinner, so that Mary cleans up and Martha can join in the discussion."

At Jesus' nod of approval, Mary spoke up. "We would have taken turns serving the meal, but we found Martha was a much better cook than I could ever be!" She rose and led Jesus to the small guest room where clean robes had been laid out for Him, and a basin of water and a towel were on the small table by the bed. "Please join us when you are ready," she said, and headed back to the courtyard.

Day 5: Thursday

A few minutes later Jesus appeared in the courtyard, refreshed and in His clean clothes. "Thank you for your hospitality," He said, settling back into His favorite chair. Mary tended to His wounds, and then poured sweet scented oil on His feet. She put the jar of oil away, and sat at His feet. Lazarus began to tell Jesus what had been happening in Bethany the last few days.

"There was a disturbance here last week," said Lazarus, his words coming slowly. "Those Temple guards have been lurking about ever since You left here. At first they held back, not showing themselves too openly, but of late they became bolder, actually searching the house, probably for some evidence against You, or for some hint of Your plans. At some point their behavior changed. We realized they were trying to kill me, but I was careful never to be out of the house alone."

"I knew they were trying to kill you when we were with you last week. They were trying anything they could to discredit Me," said Jesus. "I know they had kept up their persecution of your family."

"They were gone on the Sabbath, and the day after that," said Lazarus, "But came back on the first day of the week. They told Martha that the disciples had stolen the body of Jesus, but of course we knew that couldn't have been true. They said Your body had disappeared from the tomb. We told them we had not seen You since that Thursday morning a week ago, but we could tell they did not believe us. They searched the house again, but of course did not find You."

Lazarus took a good look at Jesus, and then went on: "But how is it, Lord, that You have risen as You raised me up four days after my death, but I see the wounds are still in Your hands and feet? We heard You had died, and the stories gave us hope that You had risen. But while I am in perfect health, You, my dearest master, appear weak." He paused. "Can you tell us what has happened – why You still appear wounded and ill?"

Jesus considered the question. "Do you remember how it was when you were dead, Lazarus?"

"I remember floating from the tomb to where You were camping, Lord. I was free from all the pain and suffering. The disease was gone, and I felt completely normal again! Well, as normal as I could feel, floating around the countryside without my physical body attached." Lazarus stopped for a moment, remembering, and then went on. "I remember hearing You say that this illness was not meant to end in death, but that it was going to bring glory to God, for it will show the glory of the Son of God."

Lazarus paused. "I knew the Son of God was somehow You, Jesus, but I still didn't understand what that meant. You said that I was asleep, and that You would go and wake me up, that You and all the disciples were going to Judea."

Mary spoke up. "I was so sick with grief that I couldn't leave the house, but Martha went to the camp where You and Your disciples were staying. She said it was maddening! No one seemed to understand what was happening! The disciples were talking about being stoned if they went to Judea, and it took Jesus saying plainly, 'Lazarus is dead' for them to realize why Martha was there, why she was so upset, why she was begging Jesus to come back and do something for our brother. Even though he was dead, we knew You had the power to heal him."

"And You did," said Lazarus. "In my strange state I could see You travel to my burial cave. I was hovering near my body when I heard You say, 'Lazarus, come forth' and at Your words I floated back into my body. All of a sudden I was breathing, and I could hear and smell and feel the linen wrapped around me. I remember walking forward. The bandages were still on my eyes, but I could tell the difference between the dark of the cave and the light outside. I was alive! And I was completely free of disease." He looked at Jesus. "But You still look as if You had just left the cross. Didn't Your body heal as mine did?"

"I have not come to heal Myself," began Jesus "I rose from the dead to show the power of our Father in heaven, to fulfill the prophecies, and to finish the ministry laid out for Me, but the healing of My body did not need to be part of that plan. The scriptures say that the Messiah will suffer before He comes into His glory. I know My suffering is temporary. Soon I will go to the Father and leave this pain behind. So, Lazarus, My experience is not quite the same as yours."

"What was it like for You?" asked Mary.

"I, also, was aware of My spirit hovering outside My body," said Jesus. "It felt good to be free of the pain, but I knew My time here was not yet over. I had died on the cross, but I still had to be resurrected on the third day, as the prophets had foretold. I still had work to do. My death on the cross and resurrection would take away the sins of the world, but the disciples and My followers still needed guidance. They needed to know what our time together was all about. They needed to know what My death and resurrection meant. They needed to know how to start their new ministry, and they needed to know to wait in Jerusalem to receive the power of the Holy Spirit."

"But the wounds," interrupted Lazarus.

Jesus looked down at His hands. "My resurrection would fulfill the prophecies, but for it to be believed, I had to retain the wounds I carried from the nails and the spear. Otherwise, no one would have believed that I was Jesus. I had to show the wounds to the disciples before they believed." He stopped, remembering His journey through death.

"It was so dark in the tomb when I awoke in my body. The pain was incredible. But I was alive. I had work to do, and I knew I had 40 days to complete it. I just prayed to my Father in heaven, that I would last that long."

At His sigh, Mary leaned her head against His knee. Lazarus appeared lost in thought, and into this quiet group Martha hustled, bringing the dishes for their meal. They gathered around the table, and Mary gave Martha a shortened version of what she had missed.

"It has been like a nightmare around here," said Martha, as she passed a dish to her brother. It's those Temple priests, sending those spies to snoop around the house until we can't even go to the marketplace alone. When you healed Lazarus, it woke up the whole countryside. Everyone was talking about it. People who we'd have sworn had never spoken Your name started calling themselves followers, claiming that Messiah is among us. I've never seen anything like it."

Lazarus interrupted again. "The Temple priests had never seen anything like it, as well, and we started hearing rumors of secret meetings among the Pharisees and Caiaphas. Someone said they heard something like, 'It is better for one man to die for the people than the whole nation perish,' but that sounded extreme, even for them."

Jesus held up a hand. "Actually, that was one of the prophecies that had to be fulfilled. One man did die for the nation, so that the whole nation might not perish. But the meaning of it was not exactly what they were thinking of." He seemed thoughtful, and Martha took the opportunity to push on.

"It seems our Lazarus was one miracle too many for those priests. Did you know they had surrounded the house while you were here a few days ago? They were lying in wait to try to kill him, so everything might quiet down again. But since Lazarus took care to never be seen alone, that little plot never came to pass." She looked pleased, and Jesus laughed, imagining the care Martha must have taken to make sure that everyone would know Lazarus was not alone.

Then He suddenly looked serious and said, "Lazarus, did you know why they wanted to kill you? They wanted to test My ability to raise you from the dead as I did before. If I could not bring you back from death a second time, they wanted to spread the word that My raising you from the dead was all a hoax."

Mary looked shocked, but Martha was nodding her head as if she had realized that already. "We heard they were threatened by the miracles You had done, that Your ministry was attracting too many of the people. They were really afraid of the Romans noticing a new power rising up in the area. They thought the Romans would take away their power in the Jewish nation, and perhaps even the Jewish nation itself." Martha almost shook her fist in righteous indignation before she remembered that Jesus had submitted Himself, with all His power, to the local Roman government.

"Well, that's what we heard, anyway," she said. "So many people were referring to You as the Messiah, and of course all they could think about was the Messiah at the head of a mighty army to rid this land of the Romans and take back what was ours." She continued, her voice sounding puzzled. "The spies from the Temple had all gone back to Jerusalem. We heard what had happened that night. No one expected the Messiah to die. They thought they had killed off a troublemaker. They thought Your miracles and what You did for Lazarus would be forgotten if You died."

Mary spoke up quickly, "And then we heard the other rumors! Rumors that You were alive! Of course we believed it! Lazarus was right here beside us as living proof that You have power over death itself. But we heard the Romans were looking for You and all Your followers again, so we knew it would be best for us to stay here. Lazarus knew You'd come to us!" She looked at her brother with shining eyes, and then turned back to Jesus. "And You did!"

"Yes," said Jesus. "I came as soon as I felt well enough to travel. I can only stay one night, but I wanted to stop here first, to see you all again. Lazarus, your story will not be forgotten; it will be told for generations to come; as well as the story of Mary anointing Me the day before we entered Jerusalem in triumph. And the priests will begin to find out that I died for the nation, but not to protect the current nation from Rome. Eventually Rome itself will be conquered and fade, but My followers, My believers, will spread throughout the world, in numbers uncounted."

Mary seemed to gaze into that future, Lazarus sat with a slight smile on his face, and Martha laughed at both of them. "Well, the dishes won't carry themselves out to be cleaned and put away, no matter what the future brings for either us or Rome." She gently nudged Mary.

"My turn to be the servant!" she laughed, jumping up and quickly gathering up the dishes. A couple of them fell from her hands in her haste, but Jesus quickly caught them before they hit the floor. They all laughed at that, and Mary carefully moved into the back room, her dishes now in perfect balance. She popped her head back in to say quickly: "Don't say anything while I'm gone!" Martha halfway rose toward her, and Mary scurried back to her dishes.

Jeremiah noticed they really didn't say anything, either from a courtesy to Mary, or just from contemplating everything that had been said already. Even Martha was silent, a slight frown on her face as she puzzled over the events.

The scene faded as Peter turned to Jeremiah. "Are you in need of some contemplation as well?" he asked.

Jeremiah felt drained of all energy, although he knew heaven was a place where no one was tired or needed sleep. "It is a lot to think about," he said. "The fig tree, Lazarus, Mary and Martha switching places, Jesus dying for a nation that did not even know Him yet . . ."

Peter pointed to the door. "Look! I think I see your guide. She will take you again to your contemplation area, and I will come for you when you are ready to begin again.

Jeremiah gratefully followed the young woman out into the beautiful city. He was noticing much more about the city than he had before. As they passed a large domed pavilion which sat on several layers of different colored stones, he stopped for a better look. As he was wondering what the precious stones were, the young woman started to name them: "The bottom later of the foundation is jasper, the second layer is sapphire, the third layer is a chalcedony, the fourth layer is emerald, the fifth layer is sardonyx, the sixth layer is sardius, the seventh layer is chrysolite, the eighth layer is beryl, the ninth layer is topaz, the tenth layer is a chrysoprasus, the eleventh layer is a jacinth, and the top layer is amethyst."

Twelve columns stood in a circle on the amethyst, and Jeremiah began to read the names inscribed at the base of each column. "Each name is one of the twelve tribes of Israel," his guide said, and pointed to the statues in the center of the building. "Here are statues of the patriarchs: Abraham, Isaac, and Jacob. Do you recognize who that statue in the middle of them is?"

Jeremiah saw the statue was holding tablets of stone. "That must be Moses!" he cried.

"You are right, Jeremiah," said the angel.

"This looks so familiar, but I cannot remember where I might have seen it, or read about it. Not the dome or the columns or the statues – it is mainly that foundation, the stacks of beautiful stones."

"You might look in Revelations 21," said the angel.

"Thank you," said Jeremiah.

"You are a follower of Jesus; I am happy to serve you, just as I served the disciples when they were living on earth." The young woman smiled at him as they walked on.

Jeremiah was shocked. He had never thought of himself in the same category as the disciples and followers of Jesus long ago. But clearly, the young woman (angel, he corrected himself) placed Jeremiah in that same company.

As his first shock eased, he realized in his heart he was a follower, and that a couple of thousand years made no difference to the angel – angels are ageless and immortal. Jeremiah had never felt so humble in his life. His gratitude for this experience welled up beyond his ability to contain it. Although he had never been much of a singer, the only way to express this was in song, and Jeremiah found himself singing an old praise song, feeling as if every word had been written for just this occasion. To his amazement, the angel joined in, and they finished the song in beautiful harmony.

There was a moment of hushed silence, and then Jeremiah shouted for joy. "I'm singing with the angels!" He gave a little leap into the air. The angel laughed, and as she did, echoes of laughter swirled around them. Butterflies danced through the air in graceful patterns and birds trilled their joyful response. Even the grass and trees seemed to wave in agreement. 'If the hills start skipping, I'm in real trouble,' thought Jeremiah, and the angel's laughter rose to new heights.

Surrounded by this joy, Jeremiah and the angel walked on into the valley beside the stream and then to the pavilion by the lake. She left him kneeling on the cushions, gazing over the lake toward the hills.

"I have given them strict orders not to skip," she said with a smile, and Jeremiah laughed again at the thought of an angel sharing a joke with him.

Then his mind went back over the day, from the fig tree to Bethany, from forgiveness and power to the bewildered priests of the Temple and the real power over death.

Day 6: Friday

Day 6: Friday: Visits Garden of Gethsemane where Peter talks about Malchus whose ear Jesus restored – explanation of blood stained sweat – Jesus sees Malchus – the Centurion and the robe that healed – soldiers who did not let themselves be changed – man who helps the ill into the healing pool – Rachel who was saved from being stoned to death – Salome, the mother of James and John – Salome who danced for King Herod Antipas

As Jeremiah rose from his cushion, he saw Peter walking toward him. "Perfect timing," said Jeremiah, and Peter grinned.

"I see you have recovered yourself," Peter waited for Jeremiah on the path back to the city. "Are you ready for day six?" Jeremiah caught up with Peter and they both moved toward the city. "Before we start the day's teaching, I'd like to do a little review so that certain events are fresh in your mind."

"What events?" asked Jeremiah?

"Today we will be visiting people who Jesus encountered on the evening He was arrested in the Garden of Gethsemane. Do you remember the servant of Caiaphas, named Malchus?"

"Isn't he the one whose ear was cut off, and Jesus restored it that night?"

"Yes, Jeremiah. I notice you are a little too polite to say it, but remember that I was the one who cut off his ear. I wasn't aiming for his ear, you know. I just didn't have much experience with handling a sword. That was probably the first one I ever had. We were all shocked at the arrival of the guards. None of us were thinking clearly. The best I can remember, I had some mad thought about drawing the sword and killing the captain of the Temple guards. I guess I thought if I killed him, the other guards would scatter."

Peter laughed at his younger self, amused at the foolish thoughts. "Looking back, I'm sure I never had a chance of mortally wounding the captain. He was so well trained I am sure he could have defended himself from such an incompetent attack. But that servant, Malchus, suddenly turned back to whisper something to the captain of the temple guards face to face, and instead of impaling the captain, the sword just cut off that servant's right ear."

Jeremiah was transfixed. He had never heard anything like this in any of the commentaries, but it made perfect sense. "So, Peter, the sword was in your right hand, and the servant suddenly turned in front of the captain. The servant actually had his back to you, which is the only way he could have been facing for you to cut off his right ear."

Peter laughed ruefully. "I'm sure a trained swordsman could have cut off any ear he chose, but I was just swinging at the captain, and that servant turned around just in time. If Jesus hadn't intervened, stepping forward to say that He was the one they wanted, and healing that servant's ear, they would have arrested all of us. Instead, the only one they arrested was Jesus. Do you remember Him saying 'put up your sword, for they who live by the sword will die by the sword'? In the middle of His arrest, He is still admonishing us from His wisdom, but we were too busy running away to think about what He was saying. We fled the scene, and you know the rest."

Peter fell silent, but Jeremiah was reminded of a mystery that had always intrigued him. "Peter, who was that young man, whose garment was taken by those who came to arrest Jesus? No one knows who he was."

"You mean the one who was wearing only a linen garment, and when those guards seized him, he fled naked, leaving his garment behind? That is only in the Gospel of Mark, but I believe our young John fits that description. Remember how hot it was that night? He had taken off his outer robe as we were praying – and napping, I admit it. We were all unprepared for what was about to happen – if we had known a crowd was going to arrest our Master that night, John would never have been caught like that."

Jeremiah laughed. Peter continued: "We all ran away – it was a wild area, full of trees and hollows in the hills – lots of hiding places. Someone must have grabbed up John's robe and given it to him; the next time we saw him, he was dressed as usual. I was focused on following our Master, and wound up in that courtyard denying Him. I guess the next time I saw John was near the cross –

he was with Mother Mary and Mary Magdalene. After our Master's death, when we saw that Joseph of Arimathea was taking care of His body, we all went back into town, staying wherever we were welcome. We knew we had to avoid being seen. I didn't even want to be with the other disciples, but John insisted I stay at the house where you saw us on that first Easter. But what I want you to remember now, is the story I told about Malchus."

They arrived at the House of Images, sat in the chairs, and the images began. Jeremiah saw Jesus leaving Bethany and heading for a place he had seen before.

"Is he going to Gethsemane?" Jeremiah was clearly excited. "We visited that on our tour. It was so beautiful. I remember there were roses, but they aren't mentioned in the Bible."

"Remember, Jeremiah, there are many things that were there, or that happened, but only the most important ones were recorded in the Bible. You will be seeing many things that have never been recorded, as John wrote in the last verses of his gospel."

Jeremiah watched as Jesus entered the garden and walked over to a large stone. He sank down, resting His back against the stone. Jeremiah noticed some darker marks on the stone, and as he was starting to ask Peter about them, the scene stopped.

"Jeremiah, those marks are the blood and sweat of Jesus from the night of His arrest nine days before. He was leaning against this very stone when He fell against it, injuring himself so that His blood mixed with His sweat, causing the blood stained sweat you have read about."

Jeremiah remembered the verses from Luke. "His sweat became like great drops of blood falling down on the ground."

Peter nodded. "He had already been sweating. We were all hot that night, but He was in such agony over His decision to surrender and begin those final days that the sweat was just pouring off Him. No wonder He slipped against the rock – I think He scraped His face on it, which would explain the blood while He was agonizing. None of us knew what He was going through that night – only Judas knew what was about to happen. It was only later that we realized he knew all about it at that last supper we had together."

The images shifted to show Jesus leaving the garden and walking past a courtyard toward the Temple steps. A man was standing on the steps, giving alms to the poor as they passed by. Peter pointed to him. "How do his ears look?" he asked.

Jeremiah peered closely. "Is this Malchus? His ears look great! I can't tell which one was cut off."

"Our Master does good work, Jeremiah. This was the last healing miracle that He did before His death and resurrection. And with that miracle He also made sure that the Temple guards would only arrest Him, and not go after His followers. By this healing act, Jesus almost certainly saved all our lives, not to mention the future ministry itself."

Jeremiah noticed the images were once again moving, and saw Jesus passing by Malchus, who didn't seem to recognize Jesus at all. Malchus was distributing alms to any who passed that way, but when he offered the money to Jesus, He shook His head and walked on. As Jesus walked toward the Sheep Gate, Malchus turned to one of the Temple guards and said, "That is the first time anyone has ever refused this money!" They both stared at Jesus, but soon turned back to their tasks.

"Now He is passing in front of the Pretoria next to the Temple," said Peter. Jeremiah had done enough research to know that was where Jesus was scourged. Several official looking men were standing around, as if they were about to be called to duty.

"Who are those men?" asked Jeremiah.

"The one in the best looking uniform is the centurion who said 'Truly this was the Son of God' as Jesus was dying on the cross." Jeremiah looked impressed, and Peter continued. "This centurion was also the one who confirmed to Pilate that Jesus was dead, and who helped to lower the body of our Lord, giving Him to Joseph of Arimathea and Nicodemus for burial in his new tomb carved from stone. The other ones are the men who won the clothes of Jesus when they cast lots for them."

Jeremiah looked at the men who had won the clothes. Their faces seemed to be shining with an inner glow or light. They had held the garments of the Son of God, and they would never be the same again. The robe was in the hands of the centurion, who was saying, "My daughter was sick, shivering with a fever for two nights. I covered her up with the robe, and her fever disappeared. She is back to normal!"

One of the other men said, "Tell about your neighbor!"

The centurion was happy to comply. "Ever since his wife died, my neighbor has never been the same. His speech was loud and erratic, and he was even foaming at the mouth. I didn't know if it would help, but I placed the robe on him. Immediately he changed – he was speaking like any other man. He looked me in the eyes, and thanked me for what I had done for him. I had done nothing – it was the robe of Jesus that had done it all. At the cross, when I said, 'Truly, this is the son of God,' I had no idea that His power would continue after His death."

"If that robe has healing powers," said one of the soldiers, "why don't we put it to more use? If we cut it up, we can let it cure many more people than it can right now."

The centurion spoke slowly, as if thinking things out. "This is not a magic robe," he said, finally. "The healing powers of this robe come from its owner, Jesus the Son of God. To cut it up feels as if we not treating it with the respect it, and its Owner, deserve. The robe will stay whole."

The soldiers grumbled a little, but the centurion outranked them all, and his word was final.

"Those three soldiers," said Peter, pointing them out, "also were the ones who scourged Him before He was crucified. They whipped Him, taunted Him, and crucified Him.

These soldiers were lounging about the courtyard. They, too, were waiting to be called to duty, but their attitude seemed completely different from the others. They seemed to be just passing time, scratching the dirt with sticks or snatching a quick nap. "I see the difference in the men," said Jeremiah, "but what does it mean?"

"These men did not touch the clothes of Jesus, or handle Him in a caring manner. For them, His trial and execution were just another day on the job. Today, as every day, they are just men waiting for orders. They don't care what the orders are, they just want to do the work and collect their pay. They didn't allow themselves to be changed by Jesus, and so they were not changed."

"They don't appear to take any notice of Jesus," said Jeremiah, watching Jesus pass by the soldiers. "They certainly would have noticed if H had been moving with His disciples."

"That is one of the reasons why He travelled alone for 40 days," said Peter.

"What is Jesus saying as He passes them?" Jeremiah leaned forward, but couldn't hear the quiet words.

"He is saying, 'Father, forgive them; for they do not know what they are doing.' He forgave them from the cross, and even on the other side of death He reaches out to forgive them."

Jeremiah was silent as he watched his Lord walk on, and then saw that He was heading toward a pool surrounded by five porches with marble columns. An elderly man was helping a child with a twisted foot toward the pool. Together they made their way into the churning pool of crystal clear water. Jeremiah stared at the man.

"Should I know that person?" he asked. "Is that the man Jesus healed by the pool, who couldn't get into the water to be healed?"

"Yes, that is the same man. He is now devoting his life to helping others get into the pool for healing. He works seven days a week." Peter waited for Jeremiah's response.

"But what about the Sabbath day? Won't he get into trouble if he is working on the Sabbath?"

Peter smiled. "Yes, he did get into trouble, but that didn't stop him. Since he was healed on a Sabbath day, he works so that others may also be healed on a Sabbath day, no matter how much the Temple priests and leaders condemn him. He tells everyone that since the Lord Jesus healed him on a Sabbath day, then why shouldn't he help others, in His holy name, on the Sabbath Day?"

Jeremiah looked at the man, obviously old but eager to help anyone get to the pool. "But Peter, he wasn't healed in the pool. He was healed by Jesus without getting into the pool."

"Right, Jeremiah, and the greater message in that healing was that it was faith and belief that is needed for healing, not some pool or special location. That is what we can take away from this story. But since this man was left here by Jesus, he began to work here, happy to have a way of making a living rather than begging for alms. Some of the people he helps are able to give him a little money in exchange, and his life is much better than when he was lame and begging."

Jeremiah noticed the images changing. Jesus was now on the outskirts of Jerusalem, walking toward a small house and garden. A beautiful young woman was drawing water from a nearby well, and Jesus walked up to her.

"That's the woman that Jesus saved from being stoned for adultery," said Peter. "Her name is Rachel."

Jeremiah remembered the story well. It was one of the many he used to preach about sins and forgiveness. The Pharisees had wanted to stone her to death for committing adultery, but Jesus stopped them by saying, 'He who is without sin should cast the first stone.' Since every man there had committed at least one sin, one by one they had dropped their stones and left. When Jesus asked her where her accusers were, had no man condemned her, she answered, 'no man, Lord.' Jesus had said to her that He did not condemn her, either, and to go and sin no more.

Jeremiah watched as Jesus asked Rachel for a drink of water. She drew up a fresh bucket and poured some into a small bowl, handing it to Him with a smile. As He drank, she looked at Him a second time, as if trying to remember something. She appeared to hesitate, then spoke, "Sir, you remind me of the rabbi who saved me from being stoned by the Pharisees."

Jesus finished drinking, and then responded, "Judge not, and you shall not be judged. Condemn not, and you shall not be condemned. Forgive, and you shall be forgiven by the grace of our heavenly Father."

Rachel seemed pleased with this extraordinary response, and ran to the man working in the garden of the nearby house. "Who is that?" Jeremiah wanted to know. "Is she still living in sin?"

Peter smiled. "No, that man is her husband – her new husband. Her original husband, the one who accused her of adultery, was happy to give her a divorce after no one had agreed to stone her to death. He was an unpleasant fellow, much older than she was, and he had a lot of influence with the Temple priests and leaders. His first wife had died, and he was wealthy enough to persuade Rachel's father to give his young daughter in marriage, for a sizeable marriage price. She was a beautiful young girl when he married her, but soon his verbal and physical abuse began to affect her – not only her looks, but also how she felt about herself."

"What a nightmare!" said Jeremiah.

Peter went on, "Her neighbor tried to be kind to her, but one thing led to another, and they were caught by her husband. He was not happy when the priests told him why they had been unable to stone her, and by that time he just wanted rid of the whole situation. He had taken his complaint to the priests, thinking that if she was stoned to death it would save him both the expense of a divorce and the annoyance of seeing her with his neighbor."

Jeremiah looked amazed. "So, who is her husband now?"

"She loved that man who had tried to be kind to her, and he loved her. Her new husband is actually the man with whom she had committed adultery. He had followed the crowd which wanted to stone Rachael to death – he was the only one without a stone in his hand. No one in that crowd knew who he was. When the crowd left, he moved away with them and stood where he could still see what was going on. When Jesus left her, she started to go back home, but he met her on the way and took her to his house. As soon as her husband gave her the divorce, they were married and moved to the outskirts of the city, away from that rich man's house. Look at them now. They are just like any young couple in love – and with a baby on the way."

Jeremiah listened to the couple. Rachel was saying, "I have seen a man who might have been the one who saved my life – our lives -- and paved the way for our happiness! Could this be the Messiah who was crucified by the same people who tried to kill me?"

Her husband said, "I did not see Him just now – but maybe He is! When I went to the marketplace today there were rumors that Jesus had been raised from the dead after dying on the cross and His body put in the tomb of a rich man. Some men from the Temple are spreading the news that the disciples came and stole the body in the middle of the night, but I don't put my trust in anyone who comes from the Temple these days."

Rachel nodded. "I think this is the same Jesus - resurrected!" They both hurried back to the well, but Jesus was gone.

The images shifted, and Jeremiah saw Jesus walking back toward the heart of Jerusalem. He stopped in front of a modest house and knocked on the door. As an older woman opened it wide,

Peter whispered to Jeremiah, 'She is Salome, the mother of James and John."

Salome stared at the man in front of her. Jeremiah could almost read her thoughts: her sons had told her about the risen Jesus, and how different He looked. Could this be that man? After a moment of silence, she spoke. "Who are you, sir?"

"Salome, you are correct in your thinking. I am Jesus. Your sons have spoken truly of me." He held out His hands. "See, the marks of the nails are still there. They are healing, but you can still see them."

She stared for a moment at His hands, and then pulled Him quickly inside. "They are still looking for You, and for all Your disciples," she said. "James and John are hiding at the home of a friend who is not connected with any of Your followers." She urged Him to be seated, and brought water for Him to bathe His head and feet. "But what can I do for you, our dearest friend and Master?"

"You are already doing it," said Jesus. "I need somewhere to rest, for the afternoon and perhaps for the night."

Salome jumped up. "I am honored that You would come to our little home," she said. "Please, let me prepare a place for You to sleep. I went to the marketplace this morning, so I can offer You fresh figs, and it will not take me long to prepare the fish and bread." She hurried out to the back room, and Jesus leaned back, closing His eyes.

As the images ended, Jeremiah turned to Peter. "So, this is the mother of the 'sons of thunder'– I never would have imagined this woman as their mother! She is so eager to help, whereas her sons were so eager to claim glory for themselves."

Peter laughed. "You cannot imagine how embarrassed they were about that argument getting into the gospels! Yes, James and John, the sons of Zebedee, whom Jesus called the 'sons of thunder' came to Jesus, and asked Him to grant them what they wanted. We were all taken aback by this, and at first wondered at Jesus' answer, but then realized He was letting this play out, seeing just how far they would go. When Jesus asked them what they wanted Him to do for them, the answer shocked us even more. We did not believe our ears! They wanted to sit with Jesus, one on each side, when He came into His glory."

Jeremiah laughed with Peter, who continued: "Of course, Jesus answered their demand with a question. It was His way. He told them they didn't know what they were asking, and then asked if they could drink the cup He drinks, and be baptized with the baptism He is baptized with. Naturally, they answered, 'we can' and for once Jesus agreed with them. He told them that indeed they would drink the cup and be baptized with the baptism, but that He was not the one assigning the seats in heaven. He said those places belong to those for whom they have been prepared."

"Did they really think that Jesus would say that they could sit with Him?" asked Jeremiah.

"James was always prone to talk before thinking" said Peter, "and John many times followed his lead – until he grew up a little more and began to realize his own spiritual gifts. But that is not our concern here. What is it you really wanted to know?"

Jeremiah looked a bit sheepish. "I am confused about their mother's name. I remember Salome dancing before Herod Antipas and asking for the head of John the Baptist. Surely she isn't this same woman."

Peter laughed. "No, of course they are not the same woman. I know it can be confusing with so many people with the same name. If you would like, we can discuss that on the way to your meditation place. I can answer your questions as we walk."

"The Salome you remember," said Peter as they walked through the heavenly city, "was the daughter of Herodias and her first husband, Philip, who was a son of Herod the Great, and the brother of Herod Antipas. Herodias divorced Philip, and was now married to Herod Antipas, but John the Baptist spoke up against this marriage, saying it was not right for Herod Antipas to take his brother Philip's wife. At the birthday feast of Herod Antipas (I know, too many Herods!) Salome danced to please the king. She did please him, and he said she could have anything she wanted, no matter what it was."

Jeremiah broke in. "Obviously Herod Antipas was expecting her to ask for gold or jewels or a villa on the coast. Even if the villa was owned by someone else, as the king, he could take it and give it to her. As the king, he was so rich he could give her any amount of gold or jewels from the treasury of the kingdom."

"I see you have done your research," said Peter. "But Herod Antipas wasn't counting on the cunning of Salome's mother, Herodias. If Salome had chosen for herself, she might have wanted something like those things you mention. But she was obedient to her mother, and her mother wanted John the Baptist killed. Herodias was still angry at John the Baptist for speaking out against her marriage to Herod Antipas, and she saw this as her golden opportunity to rid herself of his accusing mouth once and for all. She told her daughter to ask for the head of John the Baptist on a platter, and Herod Antipas had to give it to her. He had made the promise before all his guests at the feast, and so of course he had to honor her request."

"I think I remember reading that Herod Antipas did not want to kill John the Baptist, that he has taken a liking to the prophet."

"That is right, Jeremiah. He knew John the Baptist was a righteous and holy man. Herod Antipas liked to hear him talk, even when he didn't completely understand what he was hearing. Even though John spoke out against the marriage of Herod Antipas, he still protected him. But the king knew if he didn't keep his promise he would lose the support of all the guests at his feast, all those important people he needed to keep the kingdom running his way.

"Even as king, Herod Antipas knew that treachery could be around every corner. He had to have people he could trust around him. If his supporters thought he wouldn't keep his promises, how could they believe any promise he made to them? They might start supporting one of his rivals. He had to kill John the Baptist, even though he didn't want to."

"I had never considered the consequences Herod Antipas would have faced if he had refused her request," said Jeremiah, and suddenly he laughed. "Do you think he learned anything about telling young women they could have anything they wanted?"

Peter grinned. "I think rather he learned not to let young women confer with their conniving mothers before they answer the king. But really, Jeremiah, that matter is not what concerns us here. That is their story, not ours."

Jeremiah nodded. "The women shared a name, but that is all. Salome the mother of James and John followed our Lord all the way to His cross. She was one of the women who went to the tomb to anoint His body after the Sabbath. And now she is helping Him even after His resurrection, opening her home to Him." He looked up, surprised that they had arrived so quickly at the place of meditation. Jeremiah had been so focused on their conversation that he had noticed nothing about their journey.

Peter smiled and stopped on the path. "Rest here with your thoughts," he said, "and I will return when you are ready to continue with the next day's events."

Jeremiah sank down gratefully on the cushion. His mind went back to the images he had seen that day. Malchus, the Centurion, the bloody rock in the Garden of Gethsemane, Rachel with her family, and the two women both named Salome. There was much to think about, and Jeremiah closed his eyes in meditation.

Day 7: Saturday

Day 7: Saturday: Roman law applies to Roman citizens – Temple priests and keeping the peace in occupied Jerusalem – blind man healed at Siloam – Pharisees question him and his parents – he meets Jesus – as guide in Jerusalem

Jeremiah rose from his meditation cushion as Peter entered the pavilion by the lake. It was a lovely place for quiet thought, with the still waters before him, the stream sounding faintly in the distance, and the surrounding hills giving a sheltering sense of peace.

'It was good to have this space to meditate on the images,' thought Jeremiah. So much had happened that he welcomed the chance to rest, think, and absorb the teachings. It had taken a while to integrate some of the more difficult differences between these teachings and the lessons he had grown up with.

They approached the House of Images in silence, and as they sat down the images began. It was morning, and Jesus was leaving the house of Salome. She was urging Him to take a small bundle of food wrapped in cloth, and He took it with a smile. "Don't linger on the doorstep," she said, "You don't know who might be loitering about, ready to report to the Temple priests." Her eyes teared up, and Jeremiah realized she regarded Him as a son. She looked around; found the streets were clear and said, "Go along, now."

Jesus held her hands for one last moment, then turned and walked up the street. Salome looked out briefly to the right and left, then quietly closed the door.

"They really were afraid, weren't they?" asked Jeremiah. "I thought the Romans had laws – I know what they did to Jesus, but we consider them a civilized nation. Much of our legal system is based on theirs."

"Remember when Paul told the Romans who arrested him that he was a Roman citizen? And that his citizenship wasn't bought, but that he was born a Roman citizen?" Jeremiah nodded. "If you were a Roman citizen, the Roman laws protected you. If you were

71

not a citizen, you were not given the same treatment. Also, since Jerusalem was far from Rome, the rulers were able to take more liberties with the law. The senate wasn't there to witness any wrongdoing, and sometimes the authorities in Rome had so much to contend with locally that they had no time to concern themselves about their provinces so far away."

"But what about the Temple priests?" asked Jeremiah? "How could they justify hunting down the followers of Jesus? They hadn't done anything wrong."

"That's true, Jeremiah, but they were suspected of either stealing the body of Jesus or maybe even harboring the risen Jesus. Since the Temple priests were the local authority, the Romans worked with them when they needed to keep the peace. If you were a Roman in charge of this Jewish territory, who really didn't care about the locals one way or another, it wouldn't matter to you who was right or who was wrong. Your only concern would be to keep the peace without the hazard or expense of calling out the soldiers. Especially since many of these matters were based on a religion that was very strange to the people of Rome."

"It sounds as if everyone wanted things to keep calm. No rocking the boat," said Jeremiah. "Then Jesus started making waves by healing people, forgiving people, teaching things the priests found intolerable! No wonder they were so against Him."

"Would you like to see a good example of what you just said?" asked Peter. "Look at this."

The images began, and Jeremiah saw the dusty streets of Jerusalem. Near a crossroad sat a man with a rag tied around his eyes. Sometimes someone who passed by would throw a coin in his bowl, making a tinkling sound. The man would then call out something that Jeremiah thought was a blessing, or maybe just thanks. He watched this for a moment then saw a small group of men coming down the road. He recognized them as the disciples, with Jesus in the middle. They stopped before the blind man.

One of them said, "Teacher, look at this blind man. Who sinned, he or his parents, to make him be born blind?" Jeremiah thought they must have known the man for them to have known he was blind from birth and not from an accident of some kind.

"Neither," said Jesus, His voice a calming sea. "This happened to display the work of God in his life." He paused, and went on, mysteriously, "while it is day, we do the work of the One who sent Me. Night is coming, when no one can work. While I am here, I am the light of the world."

Jeremiah saw Him spit on the ground, make some mud, and put it on the young man's eyes. "Go," said Jesus to the man. "Wash in the Pool of Siloam." This action was enough to gather a crowd, and Jeremiah eagerly watched as the blind man was led to the pool, everyone jostling to be the one to help him. Jesus and the disciples trailed behind.

The pool was full of crystal clear water, and everyone watched the blind man reach down toward the water, cup a little in his hand, and begin to wash the mud from his eyes. The young man blinked and put up his hands to shade his eyes. For a minute no one knew what was happening. The man was looking at the water, his eyes growing wide in shock and joy. The water cleared, and Jeremiah could see the faces of Jesus and the young man, staring at each other in the reflecting water. They looked at each other for a long moment, and then Jesus slipped away. Slowly the man raised his face and turned to the crowd. He seemed to search for a moment, and then as his name was called by first one, then another, he responded with the person's name, recognizing them by voice. Each time he stared, as if trying to fix the combination of voice and face.

As the crowd realized what they were witnessing, they began to scatter, each one wanting to be the first to tell the news to their friends. "That's how the Pharisees knew about it," said Peter to Jeremiah. "You'll see the result of that in a moment." Jeremiah looked back at the images. The young man stood silently, closing and then opening his eyes as if to get his bearings. Jeremiah saw him turn and walk slowly away, closing his eyes at times as if he needed familiar clues to make his way home. A couple of men had stayed to help him, but he was eager to find his own way, to see Jerusalem and his own house for the first time.

The images traveled with him along his slow way home, and when he reached his house, he stopped at the door, hesitating to enter. All at once he pushed the door and slipped in. There was a moment of silence, and then Jeremiah heard the cries of the man's parents. There was a bustle in the house, and then the door opened wide, the young man leading his parents outside, pointing to everything and describing it.

The noise attracted the neighbors, who crowded around. "Isn't this the same man who used to sit and beg?" someone asked.

"No, that was someone else, it only looks like him."

But the young man had heard, and stood before them. "Yes, I am that man."

"Then how did your eyes regain their sight?" One of the neighbors sounded as if he suspected a trick of some kind.

"The man they call Jesus made some mud and put it on my eyes," said the young man. "He told me to go to Siloam and wash. So I went and washed, and then I could see."

"Where is this man?" Someone else wanted to know, but the young man shook his head.

"I don't know," he said. "I saw Him at the pool, but He left as everyone else was talking to me."

His mother interrupted them "The Sabbath is almost over, and our meal is prepared. Please, son, come in and eat." Slowly the crowd of neighbors dispersed.

The images showed night falling, and then the beginning of a new day. It was very early in the morning when Jeremiah saw some of the man's neighbors gather before the house. Pharisees from the Temple were with them. The Pharisees nodded, as if confirming a command, and one of the neighbors knocked on the door. The young man's father opened it, but it was the young man who strode out into the midst of the crowd.

"Come with us to the Temple," said the leader of the Pharisees. The man looked back at his mother standing in the doorway, and nodded to her reassuringly. She reached for her husband's hand, and together they moved forward to join him in the crowd. They all walked back toward the Temple, in a silence that told Jeremiah the Pharisees had expected some trouble and were disappointed not to find it.

At the courtyard of the Pharisees, the neighbors shoved the man forward and explained what had happened. Even though Jeremiah knew the story, he was taken by surprise when the crucial element turned out to be that the healing had occurred on the Sabbath. This was a miracle! But that seemed to take second place to the laws concerning what you could and could not do on the Sabbath, the day of rest. Jeremiah had always thought it was a strange argument, but these fellows seemed to be taking it all very seriously.

"How has this happened?" said the one who seemed to be in charge. "Tell me exactly what you did."

"The man called Jesus put mud on my eyes. He told me to wash," said the young man. "I washed, and now I see." He was calm, but his parents were clearly nervous, gripping each other's hands tightly.

"This man Jesus is not from God, for He does not keep the Sabbath," said one of the Pharisees.

Another one disagreed. "How could a sinner do such miraculous signs?"

"Pharisees were the lawyers of that era," whispered Peter to Jeremiah, who suppressed a laugh. He knew plenty of lawyers who were eager to argue about anything, anytime, anywhere.

Finally, they turned back to the young man. "What do you have to say about this man Jesus? It was your eyes which regained their sight."

"He is a prophet," said the young man. His father winced, knowing his son was just making the matter worse, but unable to stop him. Suddenly the Pharisees were dragging him and his wife forward.

"Is this your son?" they demanded. "Is this the one you say was born blind? How is it that now he can see?"

His father spoke up, "This man is our son, and we know he was born blind, but how he can see now, or who gave him back his sight, we do not know." More cautiously, he continued, "Ask him. He is of age; he will speak for himself." His wife pressed his hand gratefully. Jeremiah remembered that anyone who claimed that Jesus was the Messiah would be put out of the synagogue.

The Pharisees argued with each other a while longer and suddenly called for the young man again. "Give glory to God," they said. "We know this man Jesus is a sinner." But the man was stubborn.

"Whether He is a sinner or not, I don't know. One thing I do know: I was blind but now I see." His parents were in agony, but he stood tall, looking each of the Pharisees straight in the eyes.

They asked him again, "What did he do to you? How did he give sight back to your eyes?"

"I have told you already," the young man replied, "but you did not listen. Why do you want to hear it again?" With a grin, he added, "Do you want to become His disciples, too?"

The Pharisees shouted insults at him. The loudest one was heard to say, "You are this fellow's disciple! We are disciples of Moses! We know that God spoke to Moses, but as for this fellow, we don't even know where He comes from."

The young man was calm. "Now, that is remarkable," he said. Jeremiah wondered if the Pharisees could detect the sarcasm. "You don't know where He comes from, yet He gave me my sight. We all know that God does not listen to sinners. He listens to the godly man who does His will. Nobody has ever heard of anyone blind from birth regaining his sight. If this man were not from God, He could do nothing."

This reasoning was so logical, and so well put, that Jeremiah was surprised that not even one Pharisee agreed. The young man was arguing circles around them, but they refused to acknowledge it. "You were steeped in sin at birth; how dare you lecture us!" At a gesture from the one in charge, the younger Pharisees moved in, grasping him and bodily moving him out of the courtyard, the parents following.

It was a smaller group that went through the town on their way back to the house. The young man and his parents were first, with a few neighbors trailing behind. A couple of Pharisees followed, as if looking for more trouble. On their way back, they saw Jesus standing beside the road. The young man went up to Him expectantly, and Jesus asked, "Do you believe in the Son of Man?"

The young man was hopeful. "Who is He, sir? Tell me so I may believe in Him."

Jesus said, "You have seen Him; in fact, He is the one speaking with you now."

The young man said, "Lord, I believe." His parents watched in amazement as their son fell to the ground and worshiped this very ordinary looking man.

Jesus looked around at the little crowd and said, "I have come into the world for judgment that those who do not see may see; and that those who see may become blind."

The Pharisees on the edge of the crowd called out, "What, are we blind too?"

Jesus looked directly at them and said, "If you were blind you would not be guilty of sin, but now that you claim you can see, your guilt remains."

As the images faded Jeremiah turned to Peter. "Wow! Those Pharisees! How can anyone be so bullheaded? And the power they had. Those parents were so afraid!"

"Yes, Peter, and now can you see why all the disciples and followers were so careful to hide themselves after the resurrection? The Pharisees and the Temple priests could throw anyone out of the synagogue. They had that power, and they used it often enough to keep everyone in line. If someone was thrown out of the synagogue, they were effectively ostracized from the community. No one would trade with them, or hire them to work. Eventually they would have to move to a different area so that they could start a new life."

Jeremiah was silent as he thought about the difficulties of living in that time and place. He was startled when the images began again.

"Does this fellow look familiar?" Peter was pointing to a young man leading a party of travelers into the city.

Jeremiah peered intently at the images. The young man was happy, laughing and chatting with the head of the small group. Their route seemed to meander about the city, but Jeremiah noticed it was avoiding major groups of Pharisees, Temple guards, and soldiers. The guide seemed to know just how to dodge anyone who might detain the group on their journey. Suddenly Jeremiah said, "That's the young man who was blind from birth! And now he is a guide?"

"Jerusalem was a place of pilgrimage for many Jews," said Peter. "Simple folk from the country were often taken advantage of by soldiers or the ones in charge at the Temple. Word has gotten out that our young man is an excellent guide. Everything he does is in compliance with the law, so the Temple priests and Pharisees cannot find fault with him. His clients are happy to have a guide that knows how to spot trouble and evade it. His reward is a handsome one, and he and his parents are all doing very well."

"Look, there's Jesus!" Jeremiah pointed to a weary figure sitting on a boulder, watching the small party pass by. The young man looked at Jesus for a moment, almost paused, but continued on his way. Jesus smiled at the group, which included an old man on a donkey and some boys chasing each other around a cart piled high with rolled up bedding, bundles of food, and some young birds in a cage. The older woman bringing up the rear shouted at the boys and waved her staff as if driving a flock of errant sheep. The smile on Jesus' face flashed into a grin, and Jeremiah found himself laughing.

Peter laughed, too. "Joy happens," he said, and Jeremiah laughed even harder.

The images shifted to follow Jesus as He walked slowly toward a house not far from the palace. Jeremiah looked a little alarmed. "Isn't this a little close? Wouldn't He be safer a little more out of town?"

"I think you would call it hiding in plain sight," said Peter. "One of the followers of Jesus was Joanna, who was the wife of Chuza, Herod's steward. Chuza was a man of position and wealth, and did not concern himself with what his wife did with her portion of the household money and goods. It is to their home that Jesus is going now."

"I remember verses about women ministering to Jesus out of their substance, but I didn't realize some of the women were really wealthy," said Jeremiah. "This is a large home! Aren't they afraid some of the servants would talk?" He watched as Jesus went carefully to a side door. There was a whispered conversation and Jesus entered, the door closing silently behind Him.

"He stayed safely there all night. Joanna had several rooms of her own, that her husband and his servants never entered. And, remember, His appearance was so altered that even if He had been seen, He might not have been recognized."

"Things were certainly complicated," said Jeremiah. "And wasn't Joanna with the other women on that first Easter Sunday, when they went to the tomb?"

Peter nodded. "She was the one who provided everything they needed to finish the anointing of the body for what they thought was its final resting place. Those things were expensive, and not easy to buy on such short notice. Joanna had the contacts and the funds they needed. She was a wonderful blessing to our little community."

The images faded and Jeremiah looked over at Peter. "This is an amazing experience – and very educational! What comes next?"

"I think you'll like the next day," said Peter.

Day 8: Sunday

Day 8: Sunday: Why the disciples waited instead of going to meet Jesus in Galilee as instructed by Jesus – Jesus meets with 12 disciples – John says Thomas is not a doubter

"It is the eighth day," said Peter. "You will be watching a meeting that was not only important, but also very emotional, for all of us. First, however, we'll travel back a little so you can see the importance and the emotions building up to this."

The images showed Jesus and the disciples finishing a meal and then walking out into the night. As they walked up a hill to a grove of olives, Jeremiah realized they were headed for the Garden of Gethsemane, and that this was the night that Jesus surrendered to the Temple guards. Although it was clear that Jesus was weighed down by His decisions, He still looked more like the healthy Jesus who had healed the blind man than the resurrected Jesus tormented by His wounds.

Jesus was quoting from what Jeremiah knew as the Old Testament, talking about everyone being offended because 'I will smite the shepherd, and the sheep of the flock will be scattered,' but then He added His own words, "But after I am raised up, I will go before you into Galilee."

The images shifted to show the early morning scene of the first Sunday. Jesus was telling Mary Magdalene, "Go and tell Peter and the disciples that I ascend to my Father and your Father, to my God and to your God. Tell them to meet me in Galilee."

The image shifted again to follow the women who had been running after Simon Peter and John. Once again he watched the women see Jesus, and then throw themselves on the ground, worshipping. Then Jesus said, "Do not be afraid; go tell my brothers that they should go into Galilee, and there they will see me."

The images stopped and Peter said, "What does Jesus keep repeating here? What are we supposed to be doing?"

"He keeps saying for you to go to Galilee," said Jeremiah, "But I know the Bible says you meet Him in Jerusalem, in that little room. I saw those images from the first night, and if I remember correctly, this next meeting is also in Jerusalem. Why didn't you go to Galilee? What was going on?"

"You saw how we avoided the Temple guards and the Romans," said Peter. "That was part of it. Also, remember, on that first day when we met with Jesus, Thomas wasn't there. We couldn't convince him to go – he wasn't going to make that long trip for nothing, and we wouldn't leave without him. Thomas said, 'Until I see His wounds, I will not travel to Galilee.' The third part was sheer exhaustion, both physical and emotional – we were all on what you would call an emotional roller coaster." He grinned at Jeremiah's expression at hearing such a modern term from his ancient friend.

"We had seen our master -- our dearest friend -- taken, tortured, and put to death. I had denied Him three times. One of our own had sold Him out – we saw later how that was part of the plan but at the moment we felt that Judas had betrayed not only Jesus, but all of us. We were all utterly miserable. We hadn't slept or eaten the night of His trial or the day of His execution, and I really can't remember much about that Sabbath day at all." Peter paused, and then went on.

"And then on Sunday the women tell us that the Master has risen and they have seen Him, but of course we can't believe them – we don't dare. We can't let our hopes rise up if they are to be destroyed all over again. We couldn't take it. And then I saw Jesus, with my own eyes! He forgave me and called me Peter! And that night He appeared to us! The light has overcome the darkness. Jesus has overcome His own death. Suddenly everything is possible. And then He is gone again. When will He come back? Should we go to Galilee or wait for Him here? What if we go and He comes back to this room? No one knows where He is. Confusion falls, but at least it is a hopeful confusion." He looked at Jeremiah. "Can you see how exhausted we all were -- to go emotionally from being in the deepest hole to being over the moon with holy joy? Who could eat? Who could sleep? We really didn't know what to do next."

As Peter paused for breath, Jeremiah said slowly, "I guess we do rush though that time when we preach about it. We are so focused on the resurrection that we don't pay much attention to what you were all going through that week."

"It was an amazing time," said Peter. "You can just imagine the arguments. Of course the sons of thunder wanted to set out for Galilee right away, but we talked them out of that plan. The saner heads among us realized we needed to rest, and replenish our energy. Maybe I slept that whole week, I really don't remember. Finally, we agreed that if we did not see Jesus again within a week that we would move to the shores of the Sea of Tiberias. Most of us were fishermen, you remember, and this city life was getting to us – especially since we had to stay away from the Temple guards and Roman soldiers. We needed to get back to familiar territory, back to the sea, which of course, was in Galilee. His instructions at the time were just to go to Galilee – He hadn't said exactly where. If we went to the sea, we would at least be in the area."

"You probably were also waiting for those Temple priests and Roman guards to stop their search," said Jeremiah. "Surely if nothing else happened and everyone was lying low, the excitement would die down and you could all slip quietly away from Jerusalem."

"Yes, Jeremiah, that was part of it, also. We had been helping Jesus in His ministry, and now it looked as if it really had not ended. We didn't know exactly what was going to happen, but we didn't think us being held in prison was what Jesus had in mind. He had been very careful not to have us arrested that evening, so we thought He had something planned for us as free men."

"That makes sense," said Jeremiah.

"Most of us met for prayer, supplication and dinner each night," said Peter. "I do remember that much. We thought that since Jesus had come to us while we were at dinner, it would be a good idea to keep meeting for dinner. Also, we could report if any of us had seen Him during the day. We found out later where He had been staying in the city, but at that time, no one knew where He was. On that Sunday evening, He had eaten supper at the house of Joanna. We were all eating at that room where you saw us before." At his words, the images appeared.

83

Day 8: Sunday

Jeremiah saw that same room, with the same men crowded around the table. Automatically he counted, and came up with 12. No one seemed to be especially friendly toward Judas, but at least he was here. And the disciple that had been missing before was here: Thomas. They were finishing their meal and continuing their discussion.

"It has been a week," said James, the older son of thunder, "so tomorrow we leave for Galilee." Heads nodded in agreement, and Simon Peter took charge. "We haven't seen much military or Temple presence in the streets for the last couple of days, but we don't want to stir anything up now. We should travel in small groups, two or three together at the most, and leave at different times. Once we are far enough from Jerusalem, we can travel together – I suggest outside Bethany on the way to Ephraim." He looked at the sons of thunder. "I know you are impatient to leave, so why don't you start off first?" James and John looked pleased, and the other disciples shifted around the table, forming the small groups of two or three. Judas was with Simon Peter. They were deep in their plans when Jeremiah saw the door quietly open and an emaciated figure enter.

"Peace be with you," said Jesus, and everyone turned to stare at Him. Their startled confusion seemed to make more sense now that Jeremiah had seen the images of Jesus in His ministry with them, as hearty and healthy as any of the disciples. The man he saw now was obviously suffering from some physical ailment. He was so thin that Jeremiah wondered if He was eating at all, or if the food was somehow unable to nourish His body.

After a shocked silence, one of the men rose and Jeremiah knew he must be Thomas. Jesus held up His hands and said, "Look at the marks from the nails. Put your hand out and feel the spear wound in My side. Have faith; believe."

Without moving from where he was, Thomas cried, "My Lord and my God!" with such fervor and love that Jeremiah's eyes teared up a little.

"Thomas, you believe because you have seen Me." Jesus stretched out His arms to encompass the entire room, perhaps the entire world. "Blessed are they who have not seen, but who believe." The men were silent, and in this silence Jesus walked out of the room. The disciple nearest the door saw Him disappear into the darkness of the Jerusalem streets. It was close to midnight.

"He's gone again!" shouted James. John looked a little uncomfortable at his brother's outburst, but James was not finished – now he turned to Thomas. "He just invited Thomas to see His hands and feet! Did He come all this way just to speak to your doubt?" Thomas looked down, clearly uncomfortable, but the young John spoke up.

"Did you not hear the greater message? How many countless others will believe who have not seen? How far will His ministry reach? How far will we go to spread His message?" James backed down a little and John continued. "You speak of his doubt, but I see a man so broken by love that he dares not believe lest it not be true and the world would then turn truly black with sorrow." James sat down with an air of resignation, and Jeremiah realized that this scene had probably been repeated dozens of times, with different themes and messages, as John grew older and began to develop his own identity, separate from his brother.

John was on fire now. "Do you not remember when we were debating on returning to Bethany with Mary and Martha, when Lazarus was dead? We all knew the authorities were lying in wait for us, and that we might be stoned, at the very least. While the rest of us were trying to talk Jesus into leaving them all behind, Thomas spoke up. He said, 'Let us go also, so we may die with Him.' Do you remember how he shamed us all with his loyalty and love?" John looked around the table. "I wish to hear no more about the doubts of Thomas."

"He didn't get his wish, did he?" said Jeremiah. "But he wrote it in his gospel!"

"John was always focused on the greater lesson. He was the youngest, but he seemed to grasp the inner truth much quicker than any of us. It is true he kept that part about the doubts of Thomas in his account, but he thought it had to be there to bring the greater message that Jesus shared with us that night."

"Maybe we talk so much about 'doubting Thomas' because we have so many doubts ourselves," said Jeremiah. "We tend to put the disciples on pedestals, and talking about the doubts of Thomas brings him back down to our level."

"Well said, Jeremiah. "Perhaps you have a touch of John about you, also, discerning the inner truth so quickly."

If Jeremiah had been back on earth he would have felt a little embarrassed by the praise, as if was not worthy of such words, but here he merely felt both grateful and humble. All wisdom is from the Lord, he remembered. Then he recalled the image of Jesus slipping through the door into the dark streets. "Where did Jesus go that night? Back to the home of Joanna? And what did the rest of you do that night?"

"Jesus traveled on to the Garden of Gethsemane that night, passing through the East Gate," said Peter. "Everything had quieted down enough that He could pass through the city untroubled. We spent some time in that room finishing our plans and ended the evening with prayer. That night we slept in the upper room. We had to get enough rest so that we could travel the next day."

Day 9: Monday

Day 9: Monday: Jesus rests in the Garden of Gethsemane – a medical expert tells Jeremiah about the wounds of Jesus

"This is day 9, Monday," said Peter.

The images showed Jesus resting by the same stone where He had prayed before His arrest. His hair looked damp, as if He had washed in the stream.

"Why does He still look so run down?" asked Jeremiah. "If anything, He looks worse than ever. Is He curled up in pain?" Jeremiah looked more carefully at the thin figure. "And His weight loss! I've seen cases like this in our hospital missions when we visit severe trauma patients. Sometimes we can't even recognize them. Is this what is happening here?"

"That is right, Jeremiah. His body is changing for the worse every day. Actually, if you would like a more medical assessment of His condition, I could bring in an expert to help us."

Jeremiah looked troubled. "I want to know what is happening to His body, but at the same time, it pains me to see Him in such pain."

Peter nodded. "I know. But remember, what you are seeing happened two thousand years ago, and He suffered only a brief time in comparison with His life here in heaven."

"It would probably be good for me to see what is wrong with Him as part of my education, part of what I need to bring back to earth," said Jeremiah slowly. "Please, bring in your expert."

The door of the House of Images opened, and a man walked in, with a group of people trailing after him. The expert was tall and distinguished looking, and Jeremiah thought he looked like a medical scientist, or a surgeon emerging out of an operating room. Everyone had on their white coats, as if they were all doctors making the rounds in a hospital.

Peter spoke, "Jeremiah, may I present Dr. Cooley, the world's renowned heart surgeon. He was an expert in chest, lungs and heart injuries and diseases of all kinds and he can tell you all about these injuries. He has joined us after healing thousands of sick and training hundreds of healers under the direction of our Lord Jesus Christ. With him are many physicians who trained under him. Dr. Cooley, this is the Reverend Jeremiah, a temporary visitor here. He will be taking this information back to earth."

The doctor bowed and said, "It is always a pleasure to meet visitors to our kingdom. I understand you are looking at the condition of Jesus after His resurrection, before He ascended."

"Yes," said Jeremiah. "I have visited with patients in hospitals, and have learned something of how injuries can affect the body, but of course none of my patients have had these exact kinds of injuries."

"Since He did not undergo a medical examination at the time," said the doctor, "our findings are still on the speculative side. Jesus considers this not to be of great importance, but I know people in your time are used to information being available on anything, at any time."

The doctor stood to the side of the seated men, and the other physicians moved slightly behind and to the other side of Dr. Cooley. Images of the Roman soldier spearing Jesus on the cross came to view. The doctor pointed to a wound in the front side of the chest. He also displayed a drawing of a spear entering the body (see figure 1).

"This would be the type of wound that Jesus had," said Dr. Cooley. "The spear entered the right side of the chest cavity of the body, cutting the nerves, ribs, blood vessels, and muscles on its path. The cracks that are shown on the ribs happened after death, so the prophecy of a bone not being broken still holds true. The tip of the spear nicked the heart wrapping, which was surrounded by fluid due to the scourging. The medical name for this fluid around the heart is traumatic pericardial effusions."

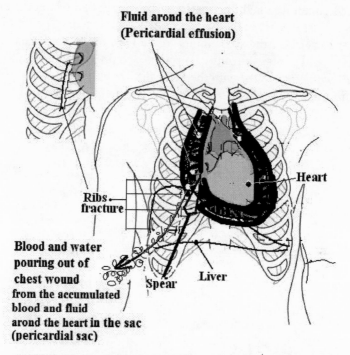

**Fluid arond the heart
(Pericardial effusion)**

Heart

**Ribs
fracture**

**Blood and water
pouring out of
chest wound
from the accumulated
blood and fluid
arond the heart in the sac
(pericardial sac)**

Spear

Liver

Diagram shows spearing of Jesus' chest to confirm His death
on the cross, and the blood and water fluid around the heart
gushing out of Jesus' chest as the spear is withdrawn.

Jeremiah was fascinated by the images before him, as if a
medical textbook had come to life. As the doctor spoke, each type
of injury was illustrated in the images before him, in a wonderful 3-
D presentation.

The doctor continued, "The spear also probably nicked the
great blood vessel, contributing to the blood and water flowing out
of the chest cavity as the spear was pulled out by the Roman
soldier. This was accurately described by Apostle John who
witnessed the event at the foot of the cross and reported, 'However
one of the soldiers pierced his side with a spear, and immediately
blood and water came out.' John 19:34"

Jeremiah watched, fascinated, as the images displayed the exact actions just described by the doctor, who continued: "The tip of the spear most likely did some injury to the food pipe (esophagus) also. This could cause an infection that would bring difficulty in swallowing associated with the fever that Jesus appears to have (see figure 2)."

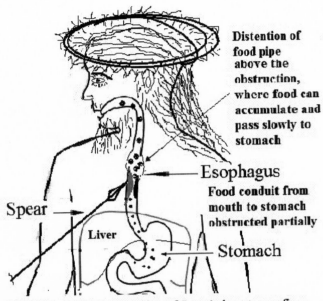

Distention of food pipe above the obstruction, where food can accumulate and pass slowly to stomach

Esophagus
Food conduit from mouth to stomach obstructed partially

Spear

Liver

Stomach

Diagram shows the spearing of Jesus' chest to confirm His death on the cross, resulting in an injury to the food passage to the stomach. Swallowed food can accumulate above the obstruction, forming a distention

"When Jesus eats, you see Him taking small bites, always followed by sips of water. Swelling has reduced the working size of the esophagus. The area of the pipe that the food travels down would have shrunk, either from swelling of the injured area of the esophagus or swelling from an infection in the middle of the chest cavity (mediastinitis). There was probably bleeding around the food pipe (esophagus), which would also put pressure on it."

Jeremiah stared at the images, trying to take it all in. "Let me see if I have it right," he said. "The spear definitely caused internal bleeding and an infection that is causing the fever. If the spear nicked the food pipe – the esophagus – that injury might be causing the swelling that causes Him to eat slowly, with small bites. The infection from the spear wound might be causing the swelling, and the infection in the chest cavity might be putting pressure on the esophagus."

"That is right," said the doctor. "You see the bleeding has stopped due to the clotting of the blood around the injured area. He is eating so slowly, and in such small quantities, that the nourishment is not enough to sustain normal body weight. In other words, He's not taking in as many calories as He is using just to live. That is why He is getting so thin. He is gradually wasting away. Note the infected pus discharging from the chest wound. The wounds in His hands and feet are healing nicely, as well as the injuries to His head from the crown of thorns." Dr. Cooley looked at Jeremiah a moment, "Do you have any more questions?" he asked.

"Actually, two questions," said Jeremiah. "First, how can He use His feet and hands with those wounds? How can He walk long distances - almost 150 miles, and prepare breakfast at the Sea of Tiberias? And second, I remember hearing something about perhaps His heart being ruptured."

"Jeremiah, those are excellent questions," said Dr. Cooley. "For the first, here is the image of His hands and feet. As you can see, the nails entered the middle of the wrist, through the small bones, and entered the feet through the tarsal bones in front of the ankle joint. The nails penetrated between the bones. There are hardly any large nerves or blood vessels at that site. The nails in the wrists pushed the large nerve and tendons away, and the nails in the feet did likewise. After the nails were pulled out, there was blood clotting with complete healing in less than 7 to 10 days. For the second question, no, there was no rupturing of the heart itself."

"Was there any damage to the bones?" asked Jeremiah. "I remember the scripture about no bone was broken."

The doctor pointed to a section of the image. "As the nails entered the middle of the wrists and feet, they did crack some small bones, due to physical force and the movement of the body up and down on the cross for three hours, using these points as a fulcrum, but there was no bone that broke into separate pieces. The long bones in the legs and arms were not broken in the middle, as prophesied. Jesus regained all His functions of His hands and feet very early after the resurrection. Do you have any more questions?"

"No, sir," said Jeremiah. "This has been a wonderful explanation of the injuries suffered by our Lord Jesus. Thank you." He rose and bowed to the doctor. It felt only right, as the doctor had bowed to them at their introduction.

The doctor bowed to them, and left the building, followed by his group of physicians. The images returned to Jesus resting in the Garden of Gethsemane.

Jeremiah found it was difficult for him to see Jesus suffering, especially now that he had more of an idea of what was happening in His body. He had sung many songs about the suffering Jesus, but none of them had affected him like this image. After a few moments he sighed and turned to Peter.

"Ready for another day?" asked Peter gently, and the images shifted again.

Day 10: Tuesday

Day 10: Tuesday: Jesus visits His tomb – Jeremiah sees Jesus brought to His tomb after His death – Temple priests and leaders ordered others to work on the Sabbath – Jesus at the cross –at His touch the title "King of the Jews" falls down – Jesus visits Joseph of Arimathea

"This is Tuesday, day 10 of the resurrection," said Peter.

Jeremiah saw Jesus rising from His place by the rock and splashing cold water from the stream on His face. Even though He was alarmingly thin, the nail wounds in His feet and hands were almost healed, with only a scab at the site of entry and exit. The wounds on His feet were healing faster than the ones on His hands, he observed, which was fortunate, as Jesus seemed determined to travel this day.

Jesus left the Garden of Gethsemane, heading north toward His tomb. When He reached the tomb, He knelt down, brushing the small stones and bits of mortar from the threshold before peering inside. Then He stood, looking around until He saw the round stone that had been rolled away from the entrance to the tomb. He gave a little nod, and then walked slowly toward His place of crucifixion.

Jeremiah sat entranced. Peter turned to him and said, "Would you like to see how they brought Jesus to the tomb after He died?" At Jeremiah's look of gratitude, the images changed again.

It was the same garden tomb, but it was late in the afternoon. The sun was about to set. Three men who Jeremiah knew must be Joseph of Arimathea, Nicodemus, and the young disciple John were carrying a body wrapped in linen. Mother Mary, Mary Magdalene, and some other women followed them. Joseph and Nicodemus carried the body of Jesus into the tomb, and placed it in the stone niche at the side of the tomb. Jeremiah knew they were preparing the body according to the Jewish rites, but he didn't really want to see any of those details, and Peter spared him those images.

"Did you notice that only Joseph and Nicodemus entered the tomb?" asked Peter. "John couldn't do it. He was completely in a state of shock. He was scarcely able to help them carry the body. Mother Mary and Mary Magdalene also did not enter. That was not the last view that a mother should have of her son."

"I agree," said Jeremiah, who had helped many mothers through family tragedies. "But who are these women coming up now? Some of them look familiar."

"They are those same women who looked after Jesus and all of us, the women who were angels but came to earth to help Jesus," said Peter. He laughed. "See how they are preventing Joseph of Arimathea from rolling the stone? Only angels would have the audacity to give an order to a man of this time and place."

Jeremiah watched as the women entered the tomb, obviously checking that everything about the final placement and burial had been done correctly, according to the traditions. They nodded to Joseph as they left the tomb, and he rolled the stone over the opening. Slowly the group walked back down the path to the town. Jeremiah could smell the scent of the Passover festivities and the see the smoke of cooking fires in the air as the group walked down the street, crossing the Pretoria and passing the entrance to the Temple to the south of town.

"The next day, on our Sabbath, the chief priests and Pharisees came to Pilate and demanded that the tomb be made secure, so that the disciples could not steal Him away," said Peter. "Remember He said He would rise after three days. If the disciples could steal the body, they could make all kinds of outrageous claims and the troublemakers could become even stronger. Pilate agreed, and gave permission for them to secure the tomb as they wished. This was done, and a watch was set."

"Wait a minute," said Jeremiah. "You said something I've never noticed before. It was the Sabbath, but the Temple priests and leaders sent masonry workers to seal the tomb, and ordered Temple guards to guard the tomb. Weren't they breaking the Sabbath laws in sending these men to work there?"

"Well done, Jeremiah! These were the same people who accused Jesus of working on the Sabbath, and they are doing the same thing themselves! It seems they only follow the law when it is convenient for them; when it is inconvenient they break it, and make others break it also. Can you imagine how the masonry workers and the temple guards felt as they were asked to work on the Sabbath, especially at the Passover festival? They had no choice but to obey their Temple leaders, but you can imagine how they felt, what they were thinking. Also, that was their only day to rest. They had a full week ahead of them. Remember, there were no weekends back then, no 40-hour work weeks. They worked from sunup to sundown and beyond, six days a week, and for many the Sabbath was a blessing."

"I have wondered about that," said Jeremiah. "They needed a day of rest, certainly, but there were so many rules about exactly what defined work, and what was too much work. We were taught that the Pharisees, as the lawyers of the Jewish nation, made sure the law was so important and difficult to understand that their own importance and place in the community was assured."

"You have been well taught," said Peter. "Are you ready to see what happens next?" At Jeremiah's nod, the images began again.

Jesus was walking toward the place of His execution. The crosses on either side of His had been removed, but His cross was still standing, the sign with the words "King of the Jews" still hanging on the top. As Jesus touched the cross, the sign fell down to the ground.

Jeremiah turned to Peter and said, "This seems really significant. What does it mean?"

Peter studied Jeremiah carefully. "What do you think it means?" he said.

Jeremiah thought for a minute, and said, "Perhaps two things. I know at the time your ministry was only to the Jewish nation. You were forbidden to have anything to do with gentiles. They were considered unclean – not as bad as lepers, but close. But now we know that Jesus died and was resurrected for everyone. Was that part of it?"

Peter nodded, and Jeremiah went on. "I'm not sure, but was part of it the idea of what Jesus as king was all about?"

"Yes, Jeremiah. There were certain expectations attached to the word Messiah. The Jewish people had come to believe that the promised Messiah would come as a king, vanquishing their enemies with a sword and sitting on a golden throne."

"I think most of us now understand that Jesus is the king of our hearts, not of our nation. He did not come to earth to sit on a golden throne, but to live in us, helping us conquer our temptations and take away our sins." Jeremiah stopped, and then went on. "We have been told that so many times that I think it is sometimes difficult to realize how different it was back then."

"Our country was occupied by Rome," said Peter. "We were supposed to hold ourselves separate from gentiles, yet they were our rulers, our oppressors. They had all the power, and cared only for collecting the taxes and seeing that we caused as little disturbance as possible. You can see how popular the idea of a Messiah who would smite our enemies and raise up an army victorious over our oppressors, would be. When it turned out that Jesus was talking about an entirely different kingdom, not an earthly kingdom, it was difficult to grasp. We were so conditioned to think otherwise."

"This is a wonderful visual image to remind me of what Jesus as king was all about," said Jeremiah.

"Are you ready to see where Jesus goes next?" asked Peter. Jeremiah nodded and the images resumed, showing Jesus walking through a small village toward a large home. The house and grounds were beautiful. The well-manicured garden was blooming with spring flowers. A side yard was filled with date and fig trees in full bloom. Jeremiah wondered whose house this was. "It is the home of Joseph of Arimathea," said Peter. Jeremiah remembered Joseph had been a member of the Sanhedrin – the Jewish ruling body who opposed Jesus -- so he had to keep his loyalty to Jesus a secret.

A servant opened the door to Jesus, but he was not invited in. After some discussion the servant disappeared back into the house, and presently Joseph himself came out. He looked intently at the thin man on his doorstep, as if trying to match the person before him with the memories of the man he knew.

Suddenly Joseph's face lit up. "Master!" he cried. "But you should not be standing outside where they could see you! Quickly, come in." The images followed Jesus as He entered, walking with Joseph through a wide passage and then into a beautiful courtyard.

A pool of water gave a hint of refreshing moisture to the air, and a profusion of flowers and greenery spoke equally of Joseph's love for beauty and his ability to provide the water to let them grow so abundantly in this arid land.

Joseph urged Jesus to sit in a large chair, spent a few moments arranging the many cushions for his guest, and then called for his servants. "Quickly, bring water to drink and to bathe His feet. Prepare a meal, but do not use too many spices. Prepare the food as you do when we visit the sick."

Jesus smiled at this detailed attention to His needs. "You are always prepared for whatever I need," He said.

Joseph looked concerned. "Master, I had heard the rumors, and of course I knew what the Temple priests were doing to dispel them. No one at the Temple knows what has really happened. You should hear the arguments! They watch me, to see if I am still connected with You and Your followers, but I have kept my distance and pretend to know nothing. I am not sure they would recognize You in Your present condition, but we will make sure you have the seclusion You need while You are here, to rest and recuperate."

"I am grateful to you and your household," said Jesus. "I am content to rest here tonight, but I have many people to visit in a very short amount of time." He paused as servants arrived with bowls of water. One servant removed His sandals and began to wash His feet. Another took a sponge, dipped it in water, and gently washed the dust from His face. Jesus washed His hands, and was handed a towel. "Bless you, dear friends," He said to the servants. They bowed, glanced quickly at Joseph, and left the courtyard.

"Water for bathing and clean clothes are being prepared for You, and whenever You are ready You can rest," said Joseph. "But look, here is our meal." Servants were approaching with covered dishes, plates, cups, and pitchers. They laid everything out on one of the tables, and the servant in charge prepared the plates for Jesus and Joseph.

As the servants left, Jesus took the bread, broke it, and said the blessing Joseph had heard so many times. "It does my heart good to hear those words again," said Joseph. "I must say, I never expected to hear them again. The last time I saw You, we were carrying you, in Your burial linen and covered with myrrh and aloe, to my tomb."

Jesus said, "I wanted to thank you for asking Pilate for My body, and for letting Me use your tomb."

"It was fortunate that Pilate and I had become acquainted in the last few years," said Joseph. "I was able to go directly to him with the request for Your body. Pilate released it as soon as he had the confirmation from the centurion. As to the tomb, I was honored that You could make use of it, even for such a short time. Especially for such a short time!" Joseph's face reflected such joy that Jeremiah knew their friendship was close, even though it had been a secret from the Sanhedrin.

"You might find this difficult to believe, dear friend," said Jesus, "but My spirit was nearby when the centurion was spearing My body. I saw him confirm My death to Pilate, and I saw you waiting to receive My body."

Joseph stared, transfixed at what his Master was telling him. "You saw all that? Even though You were dead?"

"Only My body was dead, for that short amount of time," said Jesus. "I am grateful for your friendship with Pilate – he didn't really want to be part of this at all."

"I do believe that he felt somewhat guilty," said Joseph, "that he had sentenced You to death on the cross. I feel he knew in his heart that You were innocent.

"None of them understood what was happening," said Jesus. "This is the beginning of a new ministry altogether, one about forgiveness, goodness, kindness, redemption, and new life with grace from My Father in heaven."

"I would like to hear more about that," said Joseph.

"Much of what will be taught will be based on the teachings I have been giving for the past three years – but I know you have not been able to attend most of My talks." Jesus stopped His host's sudden look of embarrassment with a gesture, and said, "My followers are in many different places, and they serve Me in many different ways. You and Nicodemus needed to be where you were during My ministry so that you both could minister to Me when I needed you – at the cross."

Joseph looked grateful for this, and Jesus continued, "Some of the teachings I repeated several times, to plant them firmly in the memory of the ones who listened, and also to give that message to as many different people in as many different places as I could. Here are some of the most important lessons: You have heard that it has been said, you shall love your neighbor, and hate your enemy. But I say to you, love your enemies, bless those who curse you, do good to them who hate you, and pray for those who spitefully use you and persecute you. If they hit you on one cheek, turn the other one. If you forgive men their trespasses, your heavenly Father will also forgive you."

Joseph sat nodding his head a little, as if taking this in. "This explains what I have heard about Your forgiveness from the cross, and Your disciples' forgiveness of Judas."

"There were other teachings that were also important," said Jesus. "Lay up for yourselves treasures in heaven, where neither moth nor rust corrupt, and where thieves do not break through nor steal. Judge not, that you not be judged, and forgive your enemy oppressors. A good tree cannot bring forth evil fruit; neither can a corrupt tree bring forth good fruit. When you follow Me, it is as if you have built your house on a rock. Even if torrential rain descends, and floods come, and winds blow and beat upon that house, it will not fall because it was founded on a rock."

As the images faded Jeremiah could see the two, talking far into the night.

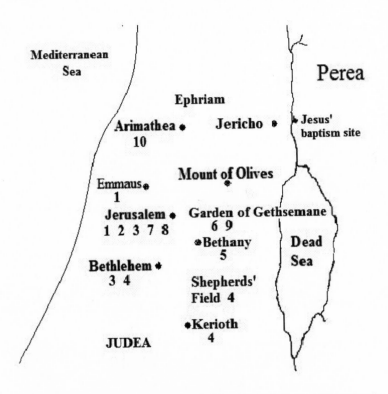

Mediterranean
Sea

Perea

Ephriam

Arimathea ◆   Jericho ◆   ◆ Jesus'
10   baptism site

Emmaus ◆   Mount of Olives ◆
1

Jerusalem ◆   Garden of Gethsemane
1 2 3 7 8   6 9

                        ◆ Bethany   Dead
                          5   Sea

Bethlehem ◆
3 4
                    Shepherds'
                    Field 4

          ◆ Kerioth
JUDEA   4

Sightings and movements of Jesus after resurrection
Days 1 - 10

Day 11: Wednesday

Day 11: Wednesday: Jesus walks partway to Jordan River – rests at Ephraim – remembers His decision at Ephraim – no one else used the tomb

Suddenly the images changed, showing Jesus and Joseph sitting at the table. It seemed to be morning now, and Jesus was wearing a new robe. Servants were just taking away the remains of what had to have been their breakfast.

"I will say farewell here," said Joseph. "It would not help either of us if we are caught outside together." He bowed his head for a blessing, and Jesus laid His hand on his head, said, "Let the grace of the heavenly Father be with you at all times."

The two men stood, and after a long look, Jesus walked back through the wide passageway and out to the road beyond, headed to the northeast.

"This is the beginning of day 11, Wednesday," said Peter.

"Where is He going?" asked Jeremiah.

"He is going to the Jordan River, where He was baptized."

"I know that place," said Jeremiah, excitedly. "On our tour we were immersed in the Jordan – they were careful not to call it a baptism, because we were baptized only once for our sins, but it was such an experience! How far is that from here?"

"About 30 miles," replied Peter. "But He will only travel half that distance today. His wounds bother Him too much for Him to travel quickly, or for too long at a time. Joseph has provided Him with food for the journey, and He will rest tonight in the hills of Ephraim. This is a place that has a special meaning for Jesus." He saw he had Jeremiah's attention, and then continued: "It was here that we came after Jesus raised Lazarus from the dead. We stayed here for days, and our Master went into the forest, in prayer, many a night. Sometimes one of us went with Him – James, John, Judas, or myself."

Peter spoke more slowly, as if remembering a crucial time, "It was there that we heard of the plot to kill Him. Nicodemus, one of the secret disciples, told our Master that the Temple priests and leaders were plotting to kill Him without a trial – you'll find that in John 7:50-52 – Nicodemus had to confront them, saying, 'Does our law condemn anyone without first hearing him to find out what he is doing?' and they replied, 'Are you from Galilee, too? Look into it, and you will find that a prophet does not come out of Galilee.' Nicodemus told us that they were determined to kill Him; that he attended a meeting of Temple priests and leaders where they said: 'Ye know nothing at all, nor consider that it is expedient for us, that one man should die for the people, and that the whole nation perish not.' You'll find that in John 11:50."

Jeremiah suddenly felt on familiar ground. "I remember this part! 'After hearing these plots, Jesus therefore walked no more openly among the Jews; but went thence into a country near to the wilderness, into a city called Ephraim, and there continued with His disciples' John 11:54. What really happened there in Ephraim? I had never attached much importance to it."

"No one does," said Peter, "but that is where our Master made His final plans to surrender to the priests at the Temple, during the yearly Passover festival. That is why He spent so much time alone, in prayer with His heavenly Father. People had been trying to kill Him for years, but remember it was His choice to lay down His life, and to pick it up again. This was the place where He made that choice, and those plans. He had no intention of being killed in some obscure place where no one would witness His death and resurrection. The Temple priests just wanted rid of Him, but He had other plans."

Jeremiah sat a minute, astonished at what he had just heard. "I remember in John 18:14 it says that Caiaphas was the one who said it was expedient that one man should die for the people. I just didn't put it together that Nicodemus might have told Jesus what they were planning. Or that the decision was made here. Our focus is always on the Garden of Gethsemane."

"But remember, He said all those words at the Last Supper, which went before His agony in the Garden," said Peter. "And He said that mysterious thing to Judas, which no one paid much attention to at the time, but later everyone talked about, that he should do quickly what he was going to do."

"And He is at Ephraim now," said Jeremiah. "Now that I know the significance of this place, I see why He would like to spend the night there, remembering His plans, and how everything actually happened."

"Yes, He probably did not plan on me going for that captain of the guard with that sword," laughed Peter, "although He was very quick to heal the ear of Malchus."

Jeremiah laughed a little also, and let his tension from hearing about Ephraim melt away. "I am glad He was able to rest at Joseph's home last night, since He is headed for a camping place now. But tell me, no one seems to really know, did anyone else ever use the tomb of Jesus? Did Joseph of Arimathea himself?"

Peter shook his head. "No, Joseph knew that was now a holy place, where the Son of God had experienced death, burial, and resurrection. Joseph gave orders for his family to bury himself away from that tomb, if possible at the Mount of Olives, and for no one ever to be entombed there."

"That is what I would have done, said Jeremiah. "Knowing what must have gone on in that tomb, how could anyone think of using it for anyone else?"

Peter nodded. "It is good to have an appreciation for holy things, Jeremiah, but it is wise to take care not to make the holy things into objects of worship. Many times that has happened in the churches of old, where the bones of an Apostle or saint were held in such esteem that people would make pilgrimages to see them. I understand that people want to cling to what they can see, whatever relic it is, rather than to trust what they cannot see."

"It is my understanding that many of those relics were used to actually make money for the towns where the relics were enshrined in the cathedrals," said Jeremiah. "With so many people making pilgrimages to see those 'holy' objects, the townspeople would have made a lot of money providing food and drink and places for them to stay."

"That is true, Jeremiah. When will people learn – it is not the relic that is to be worshipped, but Jesus! However, even having just said that, Joseph was right in not letting anyone else be entombed there. Our Lord's final resting place, the place of His resurrection, is a very holy place, next only to Bethlehem, the birth place of our Lord, and needs to be left as it is."

Day 12: Thursday

Day 12: Thursday: The Good Samaritan at Jericho

The images showed daylight filtering through the scrubby trees of a hillside of Ephraim. Jesus was lying in a small hollow, His head pillowed on one arm. Slowly He rose from the camp site, walked down the hill to a stream, and washed His face. He took up the small bundle beside Him and started the day's walk.

"This is day 12, Thursday," said Peter. "He is heading to the Jordan River, but to do that He passes through Jericho."

"Jericho, the oldest city," said Jeremiah. "At least, that is what was on our t-shirts we bought there." Peter laughed. "Is Jericho significant in some way? I only connect it with the battle in the Old Testament."

"You've heard the story in the gospels, but you don't know where it came from," said Peter mysteriously. "It is toward the end of the day as Jesus enters Jericho. It has been a long walk, and He decides to stay at an inn for the night."

The images showed Jesus entering an old inn and walking through the common room. Two men eating dinner there looked up at Him as He passed. They paused in their eating to stare at Him a minute, then resumed their conversation. Jesus sat where He could see them, and Jeremiah saw Him smile, as if pleased to see these travelers.

"Can you guess which story it is, Jeremiah? I will give you a hint. One of the men is a Jew, and one of them is not. Yet, you see them eating together in this inn by the roadside." Peter waited.

Jeremiah's brain flashed through every story he could recall. There were many incidents of Jesus consorting with gentiles, but not that many stories about two other men. Finally, he thought he had it. "Is the other a Samaritan?" he asked.

"Yes!" Peter cried.

"But I thought that was a parable. I thought it was just a make-believe story to illustrate what Jesus wanted to teach."

Day 12: Thursday

"Most of the stories Jesus used were simple ones, ones that could happen to anyone, stories of everyday life," said Peter. "Jesus lived 30 years in a normal small village in a remote area of the countryside. He saw all kinds of behavior as people lived out their lives in that rural place. Any travelers that passed that way were pressed for stories or recent events. Remember, this was before the day of TV news, or internet. Travelers were valued for their stories – many times this was the only way news was carried. In addition, His family went every year to Jerusalem for the Passover feast, and so heard many stories from fellow travelers and those who lived in Jerusalem itself. All of His experiences as a child and a young man were stored up in His memory, ready to be recalled and used to illustrate His parables and teachings."

Peter gestured toward the two men. "Here you see the Samaritan and the Jewish man who was so blessed by his actions that night. Jesus had met them before, and had heard their story. That is why they were looking at Him – He seemed familiar to them, but of course, in His present condition He was difficult to recognize. Even though the event happened several years ago, these two men meet once a year here at the inn to commemorate that experience that had became a blessing for them both. The Samaritan says that now even more than before he looks for people who might need his help."

Peter looked at Jeremiah. "What do you say about this story when you preach about it?" he asked.

Jeremiah gathered his thoughts, and began: "When an expert in the law stood up to test Jesus and asked him, 'What must I do to inherit eternal life?' Jesus answered, 'What is written in the Law? How do you read it?' The man said, 'Love the Lord your God with all your heart and with all your soul and with all your strength and with all your mind, and love your neighbor as yourself.' Jesus said that he had answered correctly, and that if he did this he would live, but the man wouldn't stop there. 'Who is my neighbor?' he asked, seeking to justify himself and his way of life.

"Then Jesus told them the story of the man who was traveling from Jerusalem to Jericho, and was attacked by robbers, who beat him up, took all his things, and left him for dead. Two men who had high standings in the Jewish community walked right by him, offering no help. Then a third man, a Samaritan, who was considered unfit to associate with Jewish people, saw him. This Samaritan took pity on him, cared for him, took him to an inn and paid the innkeeper to take care of him. There the story ends, but Jesus asks who the crowd thinks is the neighbor in the story. Of course, it is the Samaritan, who was considered to be a despised outcast among the Jews, who displayed mercy and acted to help the man. We use this story when we talk about good works, doing good and expecting no return for it.

"The name Good Samaritan is attached to many programs that help people," Jeremiah went on. "While we all applaud these programs, sometimes I think the people who name them have forgotten what the story means. It is not celebrating the fact that someone does good works. It is about the fact that of the three men who saw him, it was the most despised person who did the good works. The story means that it is the person who everyone looks down on who is the one you should call your neighbor, and who is the one who you should love as yourself. The summation of the Law into those two commandments is also in Mark:28-31, but this is the only place that tells the story of the Good Samaritan."

"Well said, Jeremiah," Peter looked especially pleased. "You have successfully put the story back in the context of the conversation, and understand how the Jewish people thought about Samaritans and gentiles. It was considered an extreme insult to call someone that, as Jesus' audience did according to John's Gospel, where they accused Jesus of being a Samaritan and having a devil."

Jeremiah grinned. That passage was well known among some of the young men of the church, who seemed to enjoy the taunting and insults. "John 8:48," he said. "'Then answered the Jews, and said unto him, 'Do not we say well that you are a Samaritan, and have a demon?' But Jesus had just called them sons of the devil, so of course they had to escalate their insults. It is amazing that he escaped that stoning."

"Jesus knew it was not yet His time – His death needed to happen in a completely different way. He angered so many crowds. Each time I expected it to be the last," said Peter. "But He knew what He was doing – none of us understood how, but He was not seized by any of the authorities until He decided it was time to lay down His life and take it up again."

"Things that seem obvious now, looking back, were probably very confusing then," said Jeremiah. "We all know those verses in John 10 about His Father loving him, because He lays down His life that He might take it up again. He says very clearly, about His life, that no man takes it from Him, but that He lays it down Himself, that He has the power to lay it down, and the power to take it again, by the commandment of His Father. When we read that on Sundays, it makes sense. But to hear that for the first time from someone you've been traveling with for three years! Did those claims seem outrageous?"

"There was much that He said that was a metaphor," said Peter. "When He talked about the shepherd and the sheep, we knew He was talking about Himself and the rest of us. When He said something we didn't understand right away, sometimes He explained to us later. From time to time, however, we assumed something was one of those metaphors, but later it turned out to be literally true. He did lay down His life, dying on the cross. He did take it up again, in His resurrection, and it was by the commandment and power of His Father."

Jeremiah tried to imagine himself in those circumstances. It was difficult to get past the lifetime of biblical study to understand these rough people in that distant time. How could they have been expected to understand things that scholars have debated on for hundreds of years?

Peter said, "At the time, we did not understand. We were fairly sure the Temple priests and leaders didn't understand, either. We only understood later, as we were preaching His gospel. It was only then that the meaning became clear to us. That understanding, and the gift of the Holy Spirit, gave us the courage to give up our lives for our Lord's cause, and to receive them back in heaven, by the mercy of Jesus. And whatever ministry we left undone on earth, we continue from heaven through other followers on the earth."

Jeremiah looked back up at the images. The Samaritan and his Jewish friend had finished their meal and were headed up to the rooms. Jesus was still at His meal, eating very slowly and sipping water after each bite. "He does stay here, right?" asked Jeremiah. "He looks too tired to go on, and He slept last night on a hillside."

"The Samaritan, recognizing a weary and wounded traveler who might be in need of help, has paid the innkeeper in advance to provide a place for Jesus to stay as long as He needed. He stays here, and continues in the morning to the Jordan River," said Peter. As if on cue, the images shifted to begin the new day.

Day 13: Friday

Day 13: Friday: Jericho, with Zacchaeus before and after Jesus – Jesus answers the same question about eternal life in three different ways – Bartimeus – Jordan River – baptism of Jesus and heavenly vision of the baptism – visions of triumphal entry into Jerusalem, Holy Spirit at Pentecost, John the Baptist

The images showed Jesus leaving the inn early in the day. Most travelers, Jeremiah realized, walked in the early morning or nearer sundown, when it was cooler. Jesus was walking through the streets of Jericho when Peter spoke.

"It is Friday, day 13. There are several incidents that happened in Jericho that you know about. Would you like to see what happened after the stories you were told?" at the eager nod of Jeremiah, Peter said, "Why don't you tell me the story of Zacchaeus."

Jeremiah began at once. For some reason, he liked this story. "Zacchaeus was a tax collector, who had grown rich by overtaxing people. The Romans couldn't be bothered with visiting each family and determining what they owed, so they relied on one of the locals to determine the tax for each family, to gather the taxes and deliver them to Rome. It was quite a common practice for tax collectors to gather more than they gave to Rome – that is how they grew rich. For that reason, the tax collectors, as you can imagine, were despised by most of their countrymen. Who would want to associate with someone who was stealing from you?

"Zacchaeus had heard about Jesus and wanted to see him. When Jesus came to preach in Jericho, there was a large crowd, and Zacchaeus was too short to see over them. He climbed a tree so that he could see Jesus and hear His teaching. I'm sure he was the most surprised person in the crowd when Jesus looked up at him in the tree and said, 'Zacchaeus, I am coming to dine at your house. Come down from that tree and prepare your household.'

111

"At the home of Zacchaeus, Jesus told him many things. The visit and the teachings of Jesus changed him. Zacchaeus repented of his sin of overtaxing the public, and gave fourfold to those whom he had cheated. He gave half of his riches to the poor and Jesus told him salvation had come to his house. That is how he became a follower of Jesus. In my sermons I urge the rich people to share with the poor." Jeremiah stopped, noticing the images before him.

"Well told, Jeremiah. Did you know that many tax collectors like Zacchaeus were corrupt? The local people as well as the Jews treated them as lepers. The disciple you know as Matthew was a tax collector at Capernaum. He was sitting at what you would call the customs entrance of the trade route when our Lord called for his ministry. Matthew's name at the time was Levi, and Jesus changed it to Matthew when He called him to follow Him."

"Once Matthew invited Jesus and the rest of us to his house for dinner, and many other tax collectors and 'sinners' were there. This was criticized by the Pharisees. 'Why does your Master eat with publicans and sinners,' they asked us, and when Jesus found out what they had said, He replied, 'the healthy do not need a physician, but they that are sick do. But go and learn what this means: I will have mercy, and not sacrifice: for I am not come to call the righteous, but sinners to repentance.' Matthew 9: 9-13 That is why Jesus went to eat dinner with Zacchaeus, a tax collector -- to bring him, a sinner, to repentance."

"So did Zacchaeus change?" asked Jeremiah.

"Look at that man in the plain robes," said Peter. "Do you see what he is doing?"

Jeremiah saw a short man in a simple robe that had seen many launderings. The man looked as poor as many of those around him, but he evidently carried a large purse somewhere within his garments, because he kept bringing out coins and dropping them into the cups of beggars, or into the hands of unsuspecting travelers. Each time the faces that had looked so tired and stressed brightened a little.

"He gave up his big house and luxurious way of life, and is now living a life of humility, faith, and obedience to the Lord Jesus. He has continued to only gather the taxes that are levied by the Romans, and as his payment to be content with the small salary they give him for his work. He distributes from his wealth to those less fortunate, and they are all blessed. Sometimes he talks about how his riches had never made him happy – that is why he wanted to listen to Jesus speak. He said that the more money he gathered, the more he wanted, until no amount was satisfying to him. Now, he has a fraction of what he used to have, but is content and happy. He often says that he is making a living from what he gets from the Romans, but he is making a life from what he gives."

"I love it!" cried Jeremiah. "His change was lasting, and benefitted not only him, but also everyone in that region. Jesus seemed to have a lot to do with rich men. But I have noticed that when they ask the same thing about what to do to inherit eternal life, Jesus gives different answers to different people. Was He being inconsistent, or is there something that was going on that was not recorded in the gospels?"

"There were many questions that were the same that Jesus answered in different ways. The question that leads to the Good Samaritan story is the same question as the one in Luke 18." said Peter. "Luke put that before the Zacchaeus story. A young ruler addressed Jesus as 'good Teacher' and asked Him what he must do to inherit eternal life. You will notice that this is the same question that one time Jesus answered with a question, 'What does it say in the Law' which the man answered correctly, but went on to ask who was his neighbor, which led to the Good Samaritan story. In Luke 18 when the ruler asks the question, Jesus first rebukes him for calling Him 'good' – 'no one is good except one – God' -- and then starts reciting the Ten Commandments. The ruler says he has kept all these since his youth, and then Jesus said, 'You still lack one thing. Sell all you have and distribute it to the poor. You will have treasure in heaven. Come, follow Me.' The man was very wealthy, and this was more than he could do. He was sad, and Jesus looked at him and said, 'How hard it is for those who have riches to enter the kingdom of God! For it is easier for a camel to enter in through a needle's eye than for a rich man to enter into the kingdom of God.'"

Jeremiah had always felt sorry for that man who could not leave his wealth to follow Jesus. "But there is hope . . ."

"Yes, Jeremiah, when asked who can be saved, Jesus replied, 'the things which are impossible with men are possible with God.'" Peter grinned. "And, of course, I had to ask about those of us who were following Him, 'We have left all we had to follow You!' and He said, 'Truly I tell you, there is no one who has left house or wife or brothers or parents or children for the kingdom of God's sake who will not receive many times more in this time, and in the world to come, eternal life.'

"At first we were as confused as you are about the different answers to the same questions, but we came to realize that Jesus knew the hearts of those who asked Him the questions, and gave them the answers they needed to hear to save their souls. The man who heard about the Good Samaritan needed to hear about his neighbor being the person that most people despise or look down on. The ruler in Luke 18 was completely attached to his money. He followed the exact commands of the law, but loved his money more than he loved a chance for a new life with God."

"One of my favorite quotes is 'Render to Caesar's the things that are Caesar's, and to God the things that are God's," said Jeremiah. "The Pharisees and Herodians tried to trick Him into saying something that would prove He was telling people to break the law, either the law of the Romans or the Law of the Jews. They said something flattering at first, so it would not look like an ambush, but went on to ask Him if it was right to pay taxes or not. If He had said, do not pay the tax, they could have arrested Him for inciting people to break the Roman law. But when He told them to look at the coin and tell Him whose portrait was on it, and whose inscription, they had to admit it was Caesar's. That's when He said, 'Give to Caesar what is Caesar's, and to God what is God's.' They were amazed at Him."

"We were all amazed at Him," smiled Peter. "He seemed unpredictable, but He knew what was in the hearts of the ones who talked with Him, and always said what they needed to hear for salvation and eternal life, whether they liked it or not. That particular time, His listeners were those who did not have much accumulated wealth. They were wage earners who had no possibility of becoming rich."

"What about Zacchaeus?" asked Jeremiah. "Jesus didn't tell him to do anything – he offered to give half of his wealth to the poor, and if he had cheated anyone he would repay them four times that amount. And Jesus said that salvation had come to his house that day. So he didn't have to give up all his wealth."

"It is not for us to know the heart of Zacchaeus," said Peter, "But from his behavior it is clear he was set free from the hold that money had over him, and he loved his new life of freedom. Did you see how delighted he was, giving money to unsuspecting people as they passed by? He truly found that it was more blessed to give than to receive."

Jeremiah felt delighted, just watching Zacchaeus. "I love these stories!"

"I think you'll like the next story, too," said Peter. "Do you remember the story of the blind man Bartimeus, the son of Timaeus? Bartimeus heard that Jesus was coming, and started calling, 'Jesus, Son of David, have mercy on me.' Evidently he was quite loud, and he must have distracted people from hearing what Jesus had to say. Everyone tried to make him be quiet, but it only made him call out even louder. Finally Jesus stood still and commanded the young man to be brought to Him. Everyone called Bartimeus, saying that Jesus was calling for him. Quickly Bartimeus rose, threw down his cloak, and came to Jesus. When Jesus asked what He should do for him, Bartimeus asked for his sight. Jesus said unto him, "Receive thy sight: thy faith hath saved thee." Immediately that happened; he was able to see, and became a follower of Jesus."

"I try to say something about sight and vision when I preach on that," said Jeremiah. "I say that the young man didn't have sight, but he had vision, the vision of healing from Jesus. Are we going to see Bartimeus now?"

Peter pointed to the images, where a man was carrying a basket of fruits and vegetables on his way to the marketplace.

Jeremiah saw Jesus and the man meet. Bartimeus gave no sign that he recognized Him, but he held up his basket. "Would you like to buy any fruits or vegetables?" he asked.

"I have no money now. My treasure is in heaven," said Jesus, and started to walk by, but the man stopped Him.

"Perhaps you do not know my story," said Bartimeus. "I was healed by the Son of David who was preaching here, and I did not pay Him anything. He never asked for payment for restoring my sight and changing my life. He was the Messiah, whose coming we were awaiting. The least I can do now is to repay Him by giving to those who do not have money to pay. Please, take some fruits and vegetables. They travel well, and you do not have to cook them."

Jesus took some figs and a few vegetables, and said, "Whatever you have done in My name for the least of these, you have done for Me. I am the bread of life; he who comes to Me shall not hunger, and he who believes in Me shall not thirst."

Bartimeus stared at Him. "When I received my sight from the Son of David, I had a vision that showed me the path to heaven. One day I will be where there is no hunger or thirst. I believe what You say. Are You the one who gave me my sight? Are You? The image of the Son of David is engraved in my vision, and I think You might be the one who healed me. The Son of David changed my life, and I have vowed to serve the needy and sick in His name until I join Him in heaven."

Jesus did not reply, but Jeremiah could see the joy on His face as He walked away with the bundle of food. Bartimeus looked after Him a long time, caught between incredulity and wonder. Finally, Jeremiah saw him take up the basket and continue to the marketplace, so lost in thought that he stumbled into at least two donkeys and a stone wall.

As Jeremiah laughed, for the sheer joy of the young man, he saw the images shift to follow Jesus as He walked to the Jordan River. As He walked, He ate the figs and vegetables that Bartimeus had given Him. When He reached the river, He stopped, and then slowly walked into it, robes and all. He immersed Himself in the river, and then stood, the water running off His hair in little streams. Jesus stood there for a moment, and then began washing His hair, bathing, and cleaning His robes from the dust, the blood, and the sweat. The river washed it all away, and Jeremiah sat entranced, seeing anew the symbolism of baptism played out before him.

Soon Jesus came back out of the river, spreading the heavier garments on the bank to dry. He stepped into the trees nearby and returned with some nuts and figs. After eating this impromptu picnic He settled into a meditative pose.

"Here's what He is remembering," said Peter, and a new set of images flowed.

Jeremiah saw a crowd of people gathered around a wild looking man standing in the river, easing an older man gently into the water. As he helped the older man up, he said, "Repent, for the kingdom of heaven is at hand and our Messiah has come. Glorify Him." He gently touched the man's forehead, guided him toward the riverbank and reached for the next one in line. "I baptize you with water for repentance, but He that comes after me is mightier than I. I am not worthy even to carry His sandals, but He will baptize you with the Holy Spirit and with fire."

Jeremiah knew he was looking at John the Baptist, and knew these words were fulfilled at Pentecost, when the Holy Spirit, appearing as tongues of flame, baptized the followers of Jesus. As the crowd parted to let a rough looking group through, Jeremiah recognized Jesus at the front. John fell suddenly silent. He stared at Jesus intently, and then motioned Him into the water. Everyone else felt the intensity, and stood back a little. As Jeremiah had just seen him do with the older man, John eased Jesus gently into the water, and then back up. But this time was different.

As Jesus came up out of the water, the blue of the sky was suddenly rent, and light poured through like a thousand suns. Suddenly the image seemed to split. Jeremiah could see what everyone else on the riverbank was seeing – Jesus in the water – but he could also something that looked like a heavenly vision.

In the image of the heavenly vision, Jeremiah saw a snow covered mountain, taller than anything he had ever seen or imagined. Jesus was at the peak, and the water was flowing from His tangled hair. This water was crystal clear, and flowed in endless streams, flowing into the mighty rivers all over the earth, on into the lakes and oceans. This holy water from Jesus encircled the whole world, giving life and joy to all the inhabitants.

Jeremiah saw the water flowing through the Palestine Valley as the River Jordan where many were baptized by John the Baptist. The water from the River Jordan flowed through the Sea of Galilee. Then Jeremiah saw the mighty Ganges River, with millions of believers in God and the sacred water, immersing themselves in the river to take away their sins, purify their souls, and give homage to the departed . It was a scene of a mass baptism giving homage to God.

Somehow amid all this life-giving water the image of a man appeared and Jeremiah knew it was King David. He bowed to Jesus, and Jeremiah saw a line of men standing behind King David, all bowing to Jesus. The last one seemed to have a little different expression on his face, and suddenly Jeremiah knew he was looking at Joseph the Carpenter. 'Those men must be the lineage of King David,' he thought. What had been just a list of names at the beginning of a gospel became real men, who had lived, died, and now beheld their descendant, who was also their Lord. As they bowed to Jesus, Jeremiah could tell they also were rejoicing, and he thought Joseph looked especially proud.

The water was still flowing in an endless stream from Jesus to the lakes and mighty oceans. Jeremiah was entranced by the men and the flowing water in this vision of heaven, but something was happening in the images of Jesus in the Jordan River. Jeremiah, and everyone else on the riverbank, saw a spirit descend like a dove, and Jeremiah knew it was the Spirit of God. As the spirit settled on the wet hair and shoulder of Jesus, a voice from heaven said, "This is my beloved Son, in whom I am well pleased." Then suddenly the dove shaped figure and the light were gone, and the sky looked as normal as ever. The other image vanished.

The crowd stirred, as if waking from a dream. As Jesus walked out of the water, John looked at Him so wistfully that Jeremiah suddenly realized John would have loved to follow Jesus, but knew his place was here. Jesus disappeared back into the crowd, and John motioned for the next man to be baptized.

The images shifted again, and even though Jeremiah saw the gates of Jerusalem, he could still hear, like a faint echo, John's message: "The Lord that is here whom I predicted is mightier than I is here at hand in front of you. He will baptize you with the Holy Spirit and with fire." A crowd of people waved palm branches and shouted "Hosanna to the Son of David! Blessed is he who comes in the name of the Lord! Hosanna in the highest!" as Jesus rode into

Jerusalem on a donkey. Jeremiah knew he was looking at the original of what the church celebrates as Palm Sunday.

Again, the images shifted and Jeremiah saw the upper room of a house in Jerusalem. Again, Jeremiah heard the echoes of the previous images as he saw a larger group of disciples filling the room. They were praying, but as the echoes of "Hosanna" died, their prayers became more audible. Jeremiah had been able to understand whatever language the people in the images had been speaking, but this time it was different. As each man spoke, obviously praising God, each language was different. Some, like Latin and Greek, Jeremiah recognized from his studies. Some of the languages were guttural, some musical, but it was clear the intent was praise, and Jeremiah felt completely awestruck as he realized he was watching the Holy Spirit descend at Pentecost.

The images shifted again, with an echo of the babble of voices lifted in praise continuing to sound as Jeremiah realized he was again looking at the Jordan River, but from the perspective of heaven. John the Baptist was there again, but in glorious robes and with such joy and vigor in his face that Jeremiah almost wept. With him was a crowd of people, all singing and praising God in their own language. John's ministry had been completed, and he could now join with the followers of Jesus in praise and worship.

"After the baptism of the Holy Spirit and fire," said Peter. "Nothing was the same. Do you see, Jeremiah, how one event led into another, all linked together like a chain? The first images were the ones that Jesus remembered, then we saw the first pouring out of the Holy Spirit on the followers of Jesus, and the last one was a vision of heaven, given to encourage Him in His last days."

Jeremiah sat as one transfixed, watching the heavenly images, and with a sigh, Peter sat back, prepared to wait it out. Presently Jeremiah sat up straighter and turned to Peter. "My soul could feast on that vision for days. But I am sure there are other lessons for me."

"Right now, only a review of the relationship between Jesus and John the Baptist," said Peter. "You remember they are cousins, and that each birth had been announced by the angel Gabriel. Mother Mary visited Elizabeth when she was pregnant six months with John the Baptist, and Mary was three months pregnant with Jesus."

Jeremiah said, "I have always felt it was interesting that they met twice, once before their birth, and the second time here on the banks of the River Jordan. And I feel especially blessed to have seen the vision of heaven, with Jesus and the water flowing throughout the world, and His ancestors bowing to Him. And I got to see Him at His baptism, with the Holy Spirit descending like a dove from heaven!"

"This is quite a lot to take in at once," said Peter. "Would you like me to take you to your place of meditation?"

"I know the way," said Jeremiah, "But I am always glad of your company. Although, I might be too lost in my own thoughts to even know you are there!"

"Then, by all means, go," said Peter. "When you are ready, return and we will start again."

As if in a daze, Jeremiah left the House of Images and made his way through the streets of the holy city to that valley with the stream rushing into the lake. Gratefully he sank down on the cushion and looked over the water to the small hills beyond. 'We began with Zacchaeus,' he thought.

Day 14: Saturday

Day 14: Saturday: Temptation of Jesus in the wilderness – Satan vanquished forever – Jesus calls His first disciples – Jesus teaches in a synagogue

Peter rose from his chair as Jeremiah entered the house of images.

Jeremiah was the first with a question. "I didn't find out where Jesus spent the night last night after remembering His baptism," he said.

"You were in a daze," said Peter. "But He just spent the night in the little forest by the Jordan River. Do you remember where Jesus went after His baptism there?"

"That was when He was in the wilderness 40 days, where He did not eat any food, and was tempted by Satan," said Jeremiah.

The images showed the resurrected Jesus heading into the scrubby forest covered hills.

"He is heading for the place where the angels ministered to Him at the end of His temptations," said Peter.

"Why would Jesus want to return to this place where He withstood the temptations of Satan for 40 days? Even though the angels ministered to Him afterwards, this place had to be a big reminder of a terrible time in His life."

"It was a crucial time in His life. He was about to transition from being known as a carpenter's son to being known as the Son of God. He had just had a most unusual baptism experience. There was a lot to think about. And then Satan came to tempt Him!" Peter pointed to the images. "Do the images show Satan now?"

"No, I see only Jesus and this beautiful setting," said Jeremiah.

"So, Jeremiah, where is Satan now?" Peter waited for an answer.

Jeremiah looked around. Was this a trick question? "He doesn't seem to be here," began Jeremiah tentatively.

Peter laughed. "All right, let's review a little. Start with what you preach about the temptations of Jesus."

Jeremiah felt on firmer ground here. "After His baptism, Jesus went to the wilderness for 40 days, without food or water. When He felt hungry, Satan came to Him, saying that if He was the Son of God, then command that these stones become bread. But Jesus answered, 'It is written, man shall not live by bread alone, but by every word that comes from the mouth of God.'

"Then Satan took Him up to the holy city and set Him on a pinnacle of the temple. Satan said, 'If you are the Son of God, then throw Yourself down, for it is written, He shall put His angels in charge of You, and they will bear you up, so that You do not dash Your foot against a stone.' But Jesus answered, 'It is written, you shall not test the Lord your God.'

"Finally, Satan took Him up a very high mountain, and showed Him all the kingdoms of the world, in all their glory, and said, 'I will give You all these things if You will fall down and worship me.' Then Jesus said to him, 'Go away, Satan! For it is written, 'you shall worship the Lord your God, and you shall serve Him only.' After our Lord rejected all the offers from Satan, he left Him, and angels came and ministered to Him." Jeremiah paused and looked at Peter for affirmation.

"Yes, Jeremiah, that was right. So what did Jesus tell Satan?"

"Jesus told Satan to be gone, to go away, the older translations say 'get thee hence' – but away from where? Away from here?"

"The battle against Satan was won here, Jeremiah," said Peter. "He was banished from the earth – forever – at that time by Jesus."

"Aren't there mentions of Satan or the devil after that, in the New Testament?" Jeremiah did not wish to be disrespectful, but if he was to bring this message back to his congregation, he had to understand it.

"Some of the mentions involve Judas, and were actually entered into those gospels later than the original writings," said Peter. "Others can be considered more of a poetic license. Remember, Jesus was talking to people who had no knowledge of psychology, mental illness, chemical imbalances in the brain, or whatever else might have been a medical cause of their 'demon possession.' Satan was defeated by Jesus, and there is a lesson here about overcoming temptations." He waited for Jeremiah to take in what he had said so far, and then continued.

"With this act, Jesus set an example to the human race to resist temptation. If you do not resist temptation, if you succumb to temptations, and therefore sin, it is the same as submitting to Satan, who some call the devil – who isn't even around anymore." He waited a moment for Jeremiah's comprehension, and then went on: "Now that Satan is banished from the earth, we can claim the victory of Jesus for our own when we battle temptations."

Jeremiah brightened. "I have preached about that! Jesus has already rescued us from sin and death, and He rescues us even from our own temptations. But we must remember this at the time that we are being tempted, and acknowledge His victory. We must live the victory every day, not falling prey to the kind of instantaneous gratification that those temptations can promise. Nevertheless, there were so many references about Satan or the devil after this time that I didn't want to tell people that he is vanquished from the earth for good. That was a little beyond my knowledge."

"Not anymore," said Peter. "Now you can tell them with authority that the devil, Satan, has been vanquished, and is banished from the earth by Jesus Christ. The devil, Satan, the Father of Lies, is no longer a threat to you. Of course, there is still plenty of temptation without the devil, but you are showing your congregation the right way to confront it. When Jesus resisted temptation, He showed us the way. And when you have the spirit of God and Jesus in your heart, you also have His power to resist all kinds of temptations, no matter how big or small they are."

Jeremiah was grateful that his teachings were on the right track. But of course, he had even more questions. "Didn't Jesus start His teaching ministry after this? Are we going to get to see it?"

"Yes, it was after Jesus conquered the devil and after the angels had ministered to Him that Jesus began His ministry. Is there something in particular that you would like to ask me, Jeremiah?"

"I had wondered about the phrase 'the time is fulfilled, and the kingdom of God is at hand: repent, and believe the gospel.' Has Jesus fulfilled something already? His ministry has just begun. I know about the word 'gospel' meaning 'good news' or 'the good messenger.'

Day 14: Saturday

"The time is fulfilled just means everything is in place for Jesus to start His ministry. It was the appointed time. John the Baptist had fulfilled his assignment - baptizing and announcing His coming - and Jesus had overcome the devil after that. It was sometime after Jesus began His ministry that John the Baptist was put in prison, and ultimately beheaded. Jesus begins by talking about repentance, as John the Baptist had done."

"Peter, my understanding is that we start with repentance because if we do not see our sins and the need for Jesus the Redeemer, none of the rest of it would have any meaning for us."

"Very good, Jeremiah. Now would you like to see Jesus begin His ministry?"

The images showed the Sea of Galilee. Several fishing boats were out on the water. Jesus was walking along the shore, and when He saw two men throwing a net into the sea, He stopped. "You!" He called to them. They looked up and stared at Jesus. "Come follow me, and I will make you fishers of men," Jesus said. The men looked at each other, and Jeremiah knew he was seeing Peter's own calling right there before his eyes. Suddenly as one they turned and walked toward Jesus, the nets forgotten in the water.

Jesus continued along the shore, until He came to a large boat pulled upon the shore, where several men sat mending their nets. Staring at each man in turn, His gaze stopped at the two brothers of the household. Jeremiah recognized James and John, the sons of thunder, with their father Zebedee. As their father and servants looked on in amazement, Jesus called them out of the boat and they left without a word.

The five men walked into Capernaum, the four fishermen and the carpenter's son. A place had been prepared for them to stay, and they began their new life in the ministry of Jesus.

"We were used to a life where we were mostly outdoors," said Peter. "We had to spend some time together to be with Jesus, to learn from Him, to learn how to learn, actually, because if you asked most of us, we would have told you we already knew what we needed to know about life. Everything He said was new, even when He quoted from the old scriptures; they suddenly had a new meaning. Then on the Sabbath day, well, watch."

The images showed a Sabbath morning at the synagogue, the men sitting apart from the women, as was the custom. The men were invited to speak (no one invited the women, and no woman dared use her voice in the synagogue) and when Jesus rose, the fishermen nudged each other, expectant looks on their faces.

"I don't remember exactly which scriptures He quoted or talked about that day," said Peter, "but what I do remember is the reaction of the congregation. Usually the speakers would begin and end their talks with phrases that indicated these were their suppositions, not to be taken as any dependable source of truth. Their talks were their opinions on the scriptures. Jesus had none of that in His teaching. He quoted the scripture, gave the meaning, illustrated it with an example, and sat down. There was silence. No one wanted to speak next. I think I remember the service continued, and maybe the women were whispering among themselves, but no man dared speak after that display of authority. Not even the scribes."

"Wow," said Jeremiah, instantly wishing he had said something more profound. Peter laughed.

"Wow is right. He had been preaching for repentance; now He was teaching the meaning of the scriptures and gathering His disciples. His ministry was off to a good start."

Day 15: Sunday

Day 15: Sunday: Jesus goes to Perea and heals a woman and a man on the Sabbath – reflections on healing on the Sabbath

"That evening Jesus rested and slept on that same hillside," said Peter. "The next day, day 15, He started walking toward Perea."

But Jeremiah's mind was still on Jesus in the synagogue. "Jesus spoke many times in the synagogues, didn't He? Did it always cause such a stir among the crowd?"

"Yes, and we quickly learned to keep an eye on Jesus at all times. We never knew when He would choose to slip quietly away or when He would stop, heal someone, and start preaching right there. In fact, it was in Perea where two of these healings occurred, both on the Sabbath."

The images showed a scene that Jeremiah recognized was from the past. Men and women were seated in a synagogue, listening to the teachings. One of the women was not sitting, but standing in an awkward position, bent double. Jeremiah knew she was the one who had been this way for 18 years, unable to straighten up. Jesus rose to speak, and as His eyes swept the congregation, He noticed the woman standing all the way in the back, doubled over as always. Glancing at His disciples, who immediately sat more attentively, He called to her. Nervously she left her place by the door, and shuffled slowly to the front of the congregation. Jesus said, "Woman, you are free from your infirmity." He put His hands on her shoulders, and immediately she stood upright.

"Praise to the Lord God," she cried, and turned this way and that, looking at everything as if for the first time. Jeremiah realized she hadn't been able to see anything from a normal position for most of her life. The rest of the synagogue was in a quiet uproar. The disciples looked poised for action, but Jesus just stood there as if waiting for something. As if on cue, the leader of the synagogue strode over to Him.

"What is the meaning of this," he almost shouted. "There are six days for work; let the ones seeking healing come on those days and be healed, not on the Sabbath day."

Jesus spoke quietly, but no one missed a word. "What a hypocrite you are. Every one of you, on the Sabbath, goes to free your ox or your ass from the stall and lead them to be watered, do you not? And shouldn't this woman, this daughter of Abraham, who had been bound by Satan for 18 years, be free from this bond on the Sabbath day? There is no difference."

As the leader of the synagogue backed slowly away, the other leaders looked down in embarrassment. The congregation seemed jubilant, greeting the woman by name and praising God. With a glance to His disciples, Jesus walked quietly through the crowd, the disciples following in His wake.

The image changed, and Jeremiah saw the resurrected Jesus passing by that same synagogue. A woman was walking down the road in the opposite direction, but stopped in sudden shock as they passed each other. She turned and spoke to Jesus.

"Sir, what did you do just now? I felt my whole body flooded with joy and wonder as you passed by me." She looked at Him more closely, but did not recognize Him.

Jesus said, "I am happy you are well and working and attending to your family."

She seemed shocked, and said, "How do You know about me and my family?"

"Your faith and belief have healed you," said Jesus, and she clutched at His robe.

"Are You the One who touched me in the synagogue a year ago?" Her voice wavered, as if she had finally found the One she had been looking for.

Jesus' smile told her everything she needed to know. As He walked on, she stared after Him. "Messiah has risen among us," she said again and again, first softly and then louder with each repetition until at last she was almost shouting with joy.

The images shifted again and Peter said, "We are still in Perea, but it is back during our ministry with Jesus. A Pharisee had invited us to dinner. Of course, it was on the Sabbath."

"Of course," said Jeremiah, and settled back to watch.

Jesus and His disciples entered a large home. The assembled guests seemed to be waiting for something, and when Jesus saw the man whose body was swollen with dropsy, He gave the disciples one of those warning glances they had come to expect. "You would call this entrapment," said Peter.

Jesus looked around at the lawyers and Pharisees and said, "Is it lawful to heal on the Sabbath day?" When they were silent, Jesus reached for the sick man, holding him by his shoulders. With a quiet word the man was suddenly healed, and Jesus released him. The man rushed out of the house, and Jesus turned back to the assembled guests. "Which of you might have an ass or an ox fall into a pit, and will not immediately pull him out on the Sabbath day?" Again, they were silent.

The images faded and Jeremiah turned to Peter. "I have counted in the gospels that Jesus healed seven times on seven Sabbath days. I know Jesus worked on all days, including the Sabbath, to relieve human suffering. I understand His message was that on the Sabbath it is good to work to heal and preach and help others. As suffering does not stop for the Sabbath, so healing does not stop on the Sabbath, either. Customs have changed since those days, and many people now work on Sunday, our Sabbath, but most businesses, especially banks, are closed on Sundays."

Peter responded, "The doctors in your country also follow what our Lord set as an example 2000 years ago -- they work all days, including Sabbath days, as needed to heal the suffering. Even in the country of Israel, the doctors work on their Sabbath and attend to emergencies to heal the sick."

"I had not heard about the doctors in Israel," said Jeremiah. "But I am glad to see them ministering to others on their Sabbath, even if they do not consider themselves followers of Jesus."

Peter agreed, and gestured to the new images before them. Two men, clearly a worker and his employer, labored in a garden. "That man there is the one who was so sick before. He is now working for the Pharisees, something he could not do when he was so ill.

Jeremiah watched as the resurrected Jesus passed by the healed man and his Pharisee employer. No words passed, but the joy on the face of Jesus told Jeremiah everything he needed to know about how Jesus felt about that days' work so long ago on a Sabbath.

Day 16: Monday

Day 16: Monday: Jacob's well – Jesus and the Samaritan woman at the well – Jesus visits with the woman and her new family – why the Samaritans were hated and despised by the traditional Jews, especially those from Jerusalem.

"It is day 16," said Peter. "Jesus is leaving Perea in the east, and crosses over the Jordan River to the west bank."

The images showed Jesus walking into the river, and then swimming.

"Why isn't He just walking on the water?" asked Jeremiah.

"He is still being as human as possible," said Peter. "He is determined not to use His divine powers for His personal benefit or comfort."

Jesus reached the other bank, climbed out of the water, and spread His outer garments to dry. He rested near the riverbank until His clothes were completely dry, then He put them on and resumed His journey to the west.

"Where is He going?" asked Jeremiah.

"You will see later," said Peter. But where He is now is quite important."

The images showed a small village in the evening. Jesus approached a well and stopped to look into it. "That well is called Jacob's well," said Peter.

Jeremiah immediately thought of the Samaritan woman who gave Jesus the water from Jacob's well. When Peter confirmed his guess, Jeremiah asked, "Why is it called Jacob's well? Can you tell me the story?"

Peter said, "In Genesis we find the story of how Jacob came to a city in the land of Canaan. He pitched his tents on a parcel of land, bought the land, and built a well, which he later gave to his son Joseph. This is the same well that the Samaritan woman used for drinking water and for her household use. After hundreds of years, it continues to provide water as it did for Jacob, his son

131

Joseph, for the Samaritans, and now for our Lord when we journeyed with Him during His ministry. Watch."

The images showed Jesus resting against the well as His disciples went into the nearby town to buy food. A Samaritan woman was walking toward the well, carrying a bucket and a large pitcher. As she drew up the water, Jesus said "Give Me a drink."

She turned to Him abruptly and said, "How is it that You, a Jew, asks for a drink of water from me, a woman of Samaria?"

Jesus said, "If you knew the gift of God, and who it is that asks you, you would have asked Him, and He would have given you living water."

The woman answered as if He had offered her some kind of magic water bucket. "Sir," she said, "you have nothing to draw with and the well is deep. Where can You get this living water? Are You greater than our father Jacob, who gave us the well and drank from it himself, as did also his sons and his flocks and herds?"

Jesus answered, "Everyone who drinks this water will be thirsty again, but whoever drinks the water I give will never thirst. Indeed, the water I give him will become in him a spring of water welling up to eternal life."

The woman said to him, "Sir, give me this water so that I won't get thirsty and have to keep coming here to draw water."

"Go, call your husband, and come back," replied Jesus.

At this, the woman blushed and said, "I have no husband."

Jesus looked at her intently and said, "That is correct. For you have had five husbands, and he who is with you now is not your husband. You have spoken truth."

The woman dropped the pitcher on the ground, her mouth open and all pretenses gone. She said, "Sir, I can see that You are a prophet. You know everything about me. Our fathers worshipped in this mountain, but the Jews say Jerusalem is the place where men ought to worship."

Jesus said, "Woman, believe me, the hour comes when you shall worship the Father neither in the Temple nor on this mountain. You worship what you do not know; we worship what we know. But the time comes, and now is upon us, when the true worshippers will worship the Father in spirit and in truth, for the Father seeks such to worship Him. God is a Spirit, and those who worship Him must worship Him in spirit and in truth."

She had followed His words intently, and said, "I know when the Messiah comes, He will tell us all things."

Jesus said, "I who speak to you am He."

"Look at all that is going on," said Peter. "This is the first time Jesus has revealed himself as the Messiah. He also says plainly that God can be worshipped everywhere, that He doesn't need a temple or churches to be built for Him. You don't need to travel to Jerusalem to a temple. God is spirit, and the Father in heaven will look for such seekers. He also knew everything about her past and present." He gestured back to the images.

The Samaritan woman seemed overcome with joy, leaving her bucket and pitcher at the well and sprinting back to the town. She told the men gathered there, "Come, see a man who told me all the things I ever did. Could He be the Messiah?" As the men slowly made their way to the well, the disciples came up, seeing the approaching crowd and urging Jesus to eat. "We all knew if He started teaching He would forget about meals entirely," said Peter. "See everyone begin to crowd around? This went on for two days."

Jeremiah watched as the images showed the people jostling about in an endless stream, each asking for and hearing details of their own lives. "They arrive skeptical, and leave believers," said Peter. "These Samaritans are the first group of people to recognize our Lord as the Messiah. We stayed there for two days before we went on to Galilee."

"One of my favorite verses is about the eternal drink which will quench thirst forever," said Jeremiah. Peter laughed.

"You would mention water," he said. "The Temple priests and leaders were furious that He had been given water by a Samaritan woman, and had actually drunk it. When they found that she had five previous husbands, and was now living with a man who was not married to her, they were even more upset. When Jesus talked with her and drank the water she offered, He broke all their rules. The Temple priests were outraged, but the people loved Him."

The images shifted to the resurrected Jesus standing in front of a house at Sychar village. "That is the house of the woman who gave Him the water from Jacob's well," said Peter.

A woman appeared at the door. "What can I do for you?" she asked.

Jesus said, "I am the Messiah, who talked with you at the well."

She scanned His face, and then her eyes lit up. "Our Messiah has returned!" she cried. "Please, Lord, enter our humble dwelling, and be welcome. I am sorry I did not recognize You at the door. You have changed since I saw You last."

Jesus walked into the house, gratefully easing into the chair offered Him and accepting the water to wash away the dust.

"Please rest there a minute while we prepare a meal for You," she begged, and ran off to the kitchen. Jeremiah laughed as he saw her dart around the small area, checking her ingredients. She mixed dough for bread, started a stew on the fire, and ran over to her neighbor's house. She ran back and forth, from her own kitchen to additional neighbors, until all the women in the neighborhood were abuzz. The woman was inviting them all to the feast, and they all promised to come.

When she returned to check on Jesus, she had her baby girl in her arms. "I never would have had the life of a wife and mother that I have now if You hadn't come to our well and spoken with me," she said. "I married that man I was living with, and now I'm as good a wife and mother as any other woman in this village. The way I behaved before, none of the other women would talk to me. You saw I was at the well alone, not gossiping with the other women in the cool of the morning. Now, they are all my neighbors. I have friends again. I would be honored if You would bless our little Miriam. I named her after Your mother, Lord." Jesus thanked her for the honor to His mother and laid His hands on the baby's head. He said a blessing, but again Jeremiah couldn't hear exactly what He said.

There was a timid knock on the door, and a group of village women entered, each bearing a dish. "Our men will be along when they have finished in the fields," one of them said, and they all began to arrange their dishes on the table, each one managing to have a quiet moment with Jesus.

Presently the men entered, some bearing wine and others small gifts that a traveler would appreciate.

When all the neighbors had gathered and the table was crowded with dishes of hearty food, Jesus' host and hostess looked to Him to bless the meal. Jesus raised His hands and said, "Our Father in heaven, holy is Your name. Your kingdom come, Your will be done on earth as it is in heaven. Give us today our daily bread, and forgive us our debts as we forgive our debtors. And do not lead us into temptation, but deliver us from the evil one."

As the blessing ended, everyone sat in silence for a moment. The Samaritan woman turned to Jesus and said, "Thank you for that prayer. I have never heard anything like it – not from any of our rabbis!" She offered a dish of stew to Jesus and her husband, and the feast began.

Jesus sat at the head of the table, enjoying the camaraderie of His hosts and their guests. He accepted the small gifts gracefully, and inquired about everyone's health and families. They all wanted to know about Him. "We heard about the crucifixion," one of them said, "But we also heard the rumors of You rising on the third day."

"We know You are the Messiah," another said, "We knew something would happen – we just did not know what it would be. Your coming here was so unexpected."

"You changed all our lives when You said we could worship from any place; that we need not go to Jerusalem, or to the mountains." The village leader's voice underlined the gratitude in his words.

The hostess clasped both of Jesus' hands in hers. "You changed everyone's lives," she said. "Anyone who doesn't recognize You as the Messiah is lost, walking in a dark tunnel with no light to show the direction to escape."

The feast was a long one, and as the last guests departed Jesus sank back in His chair, visibly exhausted. "Please, Lord, stay here with us and rest for the night. I will clean Your robes and I have some herbal healing ointment for Your wounds." The woman waited for Jesus to accept, then hurried to ready the guest room.

As the images faded, Jeremiah turned to Peter. "At one time I must have known, but I have forgotten why the Jews hated the Samaritans so much. Would you tell me?"

"Certainly, Jeremiah. The history is an old one, so I will give you the short version. Samaria was a province 42 miles north of

135

Jerusalem, whose inhabitants included both Jews and gentiles. In the long history from the founding of Samaria to the time of Jesus, many wars had been fought for that area, with much intermingling in marriage of the original Jews there with the gentiles. There was a running feud between them and the Jews in Jerusalem: not only had the Jews in Samaria married the idol worshipping gentiles, but they claimed to be Jews when it suited them, and denied their heritage when better offers came along. These Samaritan Jews even fought alongside the enemies of Jerusalem in a couple of wars. They had built their own temple on a local mountain so they could worship in whatever way they chose without having to abide by the rules of the Jews in Jerusalem."

"If they had actually fought against the Jews in Jerusalem, I can see why they would be considered enemies at the time of Jesus," said Jeremiah. "And why everyone was so shocked when Jesus was actually talking with a Samaritan woman and accepting her hospitality."

"Right," said Peter. "It wasn't only that they had defied Jewish law by marrying gentiles – these people's ancestors had raised arms against them. Blood had been shed. "

"Peter, how did the traditional Jews know Jesus had visited that Samaritan city, or accepted water, or stayed there two days? Did they have spies following Jesus around, or was it just through gossip or traveler's tales?"

"It might have been some of both," said Peter. "There were always other people around us – sometimes we knew them; other times we did not. Perhaps there were Temple spies – we certainly didn't think about that that at the time – at least, I didn't. We did a lot of traveling around: teaching and healing. Of course, at the end we returned to Jerusalem, so that everything could be done as written in the prophecies."

Jeremiah nodded. "The story of His life and teachings, of His surrender, execution, and resurrection spread from the center of Jewish power here to the entire world."

They sat in silence for a moment, thinking about how Christianity had spread from these rough fishermen and poor village folk to cover the world with the message of Jesus the Messiah.

Day 17: Tuesday

Day 17: Tuesday: Story of the ten lepers – Jesus visits the Samaritan leper

"It is Tuesday, day 17," said Peter.

The images showed Jesus rising from His bed in the guest room, and preparing to leave. When the woman of the house saw Him preparing to go, she held out her hand as if to stop Him.

"Where are You going so early?" she asked, her face a silent plea for Him to stay.

"Where I am going, you cannot come," said Jesus. "In My Father's house there are many rooms; if it were not so, I would have told you. I am going there to prepare a place for you. And if I go and prepare a place for you, I will come back and take you to be with Me that you also may be where I am."

"Oh my Lord," cried the Samaritan woman. "I long for that day, when we can be with You all the time."

"That day will come," said Jesus. "Always remember that I am the way, the truth, and the life, I am the Alpha and Omega. No man comes to the Father except by Me. If you have known Me, you have also known my Father, and from now you do know Him, and have seen His work."

The woman stood straighter and said in a firm voice "I will remember." She stopped, as if realizing again that He was leaving. She asked Him to wait a moment, went into the kitchen, and came out with two bundles. "Please, Lord, take these for the journey." She gave Jesus a bundle of dried fruit, meat, cheese, and a bag of water. "These will last for days." She looked at Him, concern in her eyes. "You have changed so much – I am worried about You, my Lord. Your suffering has been dreadful. -- I wish I could take it from You. I cannot think about what those people in Jerusalem did to You."

Jesus touched her shoulder briefly and said, "I and the heavenly Father are one, I forgave them for they did not know what they were doing. It was all part of the plan from My heavenly Father. Then He gave her a blessing and looked one last time into her eyes. Gathering up His bundle of food, He walked slowly into the street, never looking back.

After Jesus moved away from her, the Samaritan woman sighed. Hearing a cry from the other room, she ran to pick up her baby girl, holding her close. Her husband paused at the doorway and she reached out to him with her free hand. "All the happiness we have now is because of Him."

Her husband kissed the top of her head and said, "We will follow Him to the end of our lives."

The images shifted to follow Jesus. "Where is He going?" asked Jeremiah.

"He is headed northwest, to the Samarian outpost known as Sebasta. It is close to the border of Galilee and Samaria. It is a long journey, and in His physical condition, it will take Him most of the day."

The images showed a small village at nightfall, evening lights shining through the windows of an isolated home at the outskirts of the settlement.

"Do you remember the story of the ten lepers?" asked Peter.

Jeremiah laughed. "Is this that village? No one knows the name or exactly where it was located. The story is that Jesus was traveling to Jerusalem, through the middle of Samaria and Galilee. He met ten lepers near one of the villages, but they stood far away from Him, as was the custom. They lifted up their voices, crying 'Jesus, Master, have mercy on us.' When Jesus saw them, He said, 'Go, show yourselves to the priests.' As they were on their way to the priests, they were healed. I always thought that was significant – they were healed as they went. They didn't wait until they were healed to go, they went in obedience, and as they went they were healed."

"Yes, they were obedient because they had faith, and Jesus said to the one who returned to give thanks, 'Your faith has made you whole.' But why are we talking about that here? What was significant about the one who returned to give thanks?"

"He was a Samaritan," said Jeremiah. "Is this his village?"

"Yes," said Peter. "And this is his house, here at the edge of the settlement."

Jeremiah saw Jesus standing before a small house. The door had opened and a man was standing there, asking Jesus to come in, share his evening meal, and rest there for the night. "Did that man recognize Jesus as the one who healed him?"

"No, and Jesus will not tell him. It would be too dangerous. If the Temple priests found out Jesus had been here, they would interrogate that poor man mercilessly. It is better that he not know."

Jeremiah saw Jesus enter the house. The Samaritan brought a wet towel for Jesus to refresh His face, hands, and feet. As Jesus dried His face, the Samaritan set the table for the evening meal.

"Have you heard the news?" asked the Samaritan. "The Romans crucified a man for violating the laws of Moses and claiming to be the king of the Jews, They accused Him of blasphemy, but He had been to this village, and I had met Him. He was nothing like that! He was a great prophet, if not more. He had the power of God to heal!"

As he brought the food in from the kitchen, he continued to speak. "We called Him Master, because it was obvious that He was a great man. He healed ten lepers a while ago, right here in this village! I was one of them! He healed us all, instantaneously: as a bubble on the water disappears, the leprosy disappeared. He didn't have to pray for any divine intervention as many of the Law givers like Moses, and prophets like Elisha who tried for days to heal – He just healed us! I was the only one from here. The others were from Jerusalem and around that area. A couple of them were in Jerusalem when all that happened to Jesus, our healer, and when they passed through here the other day they told me all about it. Had you heard?"

"Yes," said Jesus, "I knew about that, but my understanding is that He was Jesus the Messiah, and that His suffering and death fulfilled the prophecies and predictions of the prophets of old."

"I can believe that He was the Messiah. You should have heard the authority in His voice." The Samaritan looked closely at Jesus, but did not appear to recognize Him.

Jesus continued, "Adam was the head of the human race who violated the laws of God. One man's sin brought death and destruction to our race. Moses came as a prophet to give us the Law. Many prophets came, interpreting the Law of Moses and teaching about the Messiah. Finally our Lord Jesus came to take away the sins of men and women, and also end the suffering that is the result of that sin. He came to pave the way for salvation and eternal life for all."

"I can believe He could do that," said the Samaritan. "But look, our meal is ready. Please, come to the table. I have very few visitors, and almost no one shares a meal with me. "

The host and guest sat at the table, and Jesus blessed the food with a prayer that Jeremiah knew well: "Our Father in heaven, holy is Your name. Your kingdom come, Your will be done on earth, as it is in heaven. Give us this day our daily bread, and forgive us our sins, as we forgive those who sin against us. Lead us not into temptation, but deliver us from evil. Amen."

"I have never heard such a blessing!" cried the Samaritan. "This is wonderful. I will share this word for word, to all those who believe in the One who healed me, in our village and the whole area around us. But tell me, how have You learned such a blessing?"

Jesus said, "It is from My heavenly Father." The host had a strange look on his face, as if he were wondering if this was the same man who had healed him. Jeremiah thought the man might be afraid of questioning his guest, who was obviously a very holy man. They continued the meal with Jesus summarizing many of the talks He had given, either to His disciples or to the crowd who had gathered to hear Him.

Jeremiah heard "if your right eye offends you, pluck it out, and cast it from you: for it is more profitable for you that part of your body should perish and not that your whole body should be cast into hell. And if your right hand offends you, cut it off, and cast it from you; for it is more profitable for you that one of your members should perish, and not that your whole body should be cast into hell."

The man said, "That's just how it was for me when Jesus took away my disease! My hands were painful with leprosy, but now it is all gone. When Jesus healed me, it was as if my diseased right hand had been taken off, with a new right hand coming out in its place. It was also true of my eyes. They were full of leprosy, and painful. I could hardly open my eyelids to see. As soon as Jesus healed me, it was as if my diseased eyes were pulled out of their sockets, and new eyes emerged in their places. None of this caused any pain, but restored my sight."

"You are blessed," said Jesus. "Your belief has healed you, and now you have new vision and pain-free hands."

Jeremiah also heard parts of other teachings, "with men it is impossible, but not with God: for with God all things are possible" and "all things are delivered to Me of My Father. No man knows who the Son is, but the Father, and who the Father is, but the Son, and he to whom the Son will reveal Himself."

The men talked far into the night, then the Samaritan led Jesus to a room he had prepared, and Jesus spent the night there.

Day 18: Wednesday

Day 18: Wednesday: Jesus at Nain - Stories of both Elijah and Jesus raising a widow's son from the dead at Nain – Jesus visits with the widow and her son.

"This is Wednesday, day 18," said Peter.

They watched as the Samaritan was thanking Jesus for visiting him. "Even though I have been cured of leprosy, and the priest has certified that I am clean and can worship in the Temple, only my closest relatives and a few dear friends will spend time with me or come to my home. Even when I go to synagogue, they look at me as if they do not want me there, though the rabbi has confirmed I have no leprosy. I wanted to get married and have children, but none of the parents allow their daughter to marry me. So I live a single life, contented and thanking Jesus every night for making my body whole again. Though I do not have the disease, still that stigma persists among the people around here. How can a man cured from leprosy overcome this stigma?"

Jeremiah could see the tears in the Samaritan's eyes as Jesus reached out to hug him goodbye. "Peace be with you," said Jesus, and walked out the door.

He headed out of the village, and Jeremiah asked where He was going.

"He is going northwest toward Nain." At Jeremiah's puzzled look, Peter went on, "Nain was about five miles southwest of Nazareth, on the northern edge of the Plain of Esdraelon." He paused, waiting for Jeremiah, then gave him another hint. "Two people were raised from the dead here – one by Elijah and one by Jesus."

"Now I remember Nain!" cried Jeremiah. "I remembered the story of Elijah, but not where it was."

"Before we look at what Jesus did in Nain, why don't you tell me the story of Elijah at Nain?" asked Peter.

143

Jeremiah began the story, "Elijah was staying at a poor widow's house. She had only one son, and no source of income. She only had a little flour in a jar and a little oil in a jug, but Elijah said if she would make bread for him, her flour and oil would never run out. It all happened as Elijah said, and all was well until the son of the widow became ill and died. She was stricken with grief, and cried out against Elijah. Elijah then took the boy up to his own room, cried out to the Lord, stretched out on the boy three times and cried out to the Lord to return the boy's life to him. His prayer was granted, and the boy lived. Elijah picked him up, carried him downstairs, and gave him to his mother, saying, 'Look, your son is alive!' The woman acknowledged Elijah as a man of God, speaking the true word of the Lord."

He stopped to catch his breath, and then said, "Some people have said Elijah performed what we would call cardiac resuscitation that we do to revive victims of heart attacks. Anyway, I also know that Nain is where Jesus raised a widow's son from the dead."

"Right," said Peter. "Would you like to see that?"

At Jeremiah's nod, the images began, and he saw Jesus, His disciples, and a large crowd walking toward a town. They had not yet reached the city gates when they opened. Jeremiah couldn't see anything about who was leaving the town as yet, but he knew it was a funeral procession because of the sounds of grief from the mourners. Even though Jeremiah knew these mourners were usually paid, the sounds they emitted were truly those of grief and loss.

It was a good-sized crowd coming out of the city gates, with the mourners in front, the men carrying the bier right behind, a middle aged woman following closely, and an assortment of townspeople bringing up the rear. Jesus focused on the woman, all alone behind the bier, which held a form so small that it must have been a youth.

The two crowds of people faced each other in the road. The company of Jesus had stopped when He did, watching to see what He would do. The mourners had paused; something in the face of Jesus had captured their attention, their mourning forgotten for a second. "Do not weep," said Jesus to the woman who was just behind the bier, His voice sounding even quieter in the silence after the mourners.

He walked over to the bier. The men carrying the body had stopped when the mourners did, and they, too, looked at Jesus. But Jesus had eyes only for the young form in the linen cloth. He touched the bier and said, "Young man, rise up." Immediately the young man sat up. The linen around his head fell off, and he looked around. "Mother!" he cried. The men carrying the bier carefully sat it down on the ground, and Jesus helped the youth to his feet, turning him toward his mother. She held out her arms, unable to move or speak, and held her son close. The woman began crying for joy, but the people around her were silent, as if unable to believe what had just happened.

When the woman had calmed down enough to speak, she looked around. Her eyes found Jesus. "Sir, You are a great prophet," she said slowly, reverently. Then she turned to the crowd, her voice triumphant and joyful. "A great prophet is with us! God has visited His people!" Her shouts were repeated by the crowd of townspeople, and it was a procession of triumph that turned and entered the city.

The images stopped, and Jeremiah said, "The verses go on to say that rumors of Jesus went forth throughout all Judea, and throughout the entire region."

Peter nodded. "It was one of those times when we were needed more for crowd control than anything else. Everyone wanted to meet Jesus, to see Him, to touch Him and be healed." He seemed lost in thought for a minute.

The images began, and Jeremiah saw the resurrected Jesus standing before a small house. A woman and a young man were working inside, and Jeremiah knew he was seeing the mother and her son. As they realized someone was outside, they both came out. "Can we do something for you, sir?" asked the woman, putting her hands on her son's shoulders. They didn't seem to recognize the man who made it possible for her to do just that.

"I heard something about this young man, and thought I'd see for myself," said Jesus.

The woman's face lit up and she motioned for Jesus to come inside. "Please, sir, you are not the first traveler to want to hear this tale. Even the Temple priests from Jerusalem came here with our local rabbi. They wanted to hear my story and see my boy, but they could not explain how he came back to life. They argued among themselves, and then left in a hurry, as if they couldn't wait to get back to their Temple. Please, come inside and be comfortable while I tell You about what happened on the most wonderful day of my life!"

They went in, the son making Jesus comfortable in a chair while his mother rushed to bring water for their guest. "It was a miracle, sir! A true miracle! My boy was dead. We were all in the funeral procession going out to the burial place when a great prophet came and told my son to rise up." She stopped to catch her breath. "And he did! He called for me, and then he was in my arms."

"You might not know this," she said, "but I don't have any other family. He is all I have! I have no one else to depend on, to help earn our living, or to care for me when I grow old. Without this prophet, the one they called Jesus, I would be without a son. I would be destitute and heartbroken in my old age. I would be dying without any help or hope." She hugged her son close. "He gives me hope," she said.

Jesus nodded. "You and your son were both blessed by our Holy Father."

"Yes, and we glorified God, saying that a great prophet was among us, and that God had visited His people. This prophet Jesus stayed long enough to teach us how to be followers of Him. We now know Him as the Messiah, the one we have been waiting for, for hundreds of years. He has finally come, we are witness to that!"

The boy spoke, "As I was being carried out of the town, my spirit moved out of my body. I saw the prophet Jesus in a bright white robe, light shining all around Him in the heavens. He was calling me to come back to my body, but I was so peaceful. I didn't want to come back." He reached for his mother's hand. "But then I saw my mother, crying and sobbing. The prophet Jesus told me that it is not time yet to come to heaven, and that my mother needed me on earth."

The boy looked intently at Jesus. "I saw the prophet Jesus, and as soon as He put His hand on the bier, my spirit that had been floating above my body entered back into it. Then I heard Him say, 'Young man, rise up.' And I did."

The mother said, "You cannot imagine how I felt, one moment to be mourning my son's death, the next to hold him, alive, in my arms. I cannot describe the feeling." She stared at Jesus, and then started to smile. "Something else happened recently. Our Rabbi came to see me and to tell me that he had a dream that a holy man had appeared on my doorstep. He told me to watch for him, to offer the hospitality of my home and to care for him. I believe," she said, "that You are that holy man. I was unable to thank the prophet Jesus enough, and now I have the opportunity to serve a holy man. Please stay with us this evening. We can make a bed for You in the next room."

"Blessed are they that mourn, they shall be comforted, and blessed are the pure in heart: for they shall see God," replied Jesus.

The woman clasped her hands in prayer. "You are the holy man the rabbi told us about!" she cried. "I have never heard such a blessing. I have always been pure in heart, and was blessed indeed with the prophet Jesus raised my son from the dead. I saw Him, and His power. He is the Son of God, whom I worship, walking among us."

"You have taken Him as your savior, and you will have eternal life in heaven," said Jesus.

It was the strangest evening the woman had ever spent. Her guest, the mysterious holy man whose coming had been foretold by her Rabbi, spoke in parables, gave them blessings, and was so kind, so gentle, that even though she knew He must be a very holy man indeed, she did not feel uncomfortable around Him. She made up a pallet bed for Him, and cared for His wounds. Jeremiah could see her looking carefully at the wounds, and then at the face of Jesus, and wondered if she had figured it out. She gave no sign that she had recognized her Messiah, but Jeremiah was somehow sure she knew in her heart who her holy guest was.

"It's like that old hymn, 'I love to tell the story,' she loves to tell how Jesus healed her son. Did you see? She practically dragged Him in, a stranger off the streets." Jeremiah said. "I bet that widow back in Elijah's day did the same thing."

"You're probably right, Jeremiah. They are both wonderful stories," said Peter.

147

Day 18: Wednesday

"It's a good thing I like that hymn – I can't get it out of my head," said Jeremiah, humming 'I love to tell the story' quietly to himself.

Day 19: Thursday

Day 19: Thursday: Story of Jesus as a child and growing up in Nazareth – Joseph obedient to angels – Joseph the good father – Jesus visits Nazareth – heals the old village leader who doubted Him – eats a meal with His siblings and talks with them about their brother.

"This is Thursday, day 19 of the Resurrection," said Peter. "Jesus left the widow and her son, giving them many blessings and thanks for the kindness they had shown Him. Where do you think He is going now?"

"The only village anywhere near here is Nazareth," said Jeremiah. "Would He really go back there? Is His family still there? Wouldn't they recognize Him?"

"His family is still there, but you have seen the drastic changes in His body since His resurrection. And His family had seen Him only twice in the last three years during His ministry – they have no idea how He looks now."

"I understand," said Jeremiah. "He looks so different from the Jesus I saw at the Garden of Gethsemane, or on the cross."

"The injuries on His body on Friday, the day of His crucifixion, have changed Him completely. We could not recognize Him when He appeared to us in secret. This is part of the divine plan from the Father in heaven, to let His appearance change so drastically, so that no one can recognize Him unless He reveals Himself voluntarily as He did to the Samaritans. By this physical change, Jesus was able to complete His ministry before His ascension."

"So He might be able to walk among His family and old friends without being recognized," said Jeremiah. "I wish you would tell me about His early life. There has been a lot of speculation, but the gospels are silent about most of His childhood. Some people refer to His early years as the lost years of Jesus."

"The reason the gospels are silent is because there is nothing of significance to tell," said Peter. "His birth at Bethlehem and the

149

flight to Egypt were significant, His trip to the Temple around age 12 was significant, but beyond that, He had a normal boyhood, growing into manhood in a small village. He studied with the local rabbi and learned everything He needed to help Him in His ministry later. He helped His father, mother, and siblings until He began His ministry around the age of 30.

Images began to show the young Jesus, studying the Torah with the other boys at the synagogue. "He was a good student," said Peter. "He knew the language of the Torah, and what everything meant. He knew all the prophecies and predictions that would acclaim Him as Messiah."

The images showed Jesus helping Joseph in carpentry, His part in the projects gaining in complexity as He grew older. Jeremiah saw Jesus and Joseph working on whatever construction projects were needed in the village and surrounding regions, from repairs to carpentry to building stone walls. As His younger brothers and sisters grew, they were able to help: the brothers with the family business, and the sisters with their mother's housework and cooking. Jeremiah could see Joseph aging rapidly over the years, with Jesus and His brothers taking more and more of the responsibilities. Joseph seemed to be ill sometimes, and then the youngsters worked even harder to support their family.

Jeremiah was fascinated by what he saw. "I can see now what the gospels were talking about when the people of Nazareth said, 'Is this not the carpenter, the son of Mary, the brother of James, and Joseph, and of Judas, and Simon? And are not His sisters here with us?' But why do they not mention His father Joseph? They talk about Mary and His siblings, but do not mention Joseph at all after Jesus begins His ministry."

"Joseph was older than Mother Mary. He died suddenly while working in his carpentry shop making a door and window frame for a house they were building. Jesus stayed for some time to care for the family and organize the business, assigning jobs to His siblings and helping His mother. Joseph had fulfilled his mission: to marry the young woman Mary, to journey first to Bethlehem, where the child was born, and then to Egypt, so they would be safe from King Herod. He returned to Nazareth after King Herod died, and there Jesus lived until He began His ministry. Joseph was in his mid fifties when he died. He had completed his mission, and died a few months before Jesus began His ministry."

"I know the angels appeared to Joseph, either in visions or dreams, and he obeyed them," said Jeremiah. "Each of those tasks that he carried out was in response to the direction of an angel."

"Yes, and you know from your experience as a preacher, that it takes courage to obey God, or an angel. Joseph's friends and neighbors never understood why he stayed away after he left for the census at Bethlehem, or why he came back, since he had been gone so long, but they were happy to help him set up his carpenter's shop again. The village people and neighbors welcomed his return to his work because they loved his dedication to his work and the fine products he produced from the wood."

"Joseph had faith, courage, and dedication. He did everything he needed to do to care for Mary and Jesus; and keep Him safe as He was growing up. Even though his neighbors didn't realize the significance, they could appreciate that he was a good husband and father. He was a good provider for his family. Joseph's funeral was very well attended."

"But wait, Peter," Jeremiah was struck by a thought. "You say Joseph was ill a lot. Couldn't Jesus have healed his illness? Couldn't Jesus have brought His father back from the dead? I know He had the power!"

"Jeremiah, Jesus had not yet started His ministry when His father was ill, or when he died. It was not time for Him to start working openly as the Son of God. His mission at that time was to help His ailing father and support His family. But what if He had done something miraculous for His father? What would the synagogue leaders and their neighbors in Nazareth have said? They would have suspected that He was trying to trick them, to have His father pose as a sick man who was healed or a dead man who came back to life."

"I never thought about it like that," said Jeremiah. "I suppose He didn't want His ministry to begin with doubts and rumors. And if it was the mission of Joseph to care for Jesus until He came of age, then Jesus was again doing His heavenly Father's will in letting Joseph be ill like other men, and die as he did."

"Everything was working according to the master plan of our Heavenly Father," said Peter. "Are you ready to see what Jesus does in Nazareth now?"

"Yes," said Jeremiah, and the images began to appear.

Jesus was standing in front of a house. Inside were four men and two young women. The men were stitching and gathering clothes, tents, and sleeping blankets. The women were preparing and preserving food. Jeremiah realized they were getting ready for a journey. When Jesus knocked at the door, one of the brothers opened it. "That is James," said Peter.

"What can we do for you, Rabbi?" asked James. "We are preparing for a journey to Jerusalem in a week or two, but we always have time to welcome a holy man or a stranger to our village. If you would like to share our evening meal, we eat an hour after sundown."

"Yes, thank you," said Jesus. "I would like to walk about the village and then return here to join you for your evening meal."

Jeremiah watched as Jesus wandered about the village, looking at the places He had known as a child and a youth. He looked at the houses, doors and windows He had helped His father to build, and the stone wall He had helped with. He passed by an old man lying on a wooden cot in the shade of a tree in the front yard of a small house. The man was curled up and looked deathly ill. As Jesus passed, He touched the edge of the cot.

Jesus continued to the synagogue where He had preached. Peter leaned over to Jeremiah. "This is where Aaron, one of the village leaders, had questioned His knowledge of scripture, asking where this man got this knowledge, what is this wisdom that has been given Him. 'Isn't this the carpenter?' Aaron had said. 'Isn't this the son of Mary, and the brother of James, Joses, Judas, and Simon? Aren't His sisters here with us?' It was tough for Him at Nazareth. The village leaders, and even His own neighbors didn't believe Him, or His teachings. It was true, that 'a prophet is not honored in his own country, or among his own kin, or in his own house.' Jesus had only healed a few sick people. He had been amazed at their lack of faith. It was then that He decided to move His ministry to Capernaum, 20 miles to the north."

Slowly Jesus turned and walked back the way He came. He saw the sick man whose cot He had touched on the way. The man was looking much better now, eating, and talking to his family and neighbors in a most lively fashion. As Jesus approached, one of the neighbors said, "Aaron, tell us again what happened."

The old man seemed only too happy to tell his story yet again, "As I was lying on my cot here, close to death, I saw a man, a stranger in the village, walk by. He merely touched the edge of my cot, and now I find I am completely healed. I have recovered my life! I am like a new man! Could this have been our own Jesus, the son of Joseph the carpenter, whose brothers and sisters are still with us? We heard for almost three years about His healings, miracles, and teachings, although before this day I had not believed any of them. Now we've been hearing some very strange rumors – do you think it could have really been Him? Could He have been right all along? If He is truly a man of God, then we can preach that gospel ourselves. We can bear witness to His miracles, and spread His teachings."

Jeremiah laughed at the man's exuberance, and Peter said, "It is even more ironic when you realize that man was the village leader here when Jesus was young. He was the one who did not believe someone raised in his own village could be a prophet, a man of God. But look: now he is a believer."

Jeremiah laughed again. "It took him some time, didn't it? The disciple Nathaniel got it at once."

"How do you tell Nathaniel's story, Jeremiah?"

"Philip, a disciple of Jesus, finds his friend Nathaniel. Philip says that they have found Him, the one who Moses, the Law, and the Prophets all wrote about. He is Jesus of Nazareth, the son of Joseph. Nathaniel responds with, 'Can any good thing come out of Nazareth?' And Philip, instead of arguing with him, just invites him to come and see. Of course, Jesus knew Nathaniel and his skepticism. As Nathaniel is walking up to Him, Jesus says, 'Look, an Israelite in whom there is no guile!' Nathaniel was taken aback, and asked from where He knew him. Jesus replied, 'Before Philip called you, I saw you under the fig tree.' In what is perhaps the fastest turnaround in history, Nathaniel says, 'Rabbi, You are the Son of God, You are the King of Israel.' Jesus said, 'You believe all

153

this from just Me seeing you under a fig tree? You will see greater things than this. Truly, you will see heaven open, and the angels of God ascending and descending upon the Son of Man.' And that's how Nathaniel became a disciple."

"Yes, Jeremiah, that is right."

"I have always liked Nathaniel," said Jeremiah. "His ego did not get in the way of his faith. It is too bad that it took that Aaron so long to come around."

"It took time, but he did change his mind about Jesus," said Peter. "But I think Jesus is heading toward home. Did you realize it has been 24 days since the Last Supper with the disciples? And here He is, going to have a last supper with His siblings." And with that, the images shifted to show Jesus walking on toward His old home.

He was greeted by His brother James, who gestured to a seat where His two sisters offered a basin of clean water and a towel so the traveler could refresh Himself. When He finished they all gathered around the table. Before anyone could take a bite, Jesus took bread from the basket offered by His sister Hannah and broke it. He handed out the bread, saying, "In honor of the One who died on the cross, and rose from the dead to give us eternal life, I take this bread which represents His body, and remember Him." The brothers and sisters silently took the bread and began their meal. Jesus did not eat much, and there was no conversation.

"They just didn't know what to think about that blessing," said Peter. "The usual talk at a meal with a stranger would have been news of where he had been, or the people he had seen along his way. After that blessing of Jesus, no one wanted to talk about ordinary things, and they didn't really want to talk about their brother at a meal – it was too emotional for them, remembering His death and wondering about the rumors."

At the end of the supper, Jesus took a cup of wine and said, "Drink this, all of you, as a remembrance of the blood that was shed by Jesus the Messiah on the cross for the forgiveness of sins." The sisters looked as if they were going to weep, and the brothers looked angry. Jesus spoke to their emotion, "I can see the One who died on the cross and shed His blood for the forgiveness of sins was very dear to you. I can tell you that He has risen from the dead and has been seen in Jerusalem."

James jumped up. "That is where we are going! We had heard the rumors, but have not spoken to someone who has seen Him. Can you tell us? Did you see Him?" The two sisters looked hopeful, and Jeremiah wondered what on earth Jesus would be able to say about Himself without letting them know who He was.

"I was there when He appeared to the disciples in Jerusalem," said Jesus (which was perfectly true, thought Jeremiah). "He showed the wounds on His hands and feet, and ate food with them. He visited them twice, and they talked about meeting Him in Galilee. But they also were talking about returning to Jerusalem. I do not know where anyone else is now, but they will be returning to Jerusalem – it is well that you are going there to meet Him."

James looked thoughtful, and then said, "You have not given us Your name, and I will not ask it. I see that You knew our brother and were one of His followers. We will finish our preparations and go to Jerusalem within a week or two. Perhaps we will see You there, as well."

Jesus rose from the table. All eyes were on Him as He asked His brother Simon for a bowl of water and a towel. Mystified, Simon gave Him those things, and Jesus knelt before His brother James. Jesus begins to wash the feet of James, and as all the siblings looked on, He washed the feet of everyone, even the sisters. One by one, He dipped their feet in the basin, and then dried them with the towel.

His sister Abigail was the first to find her voice. "Rabbi, why are you washing our feet?"

"You have called me Rabbi, and have invited me to be your guest. As your guest, I am washing your feet even as you, the hosts, gave me water to wash mine as I entered the house. As I have washed your feet, you also ought to wash one another's feet. Do these things and you will be blessed."

As He finished the last set of feet, He rose, setting the basin and towel carefully on the table. "Thank you for the supper," He said, and walked toward the door.

"Wait," said James. "You knew our brother – is there anything you can tell us about what has happened? We heard some of His teachings, and have recently come to believe what He said, but there is much that we missed when we did not believe He was the Messiah."

Jesus turned, as if pondering what He could say to these brothers and sisters. Slowly He sat down and they gathered around Him. "Your brother," He began, "lived and died as part of a heavenly plan. He was the Messiah promised of old, but the salvation that was promised was not for the nation of Israel from earthly oppressors, such as the Romans, but for each soul, from the oppression of evil. His ministry reached many while He was alive, but He always knew that something bigger was ahead. Finally the hour had come for Him to be glorified. The prophets had spoken of this: that He would suffer before He came into His glory. He did suffer and die at the hands of the Romans, and now He has risen from the dead as promised."

The siblings were quiet, taking this in, and then the youngest spoke. "You said something about Jerusalem," said Abigail. "We know where our mother is staying there."

James looked annoyed at the interruption, but Jesus said, "He is meeting the disciples at Galilee, and He will be returning to Jerusalem, or at least the area around there, after that. The disciples have been staying at the homes of other followers of Jesus, and the house where your mother is staying would be the best place for you to go, at least at first."

"Tell us more of His teachings," said Hannah. "And why He had to die."

"His teachings were from God," said Jesus. "God gave your brother the wisdom to speak His words. When His time on earth was almost over, He said the hour has come for the Son of Man to be glorified, that unless a kernel of wheat falls to the ground and dies, it remains only a single seed. But if it dies, it produces many seeds. The man who loves his life will lose it, while the man who hates his life in this world will keep it for eternal life. Whoever serves Me must follow Me, and where I am, My servant also will be. My Father will honor the one who serves Me."

He stopped, and then began again: "The teachings were mostly about love. Love the Lord your God with all your heart, and all your soul, and all your mind, and all your strength. And love your neighbor as yourself. If you act from love, real love, you will actually be doing more than even the law commands. If someone asks you to go with them a mile, love tell you to go with them two miles. If someone asks you for your cloak, love tells you to give them your coat, as well."

Into their silence He spoke once more, "Your brother died, but He did rise, and is alive today. He has talked about a helper that His Father will send to empower His followers. His message will be carried even farther than it could have been before. The death and resurrection of your brother freed us all from the fear of death. He said in His Father's house there are many mansions, and He will go to prepare a place for us, that where He is, we may be, also. He has also said that He would be with us all, in spirit."

The brothers and sisters were quiet. It was a lot to take in, thought Jeremiah, especially when this had been someone you had grown up with.

At last Jesus rose to leave. James asked Him to stay, but Jesus shook His head. "I must go."

"Would you bless us, Rabbi?" asked Abigail. Again, James looked exasperated at her forwardness, but Jesus seemed happy to comply.

He stretched out His hands toward them and said, "May the peace of our Father in heaven, and the love of your brother Jesus, be with you now and forever." Then He turned and walked out the door into the darkness of the village.

As the images faded Jeremiah looked at Peter. "Why didn't Jesus stay with them? He stayed in other houses."

Peter said, "Jesus did not want to extend His stay any more than that. It was enough that He had spoken with them of their brother, at great length. He was afraid of being identified, afraid that the news would spread all over Nazareth and Galilee, that Jesus of Nazareth has returned -- resurrected from the dead! He did not want that to happen."

Day 20: Friday

Day 20: Friday: Jesus talks with His brother James – the world is the family of Jesus – Jesus visits His father's grave – Jesus talks about letting the dead bury their dead.

"This is Friday, day 20 of the resurrection of Jesus," said Peter. "Jesus spent the night outdoors in a quiet area of the village. Perhaps He wanted to be alone – it was 23 days ago that He had been scourged, was crucified, and died on the cross.

The images showed Jesus walking back to the home of His siblings. As He approached the house, the door opened and James came out, carrying a bag of tools. When he saw Jesus, he dropped the bag and ran up to Him.

"Rabbi, we want to tell you something that happened yesterday. Our respected leader Aaron was on his deathbed. Aaron said some stranger walked by and touched his cot where he was laid. Now we hear the news that spread all over the village, that he is well, free of the illness that we all thought would be his death sentence. My brother has healed many by touching, we know, though we did not witness these miracles except turning the water into wine at Cana. Could it be our brother visiting us? Have you seen Him in the village?"

"I have not seen Him here," said Jesus, "but that doesn't mean He wasn't here, just that I did not see Him. What you have just told me sounds like something He would do."

James was silent for a moment, and then began again, "Rabbi, I am so glad to see You again, for more than just to tell You that news. I wanted to tell You how much we enjoyed sharing our evening meal with You last night, and hearing about our brother. We all had such a peaceful sleep afterwards! We hadn't felt that sense of peace since He was crucified. We felt that we had left Him, when He needed us most. Your words restored Him to us."

James hesitated, and then went on. "We have come to realize that even though He was our brother, He was the Messiah for all

159

people, including us. I remember one day, He was talking to the crowd, and someone from Nazareth told Him, 'Look, Your mother and brothers are over there, wanting to speak with You.' But Jesus answered, 'Who is my mother? And who are my brothers?' I remember He reached out His hand toward His disciples and said, 'Here are my mother and my brothers! For whoever does the will of my Father who is in heaven is my brother, and sister, and mother.' I did not understand why He did not want to speak to His own family, but now I know that since He is the Messiah for all of us, that the whole world is His brother, sister, and parents, and there is no difference between us and everyone else."

"You have spoken well," said Jesus. "He loved you all, and in the same way He loved all others in the world – no difference."

Jesus clasped His brother's hands in a comforting grip. James said: "My brother Simon had a dream last night. Our brother Jesus appeared as resurrected, and shared a meal with us. He did not have the injuries we have heard about that He sustained on the cross, but appeared with the shining light of many suns. He could travel with ease among the heavenly bodies. Rabbi, can you tell us what all this means?"

Jesus said, "You all have been blessed for Simon to have had such a heavenly vision. When your brother reaches heaven, He will tell them, 'and look: I see the heavens opened and the Son of Man, your brother, standing at the right hand of God.' He will be able to do this. Have faith."

James was astounded, but still remembered their tradition of hospitality. "Would you like any food or water, Rabbi?"

"No, thank you" said Jesus. "I have all I need right now. Besides, it looks as if you are preparing for that journey you mentioned yesterday."

"Yes," said James, "and I am trying to finish up some work before we go. The earnings will make our journey much easier!"

They stood a moment, and then parted, James heading toward the center of the village with his bag of tools, and Jesus walking down the road leading out of the village.

Jesus was headed toward the burial ground outside Nazareth. He stopped at a grave, and Jeremiah saw His lips move in a prayer, but couldn't hear what was said.

"That is the grave of Joseph," said Peter, "He was buried on a Friday, the same day of the week that Jesus was laid in the tomb."

"Jesus spoke several times about the dead," said Jeremiah. "Once was just after a scribe had said he would follow Him, but Jesus replied that the foxes have holes, and the birds of the air have nests, but the Son of Man has nowhere to lay His head. Then one of his disciples asked Jesus if he could first go bury his father, but Jesus said, 'Follow me, and let the dead bury their dead.' Is there any meaning there beyond what we normally preach?"

Peter said, "The first part has two meanings. Of course the obvious one is that He has no home of His own to rest in at night like others. But the other meaning is that the whole earth is His home, and that was true to the end of His life. When He died, He owned nothing. Even His clothes were stripped from His body. What does that suggest to you?"

Jeremiah shook his head. "If there is a deeper meaning there, I confess I do not know what it is."

"Jesus did not need any worldly possessions because the whole universe was His creation and belongs to Him. We are all His tenants in a way, living temporarily here until we reach our final home in heaven. We might speak of owning this land, this house, and so on, but in truth we are just stewards of our Lord's creation."

"Thank you, Peter. I have heard some teaching on that, but had not connected it to that scripture. But tell me, what did Jesus mean when He said let the dead bury their dead?"

"The word dead in that passage is used in two different ways, Jeremiah. Sometimes the Jews used the word dead to express indifference toward something, or to say that something has no influence over them. You see that in Romans 7:4, to be dead to the law, and also in Romans 6:11, to be dead to sin. Both mean that the law and sin have no influence or control over us. We are free from their influence – we act as though they didn't even exist. In this example, it is the father, the head of the family, and thus representing the family itself, who is dead. The family of origin is dead to the followers of Jesus – their family is the world. They respect their parents, of course, but their primary concern is now a larger family." Peter stopped to let Jeremiah think about that a minute.

161

"Remember also the distinction between being physically dead and being spiritually dead. So this phrase could also mean to let the ones who are 'spiritually' dead (not followers of Jesus) bury their 'physically' dead father. But none of that applies to what you are seeing now, Jeremiah. Jesus is not spiritually dead, and Joseph was physically dead and was buried years ago. What you are seeing with Jesus now is a son's natural instinct to pay His respects to His father's grave. As soon as Joseph died, Jesus buried him according to the customs and started His ministry. You could say that at that point He took up his cross, even though He did not encounter the actual cross until three years later. Have you noticed that you never hear Jesus talk about grieving or reminiscing about His father's death? Not even once? He only talked of His Father in heaven."

"Since the Bible was silent about Joseph during the years of Jesus' ministry, I never thought about Joseph being dead, so I hadn't thought about Jesus not mentioning His grief at all." Jeremiah had a logical mind, and Peter smiled at this application.

"But there is another verse about leaving loved ones behind, right after that dead burying their dead saying," said Jeremiah. "Someone else said they would follow Him, but asked first to go and say goodbye to the ones at home. Jesus replied, 'No man, having put his hand to the plow, and looks back, is fit for the kingdom of God.' What does that mean?"

"Here is a case where someone says they want to do something, but maybe in their heart they don't really want to. This might also be a reference to the prophets Elijah and Elisha, when Elijah went to the field where Elisha was plowing and put his cloak around Elisha's shoulders. Everyone knew that meant Elijah had chosen his new apprentice, but Elisha asked if it was all right to go back and kiss his family goodbye. Elijah allows him to do this, and Elisha made a sacrifice of everything he was using to plow the field: he burned the oxen as a sacrifice, and used the plowing equipment as fuel for the fire. Then he followed Elijah. The young apprentice literally burned his bridges behind him: he had no other way to make a living except from farming, and he had destroyed all of that. He was demonstrating that his choice to go with Elijah and serve God was for a lifetime."

"I never thought about that connection," said Jeremiah.

"If you put your hand to the plow and look back, if your attention is focused on where you have been instead of where you are going, you might as well stay back there. In the kingdom of God, your attention is focused on God. If your attention is not focused on God, then you are not in the kingdom of God."

"Thank you, Peter, for this insight," said Jeremiah. "But look! Jesus is going back to His resting place in Nazareth, close to the synagogue. Why would He want to stay in Nazareth?"

"He wanted to be with His family on the Thursday three weeks after His Last Supper with His disciples. Today is Friday, and three weeks ago was the Friday that He died on the cross and was entombed. His home town is a good place for Him to meditate on all that has happened, and what everything means."

"I can understand that," said Jeremiah. "Look, Jesus is now walking in front of Aaron's house. He is no longer outside on his death bed, but is in the house, surrounded by a large crowd – it looks like a feast is going on! Jesus looks pleased."

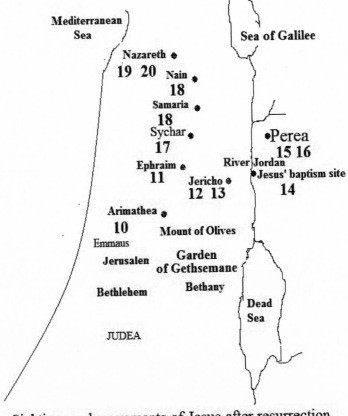

Mediterranean
Sea

Sea of Galilee

Nazareth ◆
19 20   Nain ◆
18

Samaria ◆
18
Sychar ◆
17

Ephraim ◆
11   ◆Perea
15 16

River Jordan
Jericho ◆   ◆ Jesus' baptism site
12 13   **14**

Arimathea ◆
10   Mount of Olives

Emmaus

Jerusalen   Garden
of Gethsemane

Bethlehem   Bethany

Dead
Sea

JUDEA

Sightings and movements of Jesus after resurrection
Days 10 - 20

Day 21: Saturday

Day 21: Saturday: Turning water into wine at the wedding in Cana – Jesus visits the woman who had been the bride – explanation of Jesus calling His mother 'woman' – second miracle at Capernaum – Jeremiah sees monument to Mother Mary in heaven

"This is Saturday, day 21 of the resurrection," said Peter. "Jesus is leaving Nazareth and walking toward Cana, about five miles northeast of Nazareth."

"This is where His miracles of ministry truly began," said Jeremiah. "You were there, weren't you?"

"Yes, He had called a few of us at that time. My brother Andrew was there, along with Nathaniel and Philip. Nathaniel was originally from Cana. We were all invited, along with Jesus' mother, His brothers, and His sisters for the wedding festivities."

"So Mother Mary was there, but I see you don't mention Joseph. Was this after he died?"

"Yes, Joseph had not been dead not very long when the wedding was announced. Many people in the wedding party were close friends with Mother Mary and her family, and they made a special point of urging her to come. Joseph, Jesus and His brothers had built the doors and windows for their new house, and they had all become friends. Joseph and his sons had worked on many of the building projects in Cana. Remember, Nazareth was a very small village. They worked in many of the towns and villages in the area to support their family. I think the bride and groom and their parents wanted Mary to come so she could have a break from the grief in the family and in the village itself."

"Thank you for that insight," said Jeremiah. "Can you tell me about that day, from your perspective?"

"We didn't know it was going to be the beginning of His ministry. We all just thought we were going to have a good time with Nathaniel and his friends, enjoying the good food and good wine that were always a part of a Jewish wedding. We were still

165

getting to know each other, and you have seen how competitive we could be at times. I suppose you could say we were in a festive mood."

Jeremiah laughed. He had seen young men and women gather at weddings, and had witnessed some of them having more than their share of a good time.

"When we heard the wine was running low, you could imagine our concern. And we weren't the only ones! I have no idea why the host hadn't provided enough wine – it was an expectation that was never questioned. Plenty of wine was always available for the guests. Hospitality demanded it! Of course," Peter said with a twinkle in his eye, "this was before the days of drinking and driving. Looking back, it might have been that the crowd was larger than anyone had expected – the young people were popular, and the parents were well off. Everyone expected a large feast – with plenty to drink."

Jeremiah laughed. Peter continued, "We were all surprised when Mother Mary turned to Jesus and said, 'They have no wine.' And then Jesus said something that stunned us all. He said, 'Woman, what is that to me? This is not my time.' Calling His mother 'woman' seemed the height of rudeness, and Jesus was never rude. It was only later that we understood that He was at that time separating Himself from His family of origin, from His worldly parents and siblings. The whole world became His mother and father, His brothers and sisters."

"I hadn't thought of it as sounding as shocking as it was to you," said Jeremiah.

"Mother Mary seemed not to hear. She called for the servants, telling them to do whatever Jesus commanded. Jesus asked them to fill the stone jars with water, full to the brim. As they did that, Jesus prayed to His heavenly Father for this miracle. Then He told the servants to fill flagons from these stone jars, and bring them to the head of the feast, the master of ceremonies. The servants knew they had filled the jars with water, but were now pouring wine from them into the serving flagons. No one spoke a word. They went first to the master of ceremonies, and he drank, pronounced this wine finer than the first they had tasted, and ordered the wine to be served to everyone."

"It's a great story, and it also makes a great text for a wedding sermon," said Jeremiah.

"We had planned on having a very good time with the wine at the wedding feast, but after that miracle we all decided to back off a little. Somehow getting drunk from wine that had been produced by a miracle, a miracle from the One who had called us to travel with Him in His ministry – well, we seemed to realize that was just not a good idea." said Peter. "But we should return to Jesus after His resurrection. Would you like to see where Jesus went when He arrived in Cana? Of course, it is the house of the bridal couple."

The images showed Jesus walking through Cana to the center of that small town. He stopped in front of a house where two small children were playing in the front yard. Jesus knelt down in the front yard and one child ran over to Him, climbing over Him as if He was a piece of playground equipment. The other child crawled toward Jesus. Their mother came running from the house. "I am sorry, sir if these children are bothering you," she said, reaching out to hold them back.

Jesus shook His head, called the children to come and said, "Let the little children come to Me, and do not hinder them, for the kingdom of God belongs to such as these. I tell you the truth; anyone who will not receive the kingdom of God like a little child will never enter it."

The woman looked confused. "Sir, do I know you from somewhere?"

"Yes, we have met before." Then Jesus took the children up in His arms, put His hands on them, and blessed them. The children laughed, enjoying the attention, and Jesus put the younger one on His shoulders.

"Rabbi, you speak like Jesus of Nazareth who preached all over Galilee, the Jesus who made wine from the water that we all drank at our wedding feast." She looked at the stranger, and then shook her head. "You don't look like the Jesus who changed our water into wine – forgive me, but He looked much younger and stronger – but we know Jesus suffered on the cross at the hands of the Temple leaders and Romans."

Jesus said, "All I can tell you is that I do know what happened in Cana."

When Jesus did not contradict what she was saying, she boldly continued, "We knew Jesus had died, but we have heard He was resurrected on the third day after His death. I think perhaps You are that man." She paused, then asked: "Are You the resurrected Jesus?"

"If you see with your heart instead of your eyes, you are seeing truly." At those words the woman's face lit up. Jesus continued: "You have been blessed with water made into holy wine from My Father in heaven."

"If you are the One I think you are, I know it is Your way to speak in parables and mysteries," said the woman. When Jesus made no comment she excitedly went on: "Please let me tell You about that wine and what it did for me and my family."

The two of them settled into the shade of a tree, the children still playing around Jesus, going back and forth between their mother and their new friend. The woman began, "I felt such joy, drinking that wine. All the anxiety of the wedding was gone. The wine filled us with joy! And that joy is still with me! You see these healthy children? I am certain that they were born in that joy, and continue in it. My husband's brothers and sisters were barren, and they were worried that we might be, as well."

"What a divine blessing!" said Jesus.

"Rabbi, you are right about the divine blessing! I must tell you about what happened to some of my friends who attended the wedding. First, you should know that we had many barren women in our village, not only my brothers' wives, but also some of my friends who had been married several years. They prayed at the synagogue, but there were no results. Then that mysterious wine appeared at the wedding!" She looked at Jesus, who laughed.

"Not only did the wine give us joy that lasted beyond the evening, but every one of the barren women became pregnant and they all gave birth to healthy babies! Cana is filled with many young children ever since Mary's son Jesus visited us and made water into wine for all of us to drink at my wedding feast."

"You and those who were at the wedding are blessed by our Father in heaven with children so that the miracle of the wine would multiply into other miracles," said Jesus. "Remember that whoever drinks of water given you by man shall thirst again, but whoever drinks the water given by Jesus the Messiah, even in the form of wine, shall never thirst, and will have everlasting life."

Jesus continued, "I know you have spent time up to now teaching them to walk and talk, but as they grow, teaching them love, forgiveness, and the kingdom of heaven that is within their reach will become more important. Now you know in part, but one day you will know God's love in full, and trust Him. God has a great future for you and these children."

The woman hugged her children close, and Jesus rose, put His hands on the children's heads for a final blessing, said goodbye to the woman, and walked down the road.

The woman sat for a moment, lost in wonder about His love to her children and the kingdom of God within them. She was elated with her encounter with this stranger that she had decided in her heart must be the resurrected Jesus.

She called to her husband, running inside the house to tell him all about the rabbi who had visited them. "He must be the resurrected Jesus," she insisted.

Her husband said, "Go and see if He is still nearby. We will offer Him our hospitality, whether He is the resurrected Jesus or not. What He said to you tells us He is a holy man with visions of the past, present and future."

The woman ran out of the house, peering up and down the road, but there was no sign of Jesus. Disappointment almost overcame her, but when she saw her children playing at her feet, she began to laugh and hug them. "You are our little miracles, blessed by our Lord Jesus the Messiah!" she said.

As the images faded Peter turned to Jeremiah. "Do you see the important events that took place at that wedding?"

Jeremiah said, "I know the miracle of changing the water into wine was important, and it marked the beginning of His ministry."

"Yes, and we talked briefly about the second," said Peter. "It is Jesus separating Himself from His mother, addressing her as 'woman' so it would be clear that His family was now all men and women, not just His family of origin. This addressing of His mother as woman has created a stir among many thinkers and writers."

"It still seems a little harsh not to call her mother," said Jeremiah.

"There are two other times that He does not accept His mother and siblings, that He separates Himself from His family. James the brother of Jesus just mentioned the first one, when He was in the middle of a crowd, and someone came to tell Him that His mother and brothers were looking for Him. He asked, who is my mother or my brothers, and answered by gesturing to the crowd, saying whoever does the will of God is my brother, my sister, and my mother. The other time is when He was on the cross. He saw His mother standing near the disciple John, and said, 'Woman, behold your son.' Of course, John took care of her after that. By this time, she almost felt more comfortable with the disciples than she did her own family."

Peter thought for a moment. "The statement Jesus was making was not an insult to either His mother or His brothers, but rather was a statement about His ministry. His natural family ties are severed. He is no longer Mary's son, but her savior. He is no longer the son of any human; He is the savior of humankind."

"It must have been difficult for Mary to have to share her son with the world," said Jeremiah.

"She was always so sure, so trusting with Him," said Peter. "She believed in the message of the angel who came to her long ago, and truly received a special blessing, not only to be His mother, but also to be able to let Him go, to let Him be the Messiah He was born to be."

Jeremiah was thinking about how difficult it would have been to be the mother of Jesus when Peter said, "What can you tell me about the second miracle Jesus did at Cana?"

Jeremiah was stumped. A second miracle? As he sat there thinking, Peter prompted him.

"Jesus was returning to Cana, when He met a nobleman at the edge of the town, who was rushing to meet Him."

"Right!" said Jeremiah. "The nobleman's son was sick at Capernaum and no one could cure him, not even the prayers by the local rabbi. When the nobleman heard Jesus had come out of Judaea to Galilee, he went looking for Him and met Him at Cana, running so that he was out of breath. He fell at His feet and begged Jesus to come and heal his son who was at the point of death. Jesus only said that unless you people see miraculous signs and wonders you will never believe, but that did not deter the nobleman. He asked Jesus to come before his child died. Jesus said that he may go, that his son will live. The nobleman believed Jesus, and left for his house at Capernaum. Halfway back, he saw his servants coming, literally running from his house with the news that the boy was living -- healed, and completely normal. He asked what time his son had gotten better, and the time they gave him was the time at which Jesus had said to him, your son will live. The nobleman and his entire household became believers in our Lord. It was a long-distance miracle from Cana to Capernaum."

"Very good, Jeremiah," said Peter.

"Peter, wasn't there a third miracle at Cana? I know Nathaniel was from Cana, and we had just talked about that he believed Jesus was the Son of God and the King of Israel when Jesus said He had seen Nathaniel sitting under the fig tree."

"It is true that Nathaniel was originally from Cana, but it does not say that he was living there when Philip found him and brought him to Jesus. In fact, it says that Philip, like Andrew and Peter, was from the town of Bethsaida. If you would like to think of this as a third miracle at Cana, this would not bother me, Jeremiah, but it is not recorded just where Nathaniel was sitting under that fig tree."

Jeremiah rubbed his head, and Peter looked concerned. "You have seen many days of the past since you last rested at your place of meditation," he said. "Would you like to go there now? I think there is a shrine that you might not have seen yet that we could visit on the way."

Jeremiah looked grateful, and the two men walked out of the building and into the streets of heaven. Peter led Jeremiah on a different route through the city, and again Jeremiah was astonished at the beauty and variety of the building and parks. Now he understood what Jesus meant when He said, 'In My house there are many mansions.' Near what might be the center of the city, Peter stopped and pointed toward a monument standing by itself on a small grassy hill.

Seven pillars held up a massive dome, and at the base of each pillar a name was inscribed. Jeremiah walked around the monument, looking at each name. The first one was Joseph, and then came the children: the four other sons (James, Joses, Simon and Judas) and the two daughters (Hannah and Abigail) of Mary and Joseph. Under the dome, in the center of the monument, was the most beautiful statue Jeremiah had ever seen. It was Mother Mary holding Jesus as if He had just been brought down from the cross, with all His wounds still fresh with blood.

Even with Jeremiah's limited knowledge of art, he knew the artist must be Michelangelo, and this work was very similar to the statue that he had seen pictures of in the Basilica of Saint Peter. But this statue seemed almost a living tribute to the mother and her love for her son. Tears ran down Jeremiah's cheeks as he looked at this depiction of love. There was sorrow here, but also a hit of joy to come. He had no idea how this statue could move him so deeply. Peter did not interrupt him, and after some time Jeremiah asked, 'Michelangelo?" and Peter nodded.

"He completed this just recently – you can see how his artistry has improved since he arrived here. He is a blessing to everyone."

Jeremiah took one last look at the mother and son, and walked with Peter to the place of meditation in silence.

Day 22: Sunday

Day 22: Sunday: Jesus meets the disciples at the shores of the Sea of Tiberias (Sea of Galilee) – cooks fish and bread on an open fire and feeds His disciples - Jesus has private conversations with Simon Peter, John, James and Judas – Judas leaves the group – the 11 will meet Jesus again in the mountains of Galilee, where He first selected and named His disciples

"This is Sunday, day 22 of the resurrection of Jesus," said Peter.

"Where did Jesus spend the night?" asked Jeremiah. "He left the house before they could offer Him hospitality for the night."

"Jesus spent the night along the way, as He walked northeast toward the Sea of Tiberias, which you know as the Sea of Galilee. He was used to roughing it, and still had some of the dried fruit and meat the Samaritan woman had given Him. He is traveling very slowly, as you would imagine someone would with the wounds in His chest. He had bouts of fever off and on."

"But, Peter," said Jeremiah, "How did He know exactly where to go? I don't recall any time or place being mentioned."

"That is correct, Jeremiah. He just said He would meet us at Galilee. You remember, we did wait around in Jerusalem for a week after we saw Him the first time. Then He came to us the second time, when Thomas was with us. After that, we felt it would be all right to go to Galilee, as long as we kept out of sight of the Temple priests and guards. We really didn't know how long they would be looking for us. On the way to the foothills close to Capernaum, we camped on the shores of the Sea of Tiberias."

"I sort of thought that since He was the Son of God, He would know everything about who is where and what is going to happen. I thought that He knew the site where all of you would be camping as you traveled through Galilee looking for Him," said Jeremiah.

"There has been lots of speculation about how much divine knowledge Jesus had while He was still here on earth," said Peter.

"But I can tell you, it doesn't take a genius to know where we would be, especially in times of stress. Most of us were fisherman, and several of us were from this area. This was the place where we usually went when we needed a little time away, when we needed a little relief from whatever stress we were going through."

Jeremiah laughed. "It doesn't sound so mysterious when you tell it. You can take a man out of his fishing boat, but you can't take the fisherman out of the man."

"Would you like to see what happened? Look."

The images began. A dejected looking group of men were camped on the shore of the Sea of Tiberias. John was searching for driftwood for the fire. "The youngest always got firewood duty" said Peter. All twelve disciples were there, some talking in low voices, some walking around in solitude. Simon Peter strode up and down the shore, looking at the water, then at the sky.

"What were you doing, looking at the sky and the water?" asked Jeremiah.

Peter laughed. "What any fisherman does, when they are on shore – checking the weather and other conditions for sailing."

"I see two boats there, but surely they can't be yours – you left everything to follow Jesus!"

"I knew I should have started this scene earlier," said Peter, "but much of it was not that interesting – I just wanted to get to the part where we meet with Jesus. We had arrived earlier, and while the others built the fire I headed north to where I knew some boats might be for rent. I didn't have any money with me, but somehow that did not worry me. I had gotten used to our needs being provided for." He smiled, remembering those days.

"As I walked by these boats, none of them seemed right – I can't explain it more than just that – but when I saw those boats at a dock, I knew they were for us. The owner was there on the dock, and I didn't have to approach him with an explanation or anything. He came to meet me, and invited me to look at his boats."

"Did that sort of thing happen very often?"

"That kind of thing never happened," said Peter. "Those boats were the livelihood of their owners. If they weren't using them to fish, they were renting them out to others, for a fee or for a percentage of the catch. As it turned out, this man was a follower of

Jesus. He heard Jesus when we were all in that area, and his life hasn't been the same since. He has been a believer of Jesus, and he remembered me as one of His disciples. He was happy to do what he could for us. He actually offered the boats before I had a chance to ask! And he wouldn't accept any payment, although all I could offer him was a part of the catch."

"That did a lot to help my mood," said Peter. "I took that as a sign that we were somehow on the right path. The boats had been provided for us, and I ran back to get a few of the men to help bring them back around to the campsite. So that is why you see those boats here, at this scene. The weather hadn't been right for going out on the sea, until about that time. I had started getting what you might call antsy again – I couldn't keep still – I wanted something to happen, and I wanted it to happen now. And now you are ready for the story to continue."

Jeremiah looked at the images of Simon Peter walking up and down the shore, looking at the water, then at the sky. Finally he stopped, and announced: "The sky is clearing -- I'm going fishing. I have to do something. The Lord can come to us in the boat just as well as on the shore."

The other disciples looked startled, and then relieved, as if he had voiced the feelings they all shared. "I'll go," said James, and John quickly agreed. The others began preparations, running over to the boats to make sure everything was ready. John carefully banked the fire before he ran to join the boat that held Peter. Jeremiah watched as the men launched the two boats into the water. Five were in one boat, and seven in the other. They all looked extremely wet, and he couldn't blame most of the men for shedding their clothes at the first opportunity.

Peter said, as if remembering, "I certainly do not miss the days of trying to fish in a sopping wet robe, the hem constantly lashing about your legs and the weight of the water pulling down at your shoulders. It was so much easier just to take the robes off while we were in the boat. Of course, there were no women around, so it didn't really matter what we had on."

Jeremiah nodded, but his attention was all on the fishermen and their boats, as they repeatedly cast their nets, but caught nothing they could eat. Eventually night fell, and the boats drifted silently on the water, floating gently all night long. It was a pretty picture, thought Jeremiah. The moonlight was reflected in the water and seemed to dance on the waves.

Finally it was sunrise, and on the shore stood Jesus. His outer robe or cloak was spread on the bushes as if He had washed it and laid it out to dry. Jesus was tending the fire, making the coals ready for cooking. He called out to the fishermen in the boats, "Friends, have you caught any fish?"

Though Jeremiah knew this story by heart, he was surprised when the disciples didn't recognize Jesus, responding as they would to a stranger: "No – we have fished all night, but caught nothing."

Jesus said, "Cast the net on the right side of the ship, and you will catch them." Without a word, the men cast the net, but the amount of fish that were caught in it made it impossible to draw up the net. It was just too heavy. The other boat moved in to help them, and for a moment, the stranger on the shore was forgotten in the manual labor of drawing in the net filled with fish.

Suddenly John cried out, "It is the Lord!" and immediately Simon Peter grabbed his robe, pulled it around his naked body, jumped overboard, and started swimming for the shore.

Peter laughed at his younger self. "Almost drowned myself, trying to swim in that robe," he said to Jeremiah. "But I didn't want to present myself to the Lord naked, and I couldn't wait for the boat to get to shore. John was the first to recognize Jesus. None of the rest of us knew it was Him until John told us, and we realized we had just been part of a miracle, to catch fish where there were none all night long."

"He has changed beyond recognition. But we have noticed that John usually catches onto the spiritual things before the rest of you." Jeremiah stopped. "No disrespect meant," he added.

"And no disrespect taken," said Peter. "John was the youngest, but he was always the first to catch the inner meaning behind some of those parables. And he was the first to recognize Jesus here."

They looked back at the images. The boats were nearly back at the shore, the nets dragging between them. The disciples secured the boats, and then turned to Jesus, standing by the fire. On the coals of the fire were fish and some bread. Jesus said, "Bring some of the fish you have just caught."

Peter said to Jeremiah, "None of us wanted to ask Him where He got that fish and bread. He had just performed the miracle of getting us a large catch of fish -- and it was our Master, resurrected from the dead! We did not question; we just accepted it."

Simon Peter and the other men hauled the nets by sheer muscle power up onto the shore. Jeremiah had never before known how beautiful a mass of fresh fish could be. They were still wet and trying to flop out of the net and their colors glistened in the early morning sun. Even with the weight of all the fish, the net was not torn, and Jeremiah marveled at the detail involved in this miracle – no one would have to spend any time mending a net that had been torn because of an abundance of fish.

"Come and have breakfast," said Jesus, and the men gathered around Him. No one needed to ask who He was; they all knew He was the Lord. Jesus took the bread, gave it to them, and did the same with the fish.

Peter turned to Jeremiah. "This was the first and last time Jesus ever cooked food for us," he said. He was always breaking the bread and handing the pieces around, with a blessing, but this was the first time He served us fish. He had never cooked for us; the women who took care of our everyday needs did all that, even at the last supper."

"And this was the third time Jesus had appeared to all of you after the resurrection," said Jeremiah. "The first one was the evening of the resurrection, but Thomas was not there. The second time was on the eighth day to all twelve of you, and this is the third time, here." He looked at Peter. "Was it after this meal that Jesus talked with you about feeding His lambs?"

Peter said, "Yes. And even though I was talking with the Lord who I loved more than anyone else in life, it was the most painful conversation I've ever had. He asked me the same question, three times, and I knew it was to counteract the three denials of Him that I had made the night of His arrest. I had denied Him three times, and now I affirm that I will be the shepherd for His flock three times. Would you like to see that? You'll see that I didn't really understand the connection with the denial and the need for the repetition at the time."

Jeremiah watched as the men finished their breakfast and sat around the campfire. Their mood had changed completely; the anxiety of the day before had vanished in the presence of Jesus. He looked different, but it was clear that He was Jesus, the Master they had followed. They again sat in groups of two or three, some solitary as before, but their voices were low and comfortable, with short bursts of laughter here and there. Jesus sat with the men, His eyes resting first on one, then another, as the conversation progressed. After some time He caught the eye of Simon Peter, and motioned him away from the group.

They rose and left the campfire silently. No one followed them – the disciples knew better than to intrude on a private moment. Jesus led Simon Peter far enough away so they could not be overheard, and they sat on some rocks near the shore.

"Simon, son of Jonas," said Jesus. "Do you truly love Me more than these?"

"Yes Lord," said Simon. You know I love You."

"Feed My lambs," said Jesus.

They both sat quietly for a moment, and then Jesus asked again, "Simon, son of Jonas do you truly love Me?"

He answered, "Yes, Lord, You know that I love You."

"Take care of My sheep," said Jesus.

Again the men sat quietly. Jesus spoke, "Simon, son of Jonas, do you love Me?"

It was clear from Simon Peter's expression that he felt hurt. "Lord, You know all things; You know that I love You."

Jesus said, "Feed My sheep." He sat quietly a minute, then added, "I tell you the truth, when you were younger you dressed yourself and went where you wanted; but when you are old you will stretch out your hands, and someone else will dress you and lead you where you do not want to go. Follow Me."

Peter turned to Jeremiah and said, "It was much later that I realized what He meant. You know how I died, crucified upside down, and here He was, telling me all about it long before it was going to happen. I was trying to figure it out when we saw John coming toward us. Believe me, if I had known all the unfortunate interpretations that would be put on that next question and answer, I would never have asked it. But I was still trying to work out what our Lord had just said to me – I think I just welcomed the diversion."

Jeremiah laughed as he saw Jesus and Simon Peter still sitting on the rocks, with John slowly walking up to them. Simon Peter looked at Jesus and said, "Lord, what about him?"

Jesus said, "If I want him to remain alive until I return what is that to you? You must follow Me."

Jeremiah said, "I can just imagine the rumors going around. But Jesus was basically telling you to mind your own business, not to wonder about the other disciples, but for you to focus on following Jesus."

"Yes, I finally got that," said Peter. "I know the scriptures have portrayed me as sort of a country bumpkin, rough around the edges, and many times not too bright. And you know what? They are right! At that time, I was never the first one to catch on to what Jesus was talking about. That was John. I was a little what you might call uncouth – I had never been around city folk, or well educated people, or people who were high up in society. I didn't know how to talk to those people, or how to act around those people. Matthew the tax collector was better at all that than we were; he dealt with the rich folk of the region every day, before his calling."

Peter looked at Jeremiah. "But the Lord called me to be the shepherd of His flock when He couldn't be there for them anymore. He called me Peter, the rock, and said 'on this rock I will build My church.' I didn't think I was the best man to take over the job of shepherd, but Jesus thought otherwise."

"And you were a great shepherd!" cried Jeremiah.

Peter laughed. "That was all due to the Holy Spirit." he said. "Do you remember Paul talking about God using the weak things of the world to confound the strong? I think he was talking about me that day – if it hadn't been for the power of the Holy Spirit, I would have still been the country bumpkin afraid to talk to city folk."

Jeremiah nodded.

"But we are getting ahead of ourselves," said Peter. "Let's go back to where we were near the campfire."

Jeremiah looked up and saw Simon Peter heading back to the campfire alone, and then sitting by himself on the beach. Jesus and John were talking together back at the rocks. Most of the other disciples were sleeping, exhausted from fishing all night on the boat. The fire was almost out, and Jeremiah noticed that the sleeping men had each put a fold of their cloaks over their faces so they could sleep in the bright sunlight.

When John at last returned to the campsite, he walked over to James, who was talking with Nathaniel. "He wants to see you," he said to James. The elder son of thunder quickly got to his feet and hurried to see what Jesus wanted of him.

After James had settled himself on a rock, Jesus said, "James, you were always the first to take action. Now we will be needing action of a different kind, and I know you will be the first for this, as well. You will be one of the finest leaders of the new ministry in Jerusalem. The way will be difficult, but I will send the help promised by my Father in heaven. You will have no fear, and at the end you will have the place in heaven that is appointed for you."

Jeremiah looked confused at this statement, and Peter said, "What do you know about the ministry of James?"

Jeremiah thought for a moment. "He was the first disciple to be a martyr. He was beheaded, and it was said this pleased the Jews in Jerusalem."

"Yes," said Peter. "James went from being a son of thunder to being a strong leader in this new religion of our Lord. I am sure that the words of Jesus had a lot to do with that transformation."

"This conversation was so important that it is mentioned in 1 Corinthians," said Jeremiah. "Although this is the first time we get to hear what Jesus said to him."

The images showed James returning to the campsite. He found Judas, who was walking by the shoreline, throwing pebbles into the sea. "He wants to see you," said James. Judas didn't need to ask who James had meant; he merely nodded and walked back to where Jesus was still sitting on the rocks.

"Judas," said Jesus, stretching out His hand. Judas sat on a rock near Him. "I can see in your heart that you feel restless, that you do not feel as one with us."

Judas spoke slowly, "I feel as if I do not belong here with the group anymore. I know You forgave me. I know they forgave me. But I have come to realize that forgiveness does not mean that life goes back to what it was before."

Jesus nodded. "Forgiveness is sometimes as difficult to receive as it is to give. And you are correct: sometimes what has changed cannot be undone."

"I am still Your follower," said Judas. "You know I am still Your devoted disciple." As Jesus nodded His head, Judas went on, "But I need to follow You alone, away from the other disciples and the crowds that they draw. I need a time apart to contemplate all that has happened – my actions and everything that followed. I had a vision that the other disciples were stoning and persecuting me."

He paused, and then looked straight into the eyes of his Master. "You told me in Bethany on that Saturday, the day of Your anointing, when we were talking privately, that You would tell me the mysteries of the kingdom. You said it was possible for me to reach it, but that I would grieve a great deal. You said that someone else would replace me, in order that the twelve disciples might again come to completion with their God. Lord, I am afraid that my leaving today might bring that to pass, but I need a time alone."

"You are wise to know what you need," said Jesus, "and also wise to act on your knowledge. It will not be today that another is chosen to take your place." He put His hand on the head of Judas. "Know that your part was necessary, and fulfilled many prophecies. You did what you had to do according to the will of our Father in heaven. You have participated in the liberation of My spirit from My body. You will be a shining star in My mansion. Receive the forgiveness we have given you. Go in peace."

Judas gave one last look toward the men at the campfire, looked one last time into the eyes of Jesus, and walked away.

Jeremiah sat, stunned. "I had no idea all that had happened. There is a lot of controversy about how Judas met his death, but no one has suggested that he was still one of the disciples after the resurrection."

Peter said, "All this needs more explanation than I can give you here, but you needed to see how Judas left the group. Jesus knew that Judas would soon die and would be replaced, and also that he needed this time apart now. Our focus is on Jesus and what He did during this time, and part of what He did was allow Judas the freedom to choose his own path, as a follower of Jesus, but alone."

Jeremiah thought for a few minutes. "All right, I understand our focus. There is more than enough for me to try to take in as it is. Maybe someday I'll hear more about Judas. But is there anything else you need to tell me about this day?"

"Not much more about this day," said Peter, "but you will be seeing some things that were not completely recorded in your Bible. When Jesus met us here, He knew we would be fishing in this place where we felt at home and comfortable. But for His final messages to us, His disciples, He chose the spot where He first named us as His disciples: in the mountains of Galilee."

"I do remember in one of the gospels His last message was given from a mountain," said Jeremiah, "but I had forgotten about that while we were looking at everyone here."

"That part of Galilee was of great significance," said Peter. "That was where He did much of His teaching, which you have compiled as the Sermon on the Mount or the Sermon on the Plains; this was where He did most of His miracles, and that was where most of His ministry was focused."

"Did you leave that day?" asked Jeremiah. "When did He tell you that He would be meeting with you again?"

"We spent this day talking with Jesus, either privately or as a group, and at the end He said to meet Him where He had first named us as His disciples. We had thought He would be traveling with us, but of course He had other plans. Part of it was that He was walking very slowly, and part of it was that He was planning to visit other places along the way. So, that's why in the next few days you'll see Him visiting different towns on the way to the mountains, and we spend a lot of time looking for Him as we go in the same direction."

Jeremiah felt dizzy, as if his brain was trying to process too much information. Suddenly he remembered a phrase from his youth: "Peter, I think you just blew my mind," he said.

Peter laughed. "That's how we felt, all the time, around Jesus."

Day 23: Monday

Day 23: Monday: Jesus visits Magdala – history of Mary Magdalene – three different Marys: Mary of Magdala, Mary of Capernaum, and Mary of Bethany – Gregory the Great – Mary Magdalene after the ascension – Mother Mary after the ascension.

"This is Monday, day 23 of our Lord's resurrection," said Peter. "On that day we got up from the shores of the Sea of Tiberias, and found that Jesus was gone from the campsite. We found out later that Jesus went to Magdala. Can you guess why?"

Jeremiah wasn't sure he had even heard of the town.

"It's a coastal fishing village, where Jesus and the disciples came after the feeding of the 4,000. It's also where Mary Magdalene was from," explained Peter. "She was from Magdala, so they called her Mary the Magdalene, or Mary Magdalene for short, to differentiate her from the other Marys."

"There are a lot of Marys in the gospels," said Jeremiah. "And there has been a lot of confusion about them over the years, especially about Mary Magdalene."

"Mary was Jesus' only female disciple," said Peter. "She was one of the most prominent Galilean disciples. She was really an apostle to the apostles, as Mother Mary is mother to mothers of all disciples and the Christian world."

"The first time Mary Magdalene was named in the gospels was in Luke 8:1-3, where it says that the Twelve were with him, including some women who had been cured of evil spirits and diseases: Mary (called Magdalene) from whom seven demons had come out. Who was she, Peter? Why did she have those demons?"

"Before the demons, Mary was a beautiful girl married to a very wealthy fisherman in Magdala. Her husband loved her very much and treasured her. They had a beautiful wedding, and she was dedicated to her husband. Then tragedy struck: he died in a boating accident, very early in their marriage, before they had any children."

183

"Oh, no, Peter! What a catastrophe." Jeremiah knew what widowhood meant in those days: the woman needed to marry again as soon as she could, or she had to go back to her family of origin, especially if she had no children and no financial support from her husband's estate. If she stayed with her husband's family, she was usually little more than a servant in the household, many times subjected to abuses of all kinds.

"The husband had provided for Mary, so that she did not have to go back to her family. Indeed, he managed things so that she had control over his fishing business, earning her own profits. She was a woman of great beauty, with a mind to match. She was very smart in her business dealings, and was able to give of her substance to the ministry of Jesus."

"So, along with Joanna the wife of Chuza (Herod's Steward), and Susanna, and many other unnamed ones, she had enough money of her own to give Jesus and the disciples, as needed for His ministry," said Jeremiah.

"Right, Jeremiah. None of the others you mentioned had been healed of any illness. And Mary Magdalene didn't become ill until her husband died. She really loved him, and didn't know what to do with the rest of her life."

"We would call this Post Traumatic Stress Syndrome today (PTSD)," said Jeremiah. "I am guessing that the trauma of her husband's death was too much to bear, and she became mentally ill – it was a psychosis, not a physical illness. At the time she was labeled as devil possessed."

"We did not have the knowledge of mental illness as you have today. Faced with behavior that no one could explain, the priests used the term demon possession to cover any unusual behavior. Certainly no one back then could figure out what was happening in these people who might be suffering from a chemical imbalance or unknown mental trauma or born with an abnormal brain function. So it was with Mary of Magdala. The priests had decided that she had seven devils, and when Jesus came to the village and 'cast them out' they were dumbfounded."

"I know that sometimes it is difficult for a healed person to go back to their original environment," said Jeremiah.

184

"That might have been part of why she was so willing to join our ministry, rather than just donate money," said Peter. "There was no doubt that she had suffered, and when she had been healed, her devotion was beautiful to see."

"Would you please clear up the issue of how far her devotion went?" Jeremiah was trying to ask the question in a respectful way.

"I find it amazing what some so-called scholars will write," said Peter. "We are hearing all sorts of accusations about her character. I suppose it sells a lot of books, but none of them tell the true story. Mary was beautiful; certainly, but do you remember her devotion to her husband? He was her one true love, and Jesus was her Lord and savior. It is well not to confuse the two."

"So there was no romance? The Gospel of Philip suggests otherwise."

"That gospel was written many years after the fact. A lot of it is based on the rumors of the day, and it certainly tries to discredit women as ministers in our Lord's service. I was there, Jeremiah. I would have noticed if she had behaved like that! There was no frequent touching or kissing, no romantic misbehaving, no secret marriage. Our Lord did not survive on earth past the 40th day – His injuries were too severe. There was no way He could have married and traveled far away with her, let alone fathered her child."

"So the love story part was fictional," said Jeremiah. "I am relieved to hear that. But what about her reputation? Was that completely unfounded? Pope Gregory the Great labeled her as a fallen woman in 591 AD. He described the three Marys in the gospels as all being the same woman. And the artists have certainly painted her as a wanton woman. But what was she really like, Peter? And how many Marys were there, really?"

"That's an excellent question, Jeremiah," said Peter. "There are three Marys that are confused in the bible as one and the same by many people besides Pope Gregory. Of course we are not talking about Mary the mother of Jesus; we are talking about the other ones.

"One Mary is located in Capernaum at a house of a Pharisee named Simon, where our Lord meets her and forgives her many sins, found in Luke 7:37.

"The second Mary is Mary Magdalene, who was from the village of Magdala which is located 13 miles south of Capernaum. This is where our Lord drove seven devils out of her (or cured her mental illness, whichever you prefer), found in Luke 8:1-2.

"The third Mary is the Mary of Bethany, the village located 65 miles from Magdala and 78 miles from Capernaum. This Mary was the sister of Martha and Lazarus. She anointed Jesus with ointment (John 11:2) the day before the triumphal entry of Jesus into Jerusalem (John 12:12-13) – you celebrate that now as Palm Sunday."

"When you put it that way, it does clarify things," said Jeremiah. "And I had always felt that those two women were different, since Mary Magdalene's name appears in the Bible after Jesus forgives Mary of Capernaum of her sins.

"Mary Magdalene was not a sinful woman like the Mary of Capernaum. She was devil possessed, or mentally ill. When Luke mentions the women who supported our ministry, the ones you mentioned above, he states not only that she was free of the seven devils, but also that she is in the company of respectable women who serve our Lord throughout His ministry. It is thought that she was even there at His ascension."

"Yes," said Jeremiah. All four gospel writers place Mary Magdalene as a witness to Jesus' death on the cross, His entombment, and perhaps His ascension. They also say she was the first and foremost witness to His resurrection, bringing the news of the resurrected Jesus to the disciples. This makes her one of the most significant female disciples in the gospels, apart from Jesus' own mother, Mary. I love your designation -- she is the apostle to the apostles, and the first female apostle selected by our Lord. I can see why she is symbolized with the statue in the Hall of Apostles."

Jeremiah stopped for breath and Peter laughed. "I agree with you, Jeremiah. It is unfortunate that Pope Gregory did not agree. Just between us," said Peter, "We thought the name Gregory the Great should have been Gregory the Mean and Sexist. He gave a sermon – you can find the text in the Patrologia Latina – where he stated that he believed that 'the woman Luke called a sinner and John called Mary was the Mary out of whom Luke declared that seven demons were cast' thus identifying the Marys as being one Mary. That is false."

"I know that his conclusions, even if they were false, succeeded in banning women from any position of power in the church. That was not corrected until 1969. But tell me, Peter, what did that pope say when he got to heaven and saw Mary Magdalene there?"

"Pope Gregory asked our Lord's forgiveness for labeling Mary Magdalene as a fallen woman." Peter smiled at the recollection. "And I think he was happy to see the reform in the Roman Catholic Church that gave Mary Magdalene her own feast day, ending her attack by the church."

"I can just imagine the rejoicing that was in heaven," said Jeremiah.

"There was great rejoicing," said Peter, "We were especially pleased since her reputation and good deeds were her legacy to the world. She had no children, remember, so only her devotion to our Lord lives on."

"I am curious, Peter," said Jeremiah. "What happened to her after the ascension? The Bible is silent about her. Of course there are those speculations about her marrying our Lord and perhaps having a child, perhaps traveling to a far off land such as India."

Peter said, "Since we have already talked about those stories as being invented tales to make money for the writers, and that they had no basis in fact, you can be sure that Mary Magdalene did not travel to India, or anywhere else. You have seen the wounds of Jesus, how slowly He traveled, how often He had to rest. He was in no condition to travel any great distance and set up a family."

"I know from my work with trauma patients in my prayer ministry, that there was no way Jesus could have survived those injuries He suffered on the day of crucifixion," said Jeremiah.

"What she did after the ascension was to work with Mother Mary. They continued to support the ministry of our Lord, first in Jerusalem, and then in other places as the ministry spread. She died of old age, and was received in heaven with great honors. Now she is sitting at the feet of our Lord, holding His feet as an angel. Jeremiah, do you remember what our Lord said to her when she wanted to touch and hold Him after the resurrection?"

"Yes, He told her not to touch Him, because He had not yet ascended to His Father. He also told her to go to the disciples and say to them, 'I ascend to my Father and your Father, and to my God and to your God.' But is there another reason why Jesus wouldn't let her touch him? I remember you saying that any touch might contaminate the wounds and make the infection worse."

"There was another reason, Jeremiah," said Peter. "He also did this to discredit her accusers and gossip spreaders. He was treating her as a sister. Remember when He said that anyone who does His will is His brother, sister, and mother? He does not let her touch Him to emphasize that their relationship is that of brother and sister."

"I hadn't realized that before," said Jeremiah. "May I ask one other thing? What did Mother Mary do after the ascension? You said Mary Magdalene was helping her with the work of the ministry, but there are many speculations about her life, also."

"Jeremiah, she was mainly working behind the scenes, helping the disciples in their new ministry. She also had her other six children to help, especially as they started giving her grandchildren!"

"But what about John, wasn't he supposed to take her in as a mother, when Jesus asked that at the cross?"

"Yes, Jeremiah, and when she was in Jerusalem she stayed in his home. But when she was helping her children back in Nazareth she stayed with them. It was a comfort to her that wherever she was, she had a home to stay in and people to care for her. The burial site of Joseph was also at Nazareth; she stayed close to his site of final interment and visited Jerusalem often."

"Many people pray to Mother Mary, more than to any of the saints," said Jeremiah.

"In heaven, she became a healing angel to those who pray and meditate on her, for her healing through our Lord in heaven. Her ministry actually never ended. It continues to this day with her being our Lord's ambassador for healing the ill and consoling the brokenhearted. All this is delivered in our Lord's name. When they pray to Madonna, the Mother Mary, it is the same as praying to our Lord who delivers healing to the ill and to tormented souls. The healing power of Mother Mary comes from our Lord, her first born Son."

They were silent for a minute, and then Jeremiah said, "We've had so much conversation, that I have almost forgotten to see what Jesus was doing in Magdala. If Mary Magdalene is in Jerusalem, what is He doing here?"

"He is on His way to Capernaum, but first He visits the home of Mary Magdalene. Watch, Jeremiah," and Peter pointed to the images forming before them.

Jeremiah saw Jesus walking down the street of prosperous homes. He stopped at the door of one, but did not knock. In the back of the house Jeremiah could see two men working on a fishing boat and net. Jesus put His hand on the house, and said something that Jeremiah couldn't hear.

"He is blessing the house and its inhabitants. He is blessing the fishing business and all who work there," said Peter. "Mary Magdalene has been one of His most devoted disciples, and He is honoring her and her business with His blessing and prayers."

Jeremiah watched as Jesus finished His prayers and walked down the road toward Capernaum.

Day 24: Tuesday

Day 24: Tuesday: Jesus at Capernaum – Jesus heals demon possessed man on Sabbath -- heals Simon's mother-in-law - forgives woman at Pharisee Simon's house – Jesus visits with these and other people on His journey through Capernaum

"This is Tuesday, day 24 of the resurrection," said Peter. "Today we are in Capernaum. Take a moment to think about all the events and miracles that happened at and around Capernaum."

Jeremiah thought about the madman in the synagogue, Jesus curing Simon's mother-in-law's fever, many unnamed healings, a paralyzed man, a Roman centurion's servant, the woman with the hemorrhage, and the raising of Jairus' daughter. Then he remembered the first time Jesus had brought a large catch of fish to the disciples, how He calmed the storm on the sea, walked on the water, and brought a coin out of the mouth of the fish to pay the temple tax. When Jeremiah remembered that the feeding of the 5000 also happened around this area, he laughed. "Wow, so many healings, so many miracles," said Jeremiah.

"Yes, since this was where Jesus' ministry was based at first, there were miracles after miracles and healings after healings," said Peter. "And there were many more, which have not been recorded. Since there were so many, we are going to look at this day a little differently from other days."

"What do you mean?" asked Jeremiah.

"Instead of recalling the gospel account of the miracles during that day, and then following Jesus through the day, we are going to look back in the past. We are going to see what Jesus did originally, then immediately see Him in Capernaum after His resurrection, returning to see the results of His actions. We will only see a few of the miracles and healings – the ones you are most familiar with."

"I like that idea," said Jeremiah. "I really love seeing the past, seeing Jesus working among the people."

Peter smiled, and the images began.

Day 24: Tuesday

It was the Sabbath, and everyone was at the synagogue. Jesus was teaching, and the men were astounded at His teachings: unlike the other teachers, He spoke with authority, as if He knew exactly what those words meant and could explain them to the common people. The disciples noticed that His teachings were well received, and were grateful that there would be no trouble, as sometimes happened when Jesus taught.

Just as the disciples were starting to relax and enjoy the teaching, a man jumped up from his seat. His hair was matted and dirty, his clothes were rags, and his eyes burned as if his soul was on fire. He pointed at Jesus and cried, "What do You want with us, Jesus of Nazareth? Have You come to destroy us? I know who You are – the Holy One of God!" Everyone was too startled to react immediately, but Jesus was the first one to respond.

"Be quiet!" He said, His voice stern, as to a wayward teenager. "Come out of him!" The man shook violently, started frothing at the mouth, rolling his eyes, and gave a piercing shriek as something that everyone recognized as an evil spirit came out of him.

The disciples were again prepared for the worst, but the people seemed amazed and approving of His teaching and also His treatment of the man with the evil spirit. They could see that His authority was not limited only to the scriptures, but also included power over evil spirits.

Abruptly the scene changed, and the resurrected Jesus was walking toward that same synagogue. A man was sweeping the area around the synagogue, just doing some general cleaning, and it took Jeremiah a minute to recognize that this was the same man that Jesus had commanded the evil spirit to come out of. This man's hair was clean and orderly, his robes were not new, but well tended, and his attitude was respectful to everyone who passed by.

He seemed eager to talk with anyone who would pause and listen, and his conversation was all about how Jesus had commanded the evil spirit to leave him, and it did! "He cleansed my soul from the evil spirit, and I repay His gift by cleaning the street in front of the Temple, so that all who worship here may pass easily, without any obstacles or mud to hinder them." Jesus listened to the account and congratulated the man on his new life, without the man ever realizing he was talking with the one who made that new life possible.

The images faded, and then a new one began. Jesus and the sons of thunder were leaving the synagogue and walking toward a home where Simon Peter and Andrew stood in the doorway, anxiously watching the three men approach. "Master!" cried Simon. "Come quickly! My mother-in-law is sick with a fever!"

Jesus strode into the house. The woman was lying on her bed, too exhausted to even lift her head to greet her visitors. Her daughter was holding a wet cloth to her forehead, but when she saw Jesus she quickly moved aside. Jesus knelt beside the older woman, putting one hand on her head and the other hand on her shoulder.

He did not speak, but the change in her appearance was startling. Her breathing deepened and became slower. Her shoulders relaxed and her eyes opened, focusing first on Jesus' face, then on Simon. The ravaging fever was gone. She held out her hand to her daughter, who rushed forward to hug her mother. Both women had tears in their eyes, and even Simon looked a little misty eyed. Jesus held out His hands, and the woman put both of hers in them and rose to her feet. She looked around her at the men standing there, and then laughed.

"What is this? Guests in the house, but nothing on the table to feed them? Please, sit and rest while we prepare the noon meal for you." Jeremiah laughed as she bustled around the room, arranging benches and stools so they could all sit. The daughter had hurried out to another room, and came back with cups and a pitcher of water. The older woman, who did not look nearly as old as she had five minutes ago, almost ran to the kitchen, bringing back a tray of olives and cheese. The daughter brought a platter of flat bread, still warm from the oven, and the men accepted this small feast gratefully.

As the men ate, Jeremiah saw the older woman slip out of the house and across to one of her neighbors. A few minutes later both she and the neighbor hurried out of that house, and to another one. Jeremiah realized she was telling her story to her neighbors, and remembered that the news of the healing had spread all over town.

The scene shifted a little, and Jeremiah realized he was seeing night falling. When it became dark enough to mark the end of the

Sabbath, the neighbors began arriving. Each small group brought someone who was sick or demon possessed, and Jesus stood on the doorstep, healing the ill and driving out the demons. "Do not speak!" He ordered the demons, and Jeremiah remembered the demons would have revealed who Jesus was if they had been allowed to talk. It seemed the whole town was there, and it was a very long evening.

Again the scene changed. Simon's mother-in-law was grinding some grain and giving instructions to her daughter. They looked up to see the resurrected Jesus standing in the doorway. "Oh, sir, we did not see you there. Please forgive our lack of hospitality – what may we do for you?"

"I would trouble you only for a cup of water," said Jesus. "I see you are very busy here."

Even as Jesus was speaking, the daughter jumped up and ducked into the kitchen, coming back with a cup of water and some damp towels for the guest's hands, head, and feet.

"Please sit down, sir," said the older woman, whose hands had never stopped the grinding process. "And forgive me as I work while we talk, but we are hosting a feast tonight for my daughter's husband and his friends. They have been traveling from Jerusalem to the Sea of Tiberias, and will need a hearty meal to refresh them from their travels."

She paused, as if deciding whether to continue with her tale. Something in Jesus' demeanor must have reassured her. "I had a dream the other night that Simon, my son-in-law, was going to visit me and bring his friends. And then, he sent me a message that he and his friends were coming from the shores of the Sea of Tiberias where they met their Master, the One who healed me from my high fever. Their Master had always drawn a crowd wherever He went, so I have no idea how many people Simon will be bringing with him. Best to be prepared, I always say."

Something about Jesus seemed to draw the woman to Him, and as He sat at the table, calmly drinking the water, she stopped her preparations and began talking. First she asked her daughter to bring some dates, fruit, dried fish, and bread. When those were on the table, she began asking questions. "Sir, if you have been in this area long, you must have heard the Master, at least some of His teachings."

"I have heard the teachings," said Jesus. "I saw healings and miracles. Your son-in-law might recognize Me. But what do you wish to know?"

Jeremiah almost laughed at the way Jesus fielded the questions. But the woman was serious, intent on something she had been thinking about for some time.

"The Master and His disciples were here, in and out, for many months, maybe over a year or so. He gave many teachings, but I was always too busy preparing the food, or cleaning up, or preparing for their travels to actually hear much of what He was saying." She paused, as if regretting a great opportunity. "I had thought He was like any other rabbi – even after He healed me, I should have known He was different, and maybe in my heart I did, but I still kept too busy to hear Him."

Jesus said, "You are not the first, or the last, to be too busy to listen to the words that will give you life eternal."

"That's just what I am talking about!" she said. "I've been a good woman all these years: I follow the Law, keep the Sabbath, and I have trained my daughter in these ways, also. But I have been hearing about more than just keeping the Law. I have been hearing about eternal life. The laws and the prophets do not speak about that, but the Master talked about it. Sometimes I heard Him explaining things to the men in the evenings."

"I can explain some of the things to you, right now," said Jesus. "And if you'd like to call your daughter, she can hear it all, as well."

The woman was elated. "Miriam!" The daughter came quickly to see what her mother wanted. "The preparations can wait a little while, while this rabbi tells us about the teachings of the Master, and eternal life." The daughter sat on a nearby stool and her mother turned back to this mysterious rabbi.

"The Law and the Prophets are an excellent place to begin learning about God and what He requires from you, but they had always spoken of a Messiah, someone who would come and take away the sins of Israel, and write the words of God in your hearts. No longer would you need to sacrifice animals for the forgiveness of sins, because this Messiah would suffer and die to forgive all your sins. The nation had waited many years for this Messiah, and had built up many expectations. It was thought this Messiah would restore Israel among the nations; that the country would rise up and be a strong power again."

"But God was more interested in personal relationships than with national power," He said. "The Law and the Prophets were external. The words were debated by rabbis and scholars, and interpreted by Pharisees and priests. There was no direct relationship between God and His people. The Messiah was the bridge that brought them together. His suffering, death, and resurrection atoned for the sin of Adam, and for the sins of the people, for all who believe in Him and ask forgiveness in His name."

The woman sat, stunned. This was not exactly what she had expected. She had thought there might be more rules, more things to follow, perhaps some special prayers or almsgiving.

Jesus waited while she struggled inwardly with this, eating small bites of the meal that Miriam had placed before Him. Soon He continued, "That is what it means when people asked Him about trying to get eternal life by following the Ten Commandments, or doing good works. None of those can give you eternal life. This eternal life is by the grace of God. It is a free gift through Jesus, who shed His blood for your sins. It is a free gift for all who believe in Jesus and follow Him. I think the exact words were, 'No man can come to God the Father, except through His Son. This was Jesus, who was the Messiah that no one expected. Salvation, eternal life, is possible only through Him."

"I do remember hearing those words," the woman said, "but I had no idea what they meant. When you tell me about a relationship with God, it makes more sense. When I heard that He had died, I didn't know what to think. Simon had left us to follow this man around the countryside. What would he do now? But then we heard He had risen from the dead. It was more confusing than ever."

"The Messiah had to suffer and die, and overcome death itself," said Jesus. "It was all there in the prophecies, but sometimes those poets are difficult to understand. Now that the Messiah has overcome death, He will send the promised helper to Simon, and the other followers. Then they will be ready to take up their new ministry."

"It all sounds so clear when you explain it," she said, "But I am glad I do not have to try to teach anyone else about it." She looked over at her daughter. "Miriam, I think we have had enough of this conversation. Let's get back to work!"

Jesus rose from His seat, gave the empty cup back to the daughter, and paused at the doorway. "I'm certain this meal will be a blessing to your daughter's husband and their friends," He said. "And I assure you that you and your daughter are also blessings for them." He raised His hand in farewell, and continued His journey down the road.

The women looked gratified, and sat for a moment then went back to their work with renewed energy.

'Peter, I love that," said Jeremiah. "And it helps me know more about what the disciples were doing when they came back here, after the resurrection."

"I thought you might enjoy that," said Peter. "Let us look at another."

The images shifted again and Jeremiah saw Jesus arriving at the richly appointed home of a Pharisee named Simon. Jesus joined the other guests at the table, reclining as was the custom. A woman entered through the main doorway and approached Jesus. She was carrying an alabaster jar. When she saw Jesus, she began to weep, wetting His feet with her tears and wiping them with her hair. She kissed His feet, and poured perfume from the jar onto them. The host said nothing, but stared at the ease with which his guest received these attentions. Then Jesus looked at His host and said, "Simon, I have something to tell you."

"Tell me, teacher," said Simon, but Jeremiah thought he caught a hint of challenge in those words.

"Two men owed money to a certain moneylender. One owned him 500 denarii, and the other 50 denarii. Neither of them had the money to pay him back, so he cancelled the debts of both. Now which of these debtors will love him more?"

"I suppose, the one who had the bigger debt cancelled," said Simon thoughtfully.

Day 24: Tuesday

"That is right," said Jesus. He gestured toward the woman and said, "Do you see this woman? I came into your house, but you did not give me any water for my feet. She, however, wet my feet with her tears and wiped them with her hair. You did not give me a kiss, but she has not stopped kissing my feet, from the time I entered. You did not put oil on my head, but she poured perfume on my feet. Therefore, her many sins have been forgiven, for she loved much. He who has been forgiven little, loves little."

With that, Jesus turned to the woman. "Your sins are forgiven," He said.

The other guests had been silent, watching the two men in conflict, but at this they began to talk among themselves. "Who is this who even forgives sins?"

Jesus ignored them and said to the woman, "Your faith has saved you; go in peace." She looked once into His face, lowered her eyes, and gathering her cloak around her, swept dramatically from the room. Jeremiah laughed as Jesus calmly went about eating the rest of His dinner, His host calling for more wine and the other guests whispering furtively behind their napkins.

The scene shifted to the resurrected Jesus standing outside a large home in the heart of the city. Through the windows, Jeremiah could see many young girls and women working in the house. He recognized the woman who came to the door as the woman whose many sins Jesus had forgiven at the banquet, but it was obvious that she did not recognize Jesus.

"Sir, are you traveling through this city? You are welcome to rest here, to have a meal, or to spend the night if you need a place to stay. My name is Mary, and as I have been blessed by a prophet, named Jesus, who we call the Messiah, I have made my house a blessing for holy men who are traveling through the city."

"Thank you," said Jesus. "I would welcome a meal at your table - but tell me, who are all these women and children at your house?"

"Come in and meet them," said Mary. As Jesus stepped into the house, one of the older girls motioned Him to a seat and another one brought a basin of water and some towels. A woman who was obviously their mother supervised them, nodded her approval, and then knelt to wash His feet.

Mary said, "We do not share the names of the women who live here, but this woman had been tormented and abused by her husband. When he started to turn his attention on the daughters as well, they fled to my protection. This house is for women who need a safe place to live, either escaping an abusive husband, or escaping a life of sin."

The woman washing His feet looked up at Jesus. "At first I questioned the wisdom of letting wives and mothers share the same living space with those escaping a sinful life. But I found we had much to teach each other. I have been teaching them sewing and needlework, to help them find employment in large, respectable households. They have been teaching me to think independently, to consider my needs and those of my children as things of importance, not dependent on a husband's whims."

"Since the women who rejected their former sinful ways cannot return to their previous employment, and have been rejected by their parents, we teach them new ways to earn their living. Some have become skilled weavers, cooks, even makers of jewelry. Word has spread about my rescue ministry here, but whatever jobs they have, they must return and sleep here at night. But of course, some of them have found husbands who value them as wives, and they leave with my blessing." Mary stopped for breath.

"Many of these married women are able to give money to help support my mission and rescue ministry. Since I had been forgiven by Jesus the Messiah for my sinful life," she continued, "I have begun a ministry of forgiveness and new life for other women sinners. I tell them if you repent and sin no more, your sins are forgiven as our Lord Jesus the Messiah preached and forgive my sins."

"That is a divine mission, indeed," said Jesus. "It will cleanse the hearts of many."

"That is my hope," said Mary, "But I am afraid I also have some failures. The women are welcome to stay as long as they need to, but I know that some of them return to their sinful ways when they go back to living on their own." She shook her head. "Rabbi, how many times should I forgive them and allow them back into the house?"

Day 24: Tuesday

Jesus smiled and said, "So, you are asking me, how often shall I forgive my sister who sins against me? Some say seven times, but I say seventy times seven."

Mary said, "That is wonderful! I never refuse to help. I always take everyone back and forgive their sins and failings, no matter how many times they fall. I am happy that you have confirmed my decision."

Jesus said, "Blessed are you and yours that mourn, for they shall be comforted. Blessed are those who are persecuted for righteousness sake, for theirs is the kingdom of heaven."

"I have been comforted, and I have been blessed," said Mary. "I pray that I am a blessing to others in our Lord's name. I teach the forgiveness that I have been shown, and I refuse to be resentful to those who used me. I have lost count of the number of girls and young women who have found sanctuary here since I opened this house in the name of Jesus the Messiah."

"Mary, you were once as the sheep that strayed from the flock until a Good Shepherd rescued you. Now you are the good shepherd who rescues the lost sheep. Well done."

At that moment a bell rang from somewhere inside the house, and Mary said, "That is the signal for our evening meal. Please come with me."

They joined a group of women and small children heading for a central courtyard. In this open air space, many tables were set. Mary led Jesus to the head table, and motioned Him to His place. They watched as the seats were filled. Some of the children sat at small tables, others joined their mothers at the big ones. The chattering turned to low voiced murmurs as the women saw they had a guest at the head table. When everyone was seated, Mary said, "Tonight we are blessed with a man who carries within Him the Spirit of God. He is here to bless us and share our meal with us."

Mary gestured for Jesus to begin the blessing, but He deferred to her. She said, "Eternal Father, in the name of Jesus our Messiah, I ask You to come and reach out to those who are with us sharing our meal, whose hearts ache with hurt and loneliness as mine did when You reached out to me. Father, in the name of our Lord, let these wonderful children gathered around the supper table know it is acceptable to give You the pain, loneliness and frustration that rests in their troubled hearts and souls. Permit them, through Your grace, the mercy to know You are listening to them, thinking about them, and that You care for them. Reach out to those who are in sin and seek You; comfort and guide them like the Shepherd tends the lost sheep. Redeem our body and souls. Amen."

She handed the bread to Jesus, who took it and blessed it, saying "In the name of the Father and the Son, we are breaking the bread which nourishes our body and soul." He broke the bread, passing it around to everyone at the table. Those at the other tables did the same, and the meal was served.

As they ate, Mary said, "It was at a banquet that I met Jesus our Messiah. The host, Simon, even though he had let me enter to wash the feet of Jesus with my tears, and anoint Him with my ointment, did not like the reaction from Jesus. I see now that Simon had set a trap for Jesus, by allowing me, a sinful woman, into His presence, testing to see if Jesus knew the kind of woman I was. When Jesus accepted my offering and forgave my sins, Simon was angry. He took me outside and forbade me to have anything to do with any of his guests. I told him our Lord has forgiven my sins and cleansed my soul. He said it doesn't matter, and that Jesus should not have accepted your anointing. He said Jesus should have known you are untouchable in our society. I know that Jesus was compassionate, and shared the suffering and pain of others."

Jesus interrupted her. "Mary, I have heard that when the Pharisees were critical of Jesus sharing a meal with sinners or publicans, He said that He had been sent to call the sinners to repentance, that it is not the healthy who need a doctor, but the sick who need one. He went on to quote from the scriptures that God said 'I desire mercy and not sacrifice."

"Holy man, those words could have been written just for me. He called me, a sinner, to repentance. It was at that time that I decided to spend the rest of my life in the service of our Lord, to guide those who are in darkness, like strayed sheep. It was the unconditional love of Jesus the Messiah, His compassion and forgiveness that set me free. I did not want to show merely pity, like the rich that pity the poor without showing them mercy. I wanted to show the love, compassion, and forgiveness that had been shown to me."

Their conversation branched out from there, touching on the stories of the other women at the table. "I was just one of the many prostitutes that worked the Roman garrison," said one woman. "It was not a good life, but I thought there was no other way for me. I had heard of Mary and her rescue house, but didn't think she would really let me stay with her and those respectable women."

Mary laughed. "Many of us were not respectable at one time," she said. "But now we all are. I remember persuading you that you really could have a future without depending on drunken soldiers for money. And now you're one of the most sought-after needle-workers in the house!"

The women laughed a little, and another one spoke. "I was the guilty secret of one of the high priests. What a hypocrite! Preaching purity during the day, and enjoying my bed at night. I ran off during one of the Sabbath services – the only time I could be sure he would be unable to follow me. I knew about this house, and they took me in even as I ran up to the door, Sabbath or not. The priest couldn't raise a public outcry, of course, but he managed to make his feelings known."

Mary said, "Nothing overt, of course, but we do receive donations from people who support our ministry. He made an effort to discourage that, but nothing much came of it."

Another woman chimed in, "I was married to an older man who had been divorced three times. The first week of our marriage he was as fine a husband as you would wish, but then he changed. Almost overnight, he started comparing me to his previous wives – all of them were wonderful and never made the mistakes I made. I had to work from sunup to after midnight, and any little mistake would bring abusive words and beatings. I couldn't take it anymore, and then I found him with his daughter-in-law – her husband had died a couple of years ago and she had stayed with him, helping out in his household. I caught him actually forcing her to his bed! It was all too much to take. I had thought of ending my life, but when I heard of Mary's house I felt hope return. The houses were not far from each other, and I ran away when he was asleep from too much drinking and found shelter here. The very next day he came here and demanded that Mary release his legally married wife. He told her she had no business sheltering such women. Mary was quite respectful, and asked him to come in. She served him water and told him that indeed, she had no right to shelter his wife, but that if he had treated his wives better maybe they would have stayed with him. I had never before thought about his previous divorces, but evidently Mary had. I went back with him, but ran away again at the next sign of trouble. He came for me again, and we repeated that a couple of times before he saw that I wasn't the submissive young wife that I used to be. He wound up giving me a divorce, and I moved back here for good. As the other women have said, my life has changed and now I am at peace."

"Everyone has a story," said Mary. "But we won't try to tell all of them tonight – we would be here until dawn!"

Jeremiah couldn't imagine what kind of lives those women had led. They seemed so peaceful now, sharing their evening meal and laughing gently at the day's events. When the meal was over, she invited Jesus to stay in their guest room. "We keep it just for the holy men who are traveling through Capernaum," she said, showing Him the way to a small room away from the noisy children.

Day 25: Wednesday

Day 25: Wednesday: Jesus talks with a woman He had healed from 12 years of bleeding – He heals and casts out devils – Jesus sees them both on His journey – Jesus raises the daughter of Jairus from the dead and talks with the daughter, who is determined not to marry – Jesus heals the Centurion's servant – Jesus sees the former servant, now freed and in charge of all the servants at the Garrison

"This is Wednesday, day 25 of the resurrection," said Peter. "Jesus is eating breakfast with Mary."

Breakfast was a simple meal, but Mary made sure Jesus ate enough to sustain him. Jesus told her, "Believe me, there is joy in the presence of the angels of God over one sinner who repents. You are the light of the world. A city that is set on a hill cannot be hid. Neither do men light a candle and put it under a bowl, but on a candlestick, where it gives light to all that are in the house. Let your light so shine before men, that they may see your good works, and glorify your Father who is in heaven."

"Teacher, Your blessings contain such a wealth of teaching. I know that You are sent by God, and God is within You."

Jesus said, "You were blessed when you shed tears and mourned for you were comforted by the Son of the heavenly Father." Mary's questioning look told Jeremiah that she was wondering how this man knew that she repented by mourning and shedding tears on the feet of Jesus, but He did not give her time for a response. "You are pure in heart; you shall see God. You have become as a little child; you shall enter the kingdom of Heaven. You are imparting the same message to those you have rescued who are like scattered sheep without a sense of direction." He and Mary walked toward the front door, and He walked through into the street, pausing for a last goodbye.

Mary clasped His hands in farewell. "Rabbi, I thank you for your blessing, May God go with You on your journey." She held His hands for a moment, and then let Him go.

205

As Jesus turned to walk away, a woman called to him.

"What can I do for you, daughter?" asked Jesus.

"Rabbi, the only other time someone called me 'daughter' was when Jesus who we know as the Messiah healed me when I touched the hem of His cloak as He was going to the house of Jairus." The woman saw that the rabbi was interested in her story, and said, "I'll never forget that day. Jesus the Messiah was on His way to the house of Jairus, and the crowds were pressing closely around Him. I had heard about His healing ways, and was weak from a flow of blood that had lasted twelve years. I knew He could heal me, and I knew all I had to do was touch Him – but there were so many people in front of me! The crowd was pushing and shoving, and I crawled on my hands and knees to get to Him – well, the closest I could get was the hem of His cloak, but that was enough. I felt lightening from the sky pass through me, every hair on my body stood up! I knew at the very moment, it was His healing power! The bleeding stopped immediately, Sir, and I knew I was healed. Jesus the Messiah must have felt that power come out of Him then, for He asked who had touched Him. It seemed a strange question, as the crowd around Him was thick, and it seemed everyone in town was jostling and touching Him. I knew what He meant, and I came forward, telling everyone what had happened."

She stopped for a moment, and then went on, "Sir, my affliction was doing more to me than just making me weak. Instead of the normal monthly bleeding of women, mine was constant. Since women at those times are considered unclean, they had to be purified before they could go to the Temple, be touched by men, or even prepare food for them or wash their clothes. My affliction made me always unclean, never being able to be purified. I prayed for the Rabbi in the synagogue to heal me; all the priests there had prayed for my healing also, to no avail. But after Jesus healed me, the priest certified that I was as other women, and could go to Temple, and be part of the community as all women are."

She looked at the rabbi listening so intently to her. "This healing saved my life, not only physically, but also spiritually. Can you imagine not being able to go to Temple and hear the sacred readings? Sing the sacred songs? Hear the call and response of the holy words?"

She stopped for breath and Jesus asked her what she was doing at the house of Mary.

"When the healing of Jesus saved my life, I thought about it a long time. I knew there were other souls who needed help. I couldn't heal them as Jesus healed me, but I could help them in my own way. Then I met Mary one day at the marketplace. She was buying such large amounts of everything that I had to ask her if she was giving a feast. She told her story, and I told mine. I asked her if I could help her, as I wanted to help other women, and she agreed. I became her assistant. I help her maintain the house, care for the women's needs, and also I tell them of the love and healing and forgiveness of Jesus."

She went on, "It is wonderful to have a home, and Mary and the others are like family to me now. My own family rejected me because of my affliction – they didn't want their whole household to be unclean because of me. When Jesus called me 'daughter,' it went right to my heart. Now Mary is like a young mother to me, the women here are like sisters and their children the ones I never had."

Jesus said to her, "Daughter, be comforted; your faith has made you whole. Go in peace." With these words, He walked away from the house.

The woman stood, astonished. She ran back into the house. "Mary!" she cried. "The holy man who just left your house – He said the same words to me as Jesus did when I was healed! We have heard the rumors – do you think . . ."

The women began to gather around her. One of them spoke up, "Last night, when He shared the bread around, I have never felt such joy. And I was able to sleep all night! He didn't look like the Jesus I saw once, but . . ."

Another one said, "I was able to sleep, also! And with such wonderful dreams! We have heard the rumors – perhaps He was Jesus – risen from the dead!"

Jeremiah spoke up. "This is amazing! Like ripples in a pond when a stone is thrown in, these women who Jesus healed or forgave are passing that along to other women."

Peter said, "This house of rescue that Mary founded is not called a church, but it functions as one. The word is preached, sinners are forgiven and taught new ways, and all the women support each other. Are you ready for the next one?" At Jeremiah's nod, the images began.

Jesus was walking into the synagogue, and saw a man with a withered hand. The priests were gathered around, and Jeremiah thought it looked like some sort of ambush.

"Is it lawful to heal on the Sabbath?" the priests asked Jesus.

He replied, "If your sheep fall into a pit on the Sabbath day, wouldn't every one of you lift it out, on the Sabbath day? Isn't a man worth more than a sheep? Therefore, it is lawful to do well on the Sabbath day." He looked at the man, who looked confused at the discussion. "Stretch out your hand." The man did as he was told, and his withered hand was instantly restored to health, now looking just like his other hand. Jeremiah could see the Pharisees murmuring among themselves, and knew they were starting to plot against Jesus.

The disciples looked anxiously at Jesus. The crowd seemed to be with them, but the Pharisees had disappeared, a sure sign of trouble. Jesus nodded and motioned for them to leave. They walked to the edge of town, and then beyond, into the countryside. Some of the crowd in the synagogue followed them, and they had picked up even more people as they passed through town. Jesus found a place where the crowd could gather, and began to heal the sick ones who were brought to them. To the people who were starting to call Him the Son of God, He said, "Do not tell anyone who I am."

A devil-possessed man who could neither see nor speak was brought to Jesus. The man walked with a shuffle, and his head was bowed. With a sigh, Jesus reached His hand toward the man. Jeremiah couldn't hear what Jesus said, but immediately the man jerked his head up and stared at Jesus, then around at the crowd.

His gaze returned to Jesus and he said, "That devil said You were the Son of David!" The crowd gasped as one. Not only had the dumb man spoken, but he talked about Jesus being the Son of David!

"Could this be true? Is this the Son of God?" said one.

"The Son of David! Here, among us?" another one said.

A couple of them ran back to town, where the Pharisees were gathered. Excitedly they told the story, and one of the Pharisees jumped up, angrily. "This fellow does not cast out devils on His own! He is casting them out with the help of Beelzebub, the prince of the devils! He is in league with the devil himself!" The other Pharisees agreed: they also jumped up and began talking in loud voices against Jesus.

The scene shifted and Jeremiah saw the resurrected Jesus walking toward a small garden next to the synagogue, where two men were tending the garden. Jeremiah recognized the men as the man with the withered hand and the deaf and dumb man who Jesus had healed. Jesus stopped to admire their work, and the man whose hand had been withered walked toward Him. The man carried a garland of flowers in his hand, and when he was close enough to Jesus he said, "My Lord Jesus healed me on the Sabbath day, and to honor Him I work in this garden. Since I cannot repay Jesus for His mercy, I give flowers in His name to honor those who are healers and teachers. I do not know You, sir, but You have that look about You. Would You accept this garland of flowers?"

Jesus nodded and bent down, and the man placed the garland of flowers on His head. Jeremiah thought briefly that a crown of thorns had made way for a crown of flowers.

Jesus said, "Did He not say, 'When you have done this for the least of them, you have done it for me?' Blessed are the pure in heart, for they shall see God." Then He turned and walked away.

"A crown of flowers," said Jeremiah.

The scene shifted to the outskirts of Capernaum. Jesus and the disciples were returning to the city. As they were walking, a man came running up to them. He was richly dressed, and the disciples and Jesus seemed to recognize him.

This man fell down at Jesus' feet. "Lord, please help me. I have seen Your healing miracles, and now I am in need of one. My only daughter is dying. She is only twelve years old and she is the delight of my heart. Please, come with me and heal her."

Jeremiah knew this was Jairus, and also knew he was taking a big risk: a ruler of a synagogue, asking someone who had been marked as one who consorted with devils for help. But Jesus did not delay; He and his disciples went with Jairus toward his home. People crowded around Jesus as He went, so that Jeremiah almost lost sight of Him in the crowd. Suddenly Jesus stopped, and said, "Who touched me?" and Jeremiah watched, astonished, as the woman he had seen before, whole and well, stood before the crowd, admitting to touching the hem of Jesus' cloak to be healed of her infirmity. Jairus stood by, visibly agitated, but not daring to interrupt a healing miracle, even if it was delaying his own.

Just as they turned back toward the house of Jairus, two of his servants ran up. "Your daughter is dead; do not trouble the Master to come to the house." As all hope left Jairus' face, Jesus turned to him.

"Do not be afraid. Only believe, and she shall be made whole." The procession continued, but when they reached the house, Jesus took only Peter, James, and John, along with the father and the mother of the girl. Everyone in the house seemed to be weeping, but Jesus told them, "Why are you grieving? The girl is not dead, but asleep." Then He asked everyone to leave, keeping only those who had come into the house with Him.

The parents led Jesus to where their daughter lay. He took her hand, and said, "Dear girl, I tell you, get up!" She sat up, and her mother held her close, as her father bowed low before Jesus. "Give her something to eat," said Jesus, and left quietly, His disciples following Him.

The scene shifted slightly. It was the same house, but the resurrected Jesus now stood outside. His attention was not on the house, but on an outbuilding, where a young woman was milking a cow. The young woman began telling Jesus about how she had been miraculously raised from the dead. "I have so much reverence in my heart for those who teach about the kingdom of heaven since I have returned to life. Are you a teacher like Jesus who had the power to raise the dead?"

Jesus, as usual, says nothing about who He is, but asks her why she is milking the cow, since she is obviously the daughter of the wealthy household, and not a milkmaid.

She sighed and said, "I am fifteen years old now, and my father insists that I be married to some rich man or other. There have been many offers, but I refuse them all. As a result he has ordered me to be a milkmaid until I obey and accept one of the offers to marry."

She jumped from her stool and faced Jesus. "But how can I marry? I have been raised from the dead, and I am determined to devote my life to God instead of a husband. I have had a dream in which angels told me that the children of this age marry, and are given in marriage, but they who are considered worthy of taking part in that age and in the resurrection from the dead will neither marry nor be given in marriage, and they can no longer die; for they are like the angels. They are God's children, since they are children of the resurrection. Isn't that beautiful? I have been raised from the dead! It is almost like being a child of the resurrection; I am God's child, and I will serve Him, not a husband. I respect my family, but my duty is to God."

"That does sound wonderful," said Jesus. "You are devoted to serving our Lord and carrying His message. Did you tell your father about the dream?"

"No, I knew that he would not believe it, or accept it, even if he did believe. When I have had dreams before, he never believed them, either. Finally I stopped telling him about them. We have chosen different paths. When I heard Jesus say, 'I am the resurrection and the life; he who believes in me will live even if he dies' I knew that since I had been raised from the dead that I should not be given in marriage. It is my choice, not my father's. My father thinks otherwise, as do all his friends, but I am determined in this."

She stopped, and then continued, "Sir, I do not know who you are, but I tell you that I have been raised by Jesus the Messiah who gave me eternal life. I believe in Him and will have life with Jesus after I leave this body at the end of my days here. My Lord defeated my death and gave me eternal life. The proof is that our Lord who raised me from the dead, also defeated His death on the cross and was raised from the dead on the third day as He promised."

Again she stopped, perhaps judging her visitor's possible reactions to what she was about to say. "Capernaum is full of these rumors, and even the Rabbi talked about it in one of his synagogue discussions. All the prominent members of the synagogue hierarchy gather in our house and talk about Jesus' death and possible resurrection. My father told us not to believe the rumors unless you see Him with your own eyes. Our Rabbi told us that he has heard from the messengers of the Temple priests and leaders that Jesus' body was stolen. The Temple priests and leaders sent spies came from Jerusalem looking for Him, thinking He might be hiding in the mountains or on the boat here. They left when they did not find Him. I believe that I will see Him again -- if not as resurrected here, at least when I get to heaven. My father does not understand, but I am blessed to be alive. Jesus gave me another chance to live on this earth and I want to live that life serving everyone as He did. I want to carry His message and mission to the end of my life."

She ended her speech, and then, sensing that she had not treated her guest with the proper hospitality, filled a cup with fresh milk and gave it to Jesus to drink.

He accepted this gift, and drank gratefully. Then He blessed her, saying: "Blessed are the meek: for they shall inherit the earth. Blessed are they which do hunger and thirst after righteousness: for they shall be filled". He gave her the cup and walked away. Jeremiah could see the joy on His face and the exuberance in the young Rebeka.

The images shifted to show the next day. The young woman was waking up in her room, a look of peace and joy on her face. Without pausing to think or change her night clothes, she ran to her father's room. "Father!" she cried. "I have had a dream about the stranger who was here yesterday." Her father looked tired, as if he had heard too many of these dreams. "This one is different, Father," she said. "I gave the stranger some milk to drink, and in my dream the man drinking that same milk was Jesus, who healed me. In the dream He was resurrected from His own death. He had come to visit me as a stranger, to see me again, to bless me, and to see how I was doing. He said 'For God so loved the world, that He gave His only begotten Son, that whosoever believeth in Him should not perish, but have everlasting life.' Father, I believe in Him. I know that you believe in Him – that is why you asked Him to save my life. He has blessed the path I wish to take, the path of service to Him."

Her father said, "It was Jesus who visited us yesterday, and it was Jesus in your dream?" She nodded, almost jumping up and down in her joy. "And He blessed you and your chosen path?"

"Yes, Father, I told Him all about my plans to devote my life to God, serving others, and He blessed me."

212

"Rebeka, are you sure you do not want the life of a settled, married woman? These are difficult times, and you would be secure with any of the men who have asked to marry you."

She looked at him with shining eyes. "Father, my life was saved for this."

He bowed his head for a moment, and then put his hand on his daughter's head. "If Jesus has blessed you in this, I will not hinder you. It will be done as you wish. We are both believers in our Lord, but your path is a different one than mine. I will trust our Lord Jesus to give you the security I had hoped a marriage would provide."

She stood motionless for a moment, and then flung herself into his arms. "Thank you, Father!"

The scene faded, and Jeremiah asked, "Was she the first nun?"

"No, the formalized ministry of nuns and monks came much later in the history of the church. But many women had begun this type of devotion, quite unofficially, even in the early days. Mary Magdalene and many other unnamed women spent their life following our Lord and in the service of His disciples, without marriage."

The images formed, and Jeremiah saw Jesus and some of His disciples on the way to Simon Peter's house. Before they reached it, a centurion ran up to Him. "Lord, my servant lies at home paralyzed and in terrible suffering."

Jesus said, "I will go and heal him."

But the centurion responded, "Lord I do not deserve to have you come under my roof. But just say the word, and my servant will be healed. For I myself am a man under authority, with soldiers under me. I tell this one, 'Go,' and he goes; and that one, 'Come,' and he comes. I say to my servant, 'Do this,' and he does it."

"Truly, I have not found anyone in Israel with such great faith. Go, it will be done just as you believed it would."

"My favorite part is when they found out his servant had been healed the very hour that Jesus said that," said Jeremiah. "The centurion was a gentile, but his faith was greater than that of the Jews. This was a short distance healing, compared to the healing from Cana of the illness of a boy in Capernaum."

The images formed and Jeremiah saw the garrison of the centurion. A banquet was being prepared, and the army of servants making everything ready rivaled the army of soldiers on guard outside in order and attention to duty. Jeremiah looked intently at the man in charge of the servants, and Peter nodded. "That was the servant who was healed. The centurion declared him as a free man and put him in charge of all the servants at the garrison – and you will not find a better-run place anywhere in the Roman Empire."

"Isn't something like that what happened to Joseph when he was sold into slavery in Egypt?" asked Jeremiah. "He was put in charge of Pharaoh's household."

"It was similar," said Peter. "And the centurion now has an entire command that is run as well as his own personal quarters had been run. Servants had traditionally not been much valued, but everything is so well organized that the soldiers are better equipped to do their jobs. The servants under him are enjoying a new level of respect."

The former servant of the centurion seemed to be everywhere at once, making sure all was in order and everyone was cared for. Someone called that a delivery cart was at the gate, and he went to meet it. As he was supervising the unloading, he saw a man walking along the road. Jeremiah knew the man was Jesus, but the former servant had no way of recognizing the One who had healed him from a distance. Jesus bowed, as to an equal, and the former servant returned the bow, somewhat clumsily. It was clear there were still some things he was learning about his new position. He turned back to the workers unloading the cart as Jesus walked past.

The scene shifted to a wheat field, but here Jesus and his disciples were together, walking through the field and plucking the heads of grain. They rubbed them in their hands and ate the kernels. Jeremiah was puzzled until he remembered that Jesus and the disciples got into trouble from eating grain on a Sabbath. Evidently even that amount of effort that the disciples did to get the edible part of the wheat out of the growing head was considered work under the law of the Jews.

"Why were there so many laws about what you could or couldn't do on the Sabbath?" asked Jeremiah. "I always thought those Pharisees and priests seemed just a little too fixated on that."

Peter said, "You must remember, that the defining of the laws and the administration of the laws and punishments were important parts of their power. The more complicated they could make the laws, the more difficult it was for a normal person to know how to follow them. Then the Pharisees and priests got to be all pompous and tell everyone what to do. In your modern terms they call that 'micromanagement' and it isn't an effective way to manage, either now or then."

Jeremiah said, "Jesus was talking about King David to justify what they did on the Sabbath, reminding them that even King David, the revered second King of the Jews, sinned by eating the consecrated bread, and also gave it to his companions. It was supposed to have been eaten only by the priests, but David took it when he was hungry. If the hungry King David could do that which was unlawful but necessary, and not be chastised, then the hungry Jesus could also do the unlawful but necessary and should not be chastised by the priests."

"The most profound statement Jesus made about the Sabbath was, 'The Son of Man is Lord of the Sabbath,'" said Peter.

"I always thought He was talking about the spirit of the law as opposed to the letter of the law," said Jeremiah. "The lawyers among the Jews were all about the letter of the law, wanting to define every little thing. The spirit of the law of the Sabbath is about making time to honor God in the Temple, and resting after the week's work. Surely if anyone needed help, even if it was just a sheep in a pit, you would help them, whether that was defined as work by the Pharisees or not. Our famous president Abraham Lincoln held that one has to use the spirit of the law, not the letter of the law."

"Well spoken, Jeremiah." Peter grinned. "Too bad he was not alive back then to tell those Pharisees a thing or two."

Jeremiah laughed as well. "That would have been something to see," he said. "But look, there is Jesus in the wheat field. Is that where He is spending the night?"

"Yes," said Peter.

Day 26: Thursday

Day 26: Thursday: Jesus heals blind man in Bethsaida - the two men whose demons Jesus had sent into a herd of pigs tell their story to the former blind man – Jesus gives them all a blessing.

"This is Thursday, day 26 of the resurrection," said Peter. "Jesus is going to Bethsaida. It is only a little over three miles from Capernaum. Here's what He did the last time He was there."

The images showed Jesus and His disciples walking through Bethsaida. Two men brought a blind man to meet them, begging Jesus to touch him. Evidently, Jesus had other plans, as He took the blind man by the hand and led him out of the town.

A little way beyond the city gates, Jesus stopped, spit on the blind man's eyes, and put His hands on them. Then He lifted His hands and asked the man if he could see. "I see men looking like trees walking, the man said. Then Jesus put His hands on his eyes again, and made him look up. Now the man's sight was restored completely. He could see everything clearly, and looked around, marveling at the beauty of all he saw.

Jesus said, "Go home, and do not go into the town, or tell anyone in town what has happened."

The man was too overcome to speak; he kneeled in gratitude, and his friends helped him to find his way home.

As the images faded, Jeremiah said, "Sometimes Jesus told those he healed not to tell anyone about Him. Why was that?"

Peter said, "It was all about the timing. If His popularity had peaked too soon, He wouldn't have reached the number of people He wanted. We traveled around and covered a lot of territory, for a group of men who were mainly walking everywhere. He was determined not to be taken until He was ready. Remember, it was all on His terms. When the time was right, He would go, but not a moment sooner."

"Thank you; that does clarify it. And now are we going to see what happened when He returned to Bethsaida?"

217

"Yes," said Peter, and the images began again.

Jeremiah saw the man who had been blind sitting with two other men in the shade of the wall near the gates of Bethsaida. They were drinking from their skins of water and swapping news, as any group of travelers would, and the news of the day was all about Jesus – was He resurrected, or had His disciples stolen His body as the Temple priests claimed.

The man who had been blind was finishing his tale about his meeting with Jesus. "He told me not to tell anyone, but now that He's died and been resurrected, so they say, I'm telling everyone. My name is Jacob, and if anyone asks me about Jesus, I'll be the first to say, if He can heal me, then why can't He do whatever else His follower claim He has done?"

He stared at his companions, as if inviting a challenge. "You'll get no argument from me on that," said one. They looked at each other, as if coming to a decision, and the other one spoke.

"We're actually from a place a little south and east of here: Gergesa. We also believe that Jesus came back from the dead – after what He did for us . . ." His voice trailed off and he stared into the distance.

"Don't start a story like that and stop there!" cried Jacob. "You can tell me – we're far enough from the gates that no one can hear."

The two strangers looked at each other a last time, and then the first one spoke again. "I'm Asa and this is Ram. We are merchants, and are here looking at some flax that we heard has some remarkable qualities."

"He doesn't care about that," interrupted Ram. "Get on with it."

"Well, as I said," Asa continued, "We are merchants now, but we weren't always the men you see before you." His voice lowered to a whisper, and he looked around before he said, "We were demon possessed." He waited for a big reaction, but Jacob seemed more interested than scared.

"So what kind of demon was it?" he asked. "What was it making you do?" He seemed really curious, and the two strangers seemed to relax a little.

"We were violent: mainly throwing things and attacking people," said Asa. "They tried chaining us, but we broke every chain they tried to put on us. We lived among the tombs just outside

218

of the village, and we made sure no one could walk the road beside the tombs in either peace or safety. Finally the people in that village just avoided our area completely."

"Which was inconvenient for them, since that was the best way down to the coast below," said Ram.

"So how did Jesus find you," asked Jacob. "Was He teaching with a big crowd around Him?"

"It was just Him and His disciples, coming up the coastal road," said Asa. "From what we could reason out later, they had landed their boat down at the little harbor there. Anyway, they were coming from that direction when we ran out at them.

Ram broke in, "We weren't thinking, not in those days, but I remember expecting them to be like any of the villagers who ran from us, shrieking with fright, but Jesus just stood there with His disciples behind Him."

"It was a shock when the demon inside me spoke," said Asa. "That thing seemed to recognize Jesus, and called Him the Son of God."

"Mine said, 'What do you want with us, Son of God? Have you come here to torture us before the appointed time?' I'll never forget it," said Ram, shivering a little just thinking about it.

"Mine said, 'If You drive us out, send us into the herd of pigs.' I have no idea why, but I suppose if they were spirits they needed a body of some kind." Asa was thoughtful for a moment, and then laughed. "You should have heard the squeals from those pigs after Jesus said, 'Go!' and the evil spirits went out of us and right into those pigs. That whole herd just rushed down that steep bank, it's kind of a cliff right there over the water, and they all drowned!"

Jacob joined in the laughter, picturing the herd of squealing pigs flying off the cliff into the Sea of Galilee.

Asa continued, "Well, of course, we both stood there before Jesus, as if we had been struck dumb. We had been possessed so long; we had to remember how to be men again. Whoever was tending the pigs ran off to tell their master, but someone found us clean clothes to put on, and brought us some food. Those demons didn't care much what or how often we ate, as long as we didn't die on them."

219

"When everyone from the village ran out to see what was going on," said Ram, "there we were, sitting at the feet of Jesus, eating some bread and listening to Him talk about His kingdom. You can just imagine how the owner of those pigs felt about it all. He didn't care anything about us, of course. Those pigs were his money for the coming year – drowned in the sea! He was almost too angry to speak, but he managed. 'Get out of here!' he yelled. I almost thought he was going to hit Jesus, but those friends of His looked pretty tough. The others seemed to realize what kind of power they were confronting, and just pleaded with Him to leave. So they did – they just turned around, walked right back down that coast road, and we saw their boat on its way back to Galilee."

"We had asked if we could go with them," said Asa. "We weren't so sure we would be welcome back in town, but He told us to go and spread the word of how kind the Lord had been to us."

"And that's how we became merchants," Ram added. "Everyone wanted to hear our story, and we traveled around quite a lot. We began noticing the difference in prices and quality of goods in the different towns, and since we needed to earn our living somehow, we began buying and selling. People still wanted to see us and talk with us, and if we had anything to sell, they usually bought something, if only to repay us for our time."

"But what happened back at your village?" asked Jacob. "Weren't they grateful for Jesus to have freed them from the tyranny of those demons? You two were back to normal, and the road was open for travel again."

"Yes," said Asa, "when people began to realize that the demons were gone for good, they began to appreciate what Jesus had done for them. They were able to use that road again, and were also able to honor their ancestors at the tombs, which they hadn't been able to do while we were living there, attacking everyone who tried to walk by."

"Even that man who had lost the pigs finally came around," said Ram. "His other herd multiplied faster than ever, and his loss was much less than he had feared. Everyone agreed, at last, that Jesus had blessed the village. We know that they had sent someone out to meet Jesus and thank Him, formally. I don't know if that person ever found Jesus – no one ever knew where He would turn up next. But at least they did make the effort."

Their story over, the men took turns drinking from the skin of water. Jacob was the first to notice the stranger approaching them. "Friends," he said, "does that man look familiar to you?" They all three stared as the thin man who was slowly walking toward them. Instinctively they all rose. The man coming their way was clearly no physical threat to them, but it is always best to be on your feet when meeting a stranger. Before He was close enough to hear, Jacob said, "He looks so familiar – something about His eyes. Or maybe it was that dream I had last night."

The stranger was the resurrected Jesus. "Friends," He said in greeting, and then turned to Jacob. "Can you see who I am?" he asked. Jacob was staring at the stranger as if his life depended on it. "Sir, I do not know who You are, but I think I have seen You before -- in a dream I had last night. In my dream You were feeding thousands of people with seven loaves of bread and two fish. Then the dream changed and I had a vision of You ascending to heaven, although now I see You before me. I do not understand what it means." Jacob closed his eyes, as if he could remember better without the distraction of vision. Suddenly he opened them and said, "Are you Jesus of Nazareth, who was resurrected?"

Jesus replied, "You are seeing the man who gave you sight, and drove evil spirits out of these friends of yours, and who also opened your heart to heaven with your vision of My future."

Jacob said, "I heard that the man who healed and taught about the kingdom of Heaven, Jesus of Nazareth, was crucified in Jerusalem. I also heard that this same man rose from the dead. There are so many rumors – I do not know what to believe."

"When you were blind, you lost your sight, but not your vision of servitude," said Jesus. "Because of your pure belief in the man who healed you and His message, you received your sight, and a vision of heaven, also. The kingdom of heaven is at hand and it is yours."

Asa and Ram had been silent up to this point, but now Jesus turned His attention to them. "Well done!" He said. They looked startled, and Asa was about to speak when Jesus went on, "You have indeed spread the word of the kindness of your Lord

221

throughout the region, as asked. You are witnesses of the healing power of God."

Then He paused, His gaze seeming to embrace all three men. "Go in peace," He said, and walked away slowly, leaving the men staring after Him speechless with gratitude and wonder.

Jeremiah thought Jesus was walking much more slowly than He had earlier. At a crossroads He paused, then turned toward Capernaum.

Day 27: Friday

Day 27: Friday: Sermon on the Mount and Sermon on the Plains –
the oral tradition – reaction of Simon's mother-in-law.

"This is Friday, day 27 of the resurrection," said Peter.

"Then this evening will start the Sabbath," said Jeremiah.

"Yes," said Peter, "but Jesus will not spend it with friends. He
will be alone on a mountaintop – but we are getting ahead of
ourselves. Jesus has come to this mountain for a reason; this is
where He chose the twelve disciples, and near where He gave part
of what you call the Sermon on the Mount and the Sermon on the
Plain."

"Many times on our trip to Jerusalem, the guides would say that
tradition tells us this was the place for something but that recent
archaeological finds suggest that the place was actually elsewhere.
The sermon on the mount was one of them," said Jeremiah.

"Most of those sermons are compiled from several different
events," said Peter. "The theme was common enough to string them
all together for the convenience of memory. In that age, the written
word was not as easily accessible as it is today. We were taught the
Torah, of course; the Rabbi taught us from the sacred scrolls, but it
was all memorization, the oral tradition you hear so much about.
We were not even allowed to touch the sacred scrolls. No one wrote
down what Jesus said as He was saying it – that was compiled from
memory later."

"So that might explain why several different sources tell us of
different places," said Jeremiah.

"Right," said Peter. "This was the mountainside where Jesus
spent the night praying, and then the next morning chose the twelve
of us, calling us apostles. Then He walked down to a more level
place where He could still be seen by the crowd which had
gathered, and teach. That was an exciting time. But now," he
gestured toward the images as they began to form; "there is no one
here except Jesus."

223

Jeremiah watched as Jesus climbed one of the hills near Capernaum. His steps slowed, and then stopped. He sat down, obviously exhausted.

"Is anyone coming to meet Him?" asked Jeremiah.

"We are all having the feast my mother-in-law had been preparing for days." Peter smiled at the memory. "It was a great time – we had just seen Jesus by the Sea of Tiberias, and we knew we were close to the start of a whole new ministry. Jesus had said He would meet us again, and we were all looking forward to that. If we had known He was out on that mountainside alone, we would have all gone to meet Him right there, feast or no feast. But that was His way: He would often slip away to be on His own, talking with His heavenly Father."

"Did your mother-in-law say anything about that teacher who visited her, a couple of days ago? We know it was Jesus, but she didn't." Jeremiah was curious.

"She told us about the stranger," said Peter, "and we were all excited that the Master had been here. My mother-in-law was shocked that she had been visited by Him, but not pleased that He was so secretive. 'You would have thought that He could have told me who He was,' she said. We had to convince her that He was trying not to be recognized, that it was safer if no one knew who He was, or where He was. His mission was to meet us and those whose lives He had touched."

"If He had told her, the whole countryside would soon have known," said Jeremiah. "Everyone would have swarmed around Him, wanting healing or just to listen to Him. It would have alerted the Temple priests and the Roman garrison!" said Jeremiah.

"Too true!" said Peter, and they both laughed. "When we pointed out to her that she and her daughter had enjoyed a private conversation with the Messiah Himself, who had just risen from the dead, she was actually able to laugh at herself and her pride."

"See, Peter, miracles do happen!" said Jeremiah, and they both laughed again.

Day 28: Saturday

Day 28: Saturday: The disciples leave to meet with Jesus in the mountains of Galilee.

"Today is Saturday, day 28 of the resurrection," said Peter. "Not much actually happened on this day. We had decided to see if Jesus had arrived at that place on the mountainside where He had first named the Twelve. But I am sure you know how difficult it can be to get eleven men to do one thing, at one time."

Jeremiah laughed at the idea of Simon Peter trying to get all the disciples to leave together.

"Right," said Peter. "It took some time. We weren't exactly sure what was going to happen, but we had talked with Jesus enough to know that things were going to change in a big way. As I said before, it was exciting, and we all reacted in our own way. We had arranged to leave separately, as we had been doing, and meet together at the wheat fields outside town."

The images showed the group of disciples with Simon Peter in the middle trying to get them out the door. Several were putting on their sandals, the sons of thunder were already walking down the road, and someone was still in the kitchen, coaxing a last treat from the women there. Finally they were all out the door, making their way by separate routes to the edge of town.

When they had caught up with each other at the wheat field, they went at a more leisurely pace, as those used to long walking journeys. As they walked, they kept looking about them, to each side, far ahead, and sometimes casting a look back along the road.

"We never knew where He would come from," explained Peter. "He could spring up from anywhere, and we didn't want to be taken unawares as we had in the past."

Jeremiah saw the men climb into the hills and low mountains that were on that side of the town. As dark approached, they made camp, but kept their lookout for their leader. They were alert to any sound, and even the fluttering of the leaves would bring one or another of the disciples to his feet.

On a mountainside not far away, Jeremiah could see Jesus, still alone, but resting a little more comfortably after His day in seclusion. The moon shown down on all of them, seeming to play hide and seek among the clouds that drifted by. Jesus gave a long sigh and quickly drifted off into sleep

Day 29: Sunday

Day 29: Sunday: Jesus meets and talks with the 11 disciples in Galilee – final teachings and Great Commission – He directs them to go to the Mont of Olives.

"This is Sunday, day 29 of the resurrection," said Peter.

"But, Peter," said Jeremiah, "did the disciples and Jesus get together on the mountain?"

"Yes," said Peter. "We rose early and were able to find the same place where He had first named us as His disciples. There were eleven of us now, as Judas had left to go back to Jerusalem when we were at the Sea of Tiberias. We knew we were walking in the right direction, but sometimes those hills and valleys all start looking alike. James and John were ahead of the pack, as usual, and they saw Him first, John calling out to the rest of us that they had found Him.

"We still had some supplies of food with us, and we tried to give Him a good breakfast, but He didn't eat very much. He had difficulty swallowing. Then He started talking to us. We didn't know then, but it was the last time He would speak with us until His ascension. Matthew reports part of what He said as the last paragraph of his gospel."

"I know those verses!" said Jeremiah. "Jesus said, 'All authority has been given to Me in heaven and on earth. Therefore go, and make disciples of all nations, baptizing them in the name of the Father and of the Son and of the Holy Spirit, teaching them to observe all things that I commanded you. Behold, I am with you always, even to the end of the age.' But how could He talk about the Holy Spirit – some call it the Holy Ghost - when that was not given until the day of Pentecost?"

"Did you think these words would be any easier to understand than half of what He taught us?" said Peter with a smile. "Many times He said things that confused us. Sometimes He would explain the meaning at that time, and sometimes He would explain it later.

227

This was one of the times when the meaning became clear later. At that time, we did not know how long He would be with us. He had been giving us instructions that never included Him, and He was looking worse and worse every time we saw Him. No one knew exactly what He had planned, but we knew enough to trust Him and prepare to follow His instructions."

Peter paused, remembering. "He said a lot on that mountain, but it took a long time for Him to say it. He seemed to have trouble getting enough breath, and had to pause after every sentence. But some of His words explained what had happened. He said, 'thus it is written: for the Messiah to suffer and to rise from the dead the third day, and that repentance and remission of sins should be preached in His name to all the nations, beginning at Jerusalem. You are witnesses of these things. Behold, I send forth the promise of My Father on you, but go back to Jerusalem and stay there until you have been clothed with power from on high.' You see, there's that reference to the Holy Spirit again, which at the time we did not understand."

Jeremiah said, "We use those verses in our sermons. I know those words by heart."

"Yes, I thought you would," said Peter. "Jesus also said, 'Go into all the world and proclaim the Good News to the whole creation. He who believes and is baptized will be saved; but he that disbelieves shall be condemned. These signs will accompany those who believe: in My name they will cast out demons, they will speak with new languages, they will pick up serpents with their hands; and if they drink any deadly thing, it will not harm them; they will lay hands on the sick, and they will recover.' Of course, He said much more than that, but that was all that was written down."

His voice became thoughtful as he recalled those early days. "We were about to start a new ministry, to all nations. Remember, we were about to be sent out on our own. With the help of the Holy Spirit, of course, but there were many things to talk about: leadership, the discernment of true seekers from those who were just wishing for a diversion from their lives, the details of our mission and how we were to accomplish it."

Jeremiah looked amazed at this. "I had never thought about the planning that must have gone on before the action started."

"When Jesus was still with us, He was our leader. He planned everything. We did whatever He said, followed Him wherever He went. He even provided for our everyday needs, through the women who accompanied us. Suddenly we needed to make our own plans. To use a sports analogy, our quarterback was gone, but was acting as head coach. I had been appointed the new quarterback, and I still had a lot of learning to do."

Jeremiah laughed. "My congregation will love the sports analogy, and I do, too. Did He stay with you long, teaching, and planning?"

"I think we talked together most of the day. Even though He was just talking with us, He had to stop and catch His breath at times. His appearance was dreadful. Yellow fluid (pus) was oozing out of the wound in His chest. We begged Him to rest that evening, but He said He had to start on His way, as He was going to meet us at the Mount of Olives, and His journey would take longer than ours. After that He told us to stop at Bethany and let His friends know what we were doing, and He blessed us and walked away slowly – I think He was headed south and eastward. It was the last time we would see Him until His ascension, but we didn't know that, then."

Day 30: Monday

Day 30: Monday: Jesus travels separately from the disciples, headed toward the Mount of Olives

"This is Monday, day 30 of the resurrection," said Peter. "Jesus had said to meet Him at the Mount of Olives and to travel through Bethany to talk with His friends. Once He went into the woods, we could not find Him. We traveled separately from Him, but wished at every step that we could have been with Him."

"Did He tell you why you were traveling separately?"

"No," said Peter. "At the time we thought it was just to make sure we would not all be caught together by the Romans or Temple spies. It was only later that we heard He had been going to the same places and seeing the same people we had visited during our three year ministry. I'm not sure He could have been recognized, the way He was looking so different. If He had been seen with us in a group, He might have been recognized."

"I can't tell you how shocked I am to see Him looking like that," said Jeremiah.

"The other reasons were about us taking on our own leadership, separate from Him. I had to practice being a leader, and I needed all the practice I could get! It was much easier those first few days to try on our new roles without having to deal with townspeople or temple priests, or even our kin, as much as we love them."

"And it probably also helped solidify the understanding of your message," said Jeremiah.

"Yes, our conversation was all about what we would be teaching, going over the plans, and wondering what would happen to our ministry. And we did not know what was going to happen with Him, either. We knew He would not be with us, but did not know anything beyond that."

"It seems so straightforward when we read about it," said Jeremiah. "I am sure it was all much more confusing to live through it."

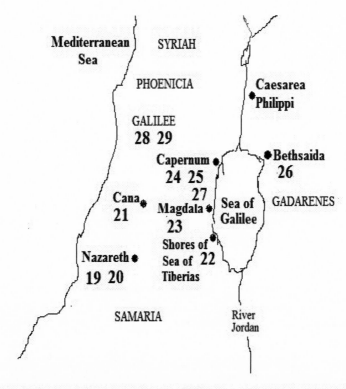

Sightings and movements of Jesus after resurrection
Days 20 - 30

Day 31: Tuesday

Day 31: Tuesday: The disciples spend night on Mount Tabor – talk about the Transfiguration.

"This is Tuesday, day 31 of the resurrection," said Peter. "Jesus had started us on our way, but we were still hoping to catch a glimpse of Him. I must confess we spent some time searching in the hills to see if we could find Him before we actually did much traveling. We looked around the hills of Galilee, the wilderness, and even towards Capernaum."

"It sounds as if this was both an exciting time and a scary time," said Jeremiah.

"Everything was new," said Peter. "We couldn't stop talking about it. But then as it was getting toward evening we arrived at Mount Tabor. Of course those of us who were at what you call the Lord's Transfiguration had to share the experience with the others. I used to wonder why the three of us were chosen: the other two were James and John. Now as I look back, I see that James was always the one to leap into action first, and John was the one to think through a situation and to grasp the inner meaning. They were a good balance for each other. I think I was there as the future leader of our little group. I certainly felt out of my depth on that day!"

"We love it when the disciples act like ordinary men," said Jeremiah. "Then we can identify with them more, and believe that we can be more like them. Would you tell me about it now, as you told the other disciples then? What was it like?"

Peter said, "Here's what it was like for us. James, John and I had all walked up the mountain with Jesus, and we were praying at the top, when suddenly His face changed. I can't say exactly how it was different, but we knew something momentous was starting. His clothes became as bright as a flash of lightning and shone with a very bright light. We couldn't really look at Him, He was so bright. Suddenly two men were standing there, and we knew they were Moses and Elijah."

Day 31: Tuesday

"But Peter, I always wondered how you knew the other men were Moses and Elijah." Jeremiah said. "I know there were no name tags!"

Peter laughed. "And there were no introductions, either. All of a sudden those passages from the Torah that spoke about those men were alive in our minds, and we just somehow knew who they were. They wore bright robes, almost too bright to look at, and they spoke with Jesus about what was about to happen. We stared at them, but they were so bright to look at that it seemed to have a strange effect on us, and the next thing we knew, we were waking up. We didn't even remember falling asleep! We were tired, from the mountain climb, but this was something else entirely." He stopped for a moment, as if even the memory had power.

Peter went on: "As I said, we were beginning to wake up, and we did become fully awake in time to hear part of their talk and to see them leave. They were talking about what Jesus was about to go through, with His trial and crucifixion, but of course none of that made any sense to us. As they were leaving, I said to Jesus, 'Master, it is good for us to be here. Let us put up three shelters, one for You, one for Moses, and one for Elijah.' I really should have just kept my mouth shut, as this whole experience was obviously beyond my understanding, but of course I felt I needed to say something. And then God spoke!"

Peter stopped, as if remembering this moment. "A cloud appeared, all around us, and you can believe we were afraid as that cloud shut out everything else from our view. Then we heard the voice, just coming out from the cloud. It said, 'This is my Son, whom I have chosen, Listen to Him.' Then somehow the cloud was gone and Moses and Elijah were both gone, as well. We were all speechless by that time, and perhaps blessedly so. When Jesus told us not to speak of any of this until He had been raised from the dead, I was only too happy to obey."

Jeremiah said, "We were taught that Moses represented the Law, and Elijah represented the Prophets, and that Jesus had come to fulfill and embody them both. He was both the message and the messenger. That was why there was no more need for prophets after Jesus: all the prophecies pointed to Him."

"Right, Jeremiah. It was afterwards, on our way back down the mountain, that Jesus told us not to tell anyone about it until He had risen from the dead. Now that He had risen, we were glad to spend a little time there, telling the rest of the disciples about it. We stayed there that night. I remember the moon was bright and the stars were beautiful."

"And where was Jesus all this time, when you were looking for Him, and traveling?"

"He was walking very slowly toward Mount Tabor. He was probably behind us; somehow, we must have missed Him in our search. He was moving very slowly."

Day 32: Wednesday

Day 32: Wednesday: Jesus finds it too difficult to climb Mount Tabor – He rests at the old campsite in the foothills where Peter, John and James camped on the night of the Transfiguration.

"This is Wednesday, day 32 of the resurrection," said Peter. "We rose early and left our night camp at Mount Tabor to continue on our way to the Mount of Olives."

"I have heard some discussion about where the Transfiguration took place," said Jeremiah. "I have heard it might have been Mount Nebo or Mount Harmon, although Nebo is really too far away to actually be considered."

"It was Mount Tabor," said Peter, "but you know, the exact spot is not what is important. The event and the meaning of it is always more important that the actual place."

"I feel that is true," said Jeremiah, "but you know how people like to pin things down, trying to find the historically accurate places. Sometimes I think they focus on the 'where' as a distraction so they don't have to think about the 'why' – the meaning of the event, why it happened at all."

"It has seemed that way to me, also," said Peter.

"But what is Jesus doing today?" asked Jeremiah.

The images formed in answer, and Jeremiah saw Jesus resting in the wilderness near Mount Tabor. He rose and began walking slowly up the mountain, stopping many times to rest. He appeared to be trying to the reach the top, where He had met with Moses and Elijah, but after one particularly long rest He sighed and started back down the mountain.

He found the foothills of the mountain, where they had camped on the way back from the Transfiguration. With difficulty, He lowered Himself onto the ground, resting His back against a rock, the branches of the bush making a sort of pillow for His head. He looked around at the fresh growth of spring, enjoying the breeze from the mountain. The birds appeared to enjoy it, as well, for they

Day 32: Wednesday

burst out in song. Jesus sighed, and settled in for the night. The moon was again bright, lighting up the top of the mountain.

Day 33: Thursday

Day 33: Thursday: Jesus heals a shepherd's son after the Transfiguration – preaches to His disciples about faith and belief - Jesus talks with the man about his experience.

"This is Thursday, day 33 of the resurrection," said Peter. "Jesus is going to come down off the mountain. Let us see what happened the last time He was there, as we were returning from the Transfiguration."

The images showed Jesus, Peter, James and John walking down the mountain. As they approached the valley, a crowd gathered around them, along with the other disciples. One of the men in the crowd stepped forward. "Teacher, I beg of you to look at my son, for he is my only child. A spirit seizes him and he suddenly screams; it throws him into convulsions so that he foams at the mouth. It scarcely ever leaves him and is destroying him. I begged your disciples to drive it out, but they could not."

Jesus glanced at the disciples. Some were looking at the ground, as if embarrassed that they could not do this healing, and others were looking at Jesus as if for guidance. "O unbelieving and perverse generation," said Jesus. "How long will I stay with you and put up with you?" To the man he said, "Bring your son here."

The man took the boy by the hand and led him to Jesus, but they were only halfway there when the boy was thrown suddenly to the ground in a convulsion, almost knocking his father down with him.

Jesus raised His hand and said, "Go out of him!" and immediately the spirit left. The boy was healed, and Jesus lifted him up on his feet again and turned him to face his father. "Here, your son is whole again."

The crowd had been silent during this, but now began to speak with excitement, amazed at the greatness of God in their presence.

Peter said, "It was after that miracle that Jesus said one of those things that at the time mystified us, but later made perfect sense:

'Listen carefully to what I am about to tell you: The Son of Man is going to be betrayed into the hands of men.' It was only later, after everything happened that we understood what He had said. He knew the time for His trial and crucifixion was coming closer – but look, here is the boy now."

The images changed and Jeremiah saw that same man and boy – they were shepherds, standing with their flock in the valley below Mount Tabor. Jesus was walking down the mountain, and as He approached them, the man stepped forward. "Sir, pray forgive me for stopping You, but I saw You come down from that mountain. Sir, something happened on that mountain last year, and whenever I see someone coming down from the mountain, I always ask them if they have seen anything unusual there."

"I have seen nothing unusual last night," said Jesus. "But tell me, what happened last year that you are still looking at that mountain?"

The shepherd paused a moment to gather his thoughts, and spoke, "Last year, about nine months ago, we were out with our flocks and gazing at the stars. Suddenly a light, bright like many suns, was shining from the top of the mountain. We have never seen such a light before, on the mountain or anywhere else."

The shepherd paused for breath and then went on: "Now I look at the mountains every night. I have not seen anything like that since. The day after we saw that light, four men came down from that mountain. One was a rabbi, and when He found that His followers were not able to heal my son – I had taken him to some travelers who were going about the countryside, teaching and healing in the name of God -- He did it Himself – my son had a bad spirit in him that threw him to the ground in fits. That rabbi healed my son, and that rabbi had been on the mountain the night that the bright light shone out. So I always ask anyone I see coming from the mountain – did you see anything unusual there.

Jesus said, "Your faith and dedication to God made your son well. The light from the mountain was a divine light, but it will not come again."

The shepherd looked a little sad at that – this event had given him something to look forward to every night, but he suddenly remembered the tradition of hospitality. "Sir, I see that You must be a rabbi Yourself, and we would be honored if You would stay the night with us and take Your evening meal here, as well. We have some festivities planned: it has been almost nine months since the rabbi they called Jesus healed my son. Some Jews and even some gentiles claim that He is the Messiah, and we are celebrating tonight in the name of the Lord Jesus who healed my son. We are inviting all our neighbors, and would like You to share the feast, as well."

Jesus said, "I am honored, but I cannot stay with you. I must continue to Jerusalem, and it is a long, slow walk for Me. But be sure that My blessings are on you, and your son, and all that are in your household."

Jesus turned and walked down the road toward Jerusalem, leaning heavily on His staff at each step. The shepherd held his son close, watched for a moment, and then they turned back to their sheep. "I am sure that was the rabbi who healed you," said the shepherd to his son. "And He gave us all another blessing!"

Day 34: Friday

Day 34: Friday: Jeremiah finds out what Judas has been doing after leaving the 11 other disciples at the Sea of Tiberias.

"This is Friday, day 34 of the resurrection," said Peter. "Jesus continues walking to Jerusalem, going more and more slowly as His wounds and fever become worse. The rest of us were also walking to Jerusalem, but at a faster pace. We wasted some time searching for Jesus along the way, but we still arrived there before He did."

"Since we have some time," said Jeremiah, "Can you show me what Judas is doing? I know there is controversy about his role in the plans of Jesus."

"What Judas did, his birth, mission and death, are a subject for a whole book," said Peter, "Judas left the Sea of Tiberias and reached Nazareth on the 24th day of the resurrection. I can show you Judas leaving the Sea of Tiberias, traveling toward Nazareth, and what happened there that day and the days after that."

"Yes, that is just what I wanted to see!" said Jeremiah.

The images showed Judas leaving the others and heading toward Jerusalem. He stopped at some of the same places that Jesus had stopped during His resurrection journey. Judas seemed to be keeping quietly to himself; he didn't start many conversations, and didn't seek out other companions as he was walking from town to town.

At Nazareth he visited the home of Jesus, where His brothers and sisters made him welcome as they would any traveler. They never asked his name, and he didn't give it. They told him about the rabbi who had visited them about four days ago and who had shared their evening meal. They said that they had been skeptical at the beginning about Jesus, but by the time of His trial and crucifixion had become believers. Mother Mary, of course, had never doubted. The siblings were going to Jerusalem, and were happy to hear a confirmation from this stranger that claimed to be an eyewitness to the resurrection of both the crucifixion and the resurrection of Jesus.

Judas also saw Aaron, the old village leader who had doubted Jesus' ministry, but who had changed his opinion after the resurrected Jesus had healed him by touching his cot. Somehow they managed to strike up a conversation, and he told Judas all about his healing and about Jesus, who grew up in Nazareth, and began His ministry not far from here. "We have heard a lot of rumors about Jesus. We were told that He was arrested by the Temple priests and guards, and charged with blasphemy. They asked the Roman ruler Pontius Pilate to sentence Him to death, and that was done."

Judas said, "All you have said is true. I was there when all these events happened. I was in the city celebrating the Passover with Jesus, and I was also there when He appeared, resurrected, to the disciples."

The old man said, "We heard that the Temple priests and leaders are telling everyone that Jesus' body was stolen from the tomb and hidden by His disciples."

"Why would they do such a thing?" asked Judas.

"The rumor has it that the disciples want to claim that Jesus walked out of the tomb as resurrected. That is what He was saying throughout His ministry. The Temple priests and leaders wanted to make sure they could explain an empty tomb: that Jesus did not walk out, alive, but was carried out, dead."

Judas was clearly shocked. "Jesus preached truth and forgiveness all His life. Why would some disciples steal His body or believe that His body is stolen and spread that false information to the public?"

Aaron said, "I have no idea. But you can be sure that money is at the center of whatever is going on; it always is. Every time we went to Jerusalem to celebrate at the Temple, we had to pay, spending all our savings and even borrowing money to attend the religious ceremonies. We had to change our money for special 'temple money' at an outrageous loss, and buy their own sacrificial animals at their high prices – ours were, of course, never good enough for the Temple priests and leaders."

"You are right, there," said Judas. I was there when Jesus said that it was written, My house is a house of prayer, but you have made it a den of thieves."

Aaron sighed. "When He first began His ministry, His mother came to us after the wedding at Cana, and told all of us how He turned the water into wine. I wanted to believe her, but it was difficult for me to accept that a boy who grew up here in our village could be who He said He was! My selfishness and bias blocked me from believing, and I have repented only recently."

"You said you wanted to believe Mother Mary, but did you?" asked Judas.

"The entire village knew that Mary would never tell a false story. She was the most trusted and revered woman in Nazareth. She is certainly the most pious woman in Nazareth, and probably in the whole land of Galilee."

"And you now believe?" asked Judas.

"Now I do," said Aaron. "I have read the Torah. There is no prophet who has fulfilled all these prophecies and predictions, especially at such a young age, and in such a short time, as our own Jesus. His words clarified and simplified the laws of Moses, and especially the many layers of law and tradition that had been built up over the years. I now believe that Jesus is the Son of God, the Messiah we have been waiting for. I prayed for His forgiveness, and I also prayed in my heart for His healing. And it did happen."

"This is wonderful," said Judas. "This shows that it is never too late to repent, ask for forgiveness, and believe in His divinity, even on your deathbed."

"I told you about my healing, and that is what made me a believer," said Aaron. "That rabbi who touched my cot did not look like the Jesus we knew, but after all, He had died and returned from the dead. That could do a lot to change a man. His injuries on the cross, from the nail wounds to the spear wound, probably did much to make Him look different from how He looked before. I believe He was the resurrected Jesus, visiting His old home, forgiving and healing the doubter. He is truly the Son of God, no matter how different He looks."

"He did look different; no one recognized Him at first," said Judas.

"I would have asked His name, but I was too sick at first, and then by the time we knew what had happened, He had left. I sent my children down the street to find Him, but He had gone." Aaron looked disappointed. "I was on my deathbed, and now look at me! I could travel anywhere, even to Jerusalem, if I wanted to. Of course, now that we know we do not need to travel to Jerusalem, I don't need to go. I am going to follow Him right here in Nazareth."

Judas said, "I believe you were healed by Jesus the Son of God. You are truly blessed!" The men bowed to each other, and Judas went on his way down the street.

After leaving Nazareth he went to other sites of his Lord's ministry: Nain, Samaria, Mount Tabor, Perea, Jericho, and the Jordan River. He immersed himself in the river and rested a day or two on the riverbank, thinking about John the Baptist and the baptism of Jesus. He then went through Bethany to Jerusalem, passing through the Mount of Olives and the Garden of Gethsemane on the way. During this entire journey, he did not see Jesus or any of the other disciples.

Finally, at Jerusalem, he went to the Temple, but there was no one there to talk with. He remembered throwing the 30 pieces of silver on the Temple floor on the Friday that Jesus had died. Judas then went out of the temple, headed south. He talked to someone who appeared to be of some importance, and the two men walked outside the city walls to a piece of land. This scenario looked familiar to Jeremiah, and he suddenly realized this was a land owner showing a piece of land to Judas. After a lot of bargaining and looking over the property, Judas paid the man.

The images stopped, and Jeremiah felt a little dizzy. So much had happened! "What day was that, when he was buying that land?" he asked.

"It was the thirty-sixth day of our Lord's resurrection," said Peter.

Day 35: Saturday

Day 35: Saturday: Jesus continues His travels towards Bethany and the Mount of Olives – the disciples reach Bethany.

"This is Saturday, day 35 of the resurrection," said Peter. "Again, everyone is continuing their journey. Jesus is slowly making His way toward the Mount of Olives. We have reached Bethany and stay there overnight as guests of Mary, Martha and Lazarus. The four sons of Mother Mary are starting their journey from Nazareth. They left their sisters behind to tend to the animals. The sisters were not happy to be staying, but were told that they were too young to make the journey, and that the brothers would be back with their mother within two weeks at the most."

Day 36: Sunday

Day 36: Sunday: The disciples talk with Mary, Martha, and Lazarus at Bethany – the disciples see the revived fig tree – the disciples arrive at Jerusalem

"This is Sunday, day 36 of the resurrection," said Peter. "We had been too tired for conversation when we arrived at the house of Mary, Martha and Lazarus, but during breakfast they told us about the visit from Jesus, and we told them about the times Jesus had talked with us. The group in Bethany was glad that that we had been able to meet with Jesus so many times. We told them about the plans to meet at the Mount of Olives, but no one knew exactly when. The women said they would nurse Jesus if they saw Him, and understood that He looked even less like Himself than before. Everyone said their goodbyes, and we all left."

The images showed the disciples walking toward Jerusalem. Slightly ahead and to the right was a fig tree, full of fruit. Birds were perched on the limbs, taking an occasional bite from a fig, and the butterflies and bees swarmed around it. Simon Peter pointed it out to the other disciples. "Look, here is the fig tree that the Master had cursed and withered, but now it is full of fruit. He was here, and revived the fig tree!"

The disciples gathered around, eating the fruit and talking about Jesus. Refreshed, they resumed their journey to Jerusalem. As they entered the city, they split up in groups of two or three, careful to avoid any Temple or Roman guards.

Finally, they stopped at a home that Jeremiah recognized. It was the house where the disciples were gathered when Jesus visited them on Sunday, the evening of His resurrection, and the following Sunday, when Thomas was present. Mary Magdalene and Mother Mary have been staying there since the crucifixion. They were delighted to hear all that has happened in Galilee and Mother Mary was especially happy that her children were preparing to come to Jerusalem.

Day 37: Monday

Day 37: Monday: Judas inspects his land purchase - death of Judas.

"It is Monday, day 37 of the resurrection," said Peter. "The disciples are at Jerusalem and our Lord is slowly making His way towards Bethany. Would you like to see the rest of the life of Judas?"

"Yes, Peter," said Jeremiah. "His story is more thought-provoking that I had thought it would be."

The images showed Judas inspecting his new land. It was afternoon and raining; perhaps he had planned to come in the morning but was waiting for the rain to stop. Everything looked wet and slippery. The lot was not a level one; it was located on a steep slope outside the walls of Jerusalem. As Judas was walking downhill, he fell on the slippery slope.

Peter said, "It was Luke the physician who got the story right in his gospel. Luke tells us: 'Now this man obtained a field with the reward for his wickedness; and falling headlong, his body burst open, and all his intestines gushed out.' Although it did not kill Judas outright, he was instantly paralyzed from the neck down."

Jeremiah couldn't see what had caused it, but he could see Judas' flesh had been ripped open in the midsection. After a minute of confusion, Jeremiah realized he was actually looking at the intestines and bowels of Judas, and quickly looked away, then back again, determined to learn everything he had promised to.

Judas was lying on the ground, alone. No one was around. No one came to help. His face was the only part of his body that had movement, and he seemed to be praying. Jeremiah thought he looked as if he were at peace. Finally his eyes closed for the last time. Jeremiah found his own eyes getting a little misty, and was glad for the tissue in his pocket.

Day 38: Tuesday

Day 38: Tuesday: Jesus does not stop at Bethany on the way to the Mount of Olives.

"It is Tuesday, day 38 of the resurrection," said Peter.

They watched as the images showed Jesus moving slowly toward Jerusalem. As He neared Bethany, Jeremiah was surprised to see that He did not stop and visit with His friends.

"He had to focus, to concentrate all of His being on just getting to the Mount of Olives," said Peter. If He had entered that house, as ill from His wounds as He was, very likely the women there would not have let Him leave."

Jesus moved slowly but steadily toward the foothills of the Mount of Olives. He paused, looked around, and settled down to camp there overnight.

The four brothers of Jesus reached the house where Mother Mary was staying, with Mary Magdalene, some of the disciples, and some women from Galilee. They were all glad to see the travelers. Mother Mary hugged her children and asked about her daughters. The sons told her what had happened in Nazareth, with the visit of the rabbi who was also a follower of their brother, and the healing of Aaron who had been on his deathbed. When they told their mother about the rituals at the meal they had with the rabbi, she said, "It was Jesus!" Her eyes shone and her face was almost radiant with happiness.

Her sons seemed taken aback at this. "He did not look like Jesus," one said. "He was tired, thin, obviously suffering from some ailment."

Another brother said, more thoughtfully, "There would have been no way for us to recognize Him as our brother unless He revealed that He was."

Mother Mary, though happy to have heard news of her firstborn, was concerned for His health. "She told me later that she had a feeling that His life on earth as they knew it was about to come to an end," said Peter. "She was longing to see Him once more, and hoped she would be able to see Him before whatever she had heard the disciples talking about happened. None of us knew what was going to happen, but of course she heard some of us talking about the plans He had helped us make – plans that had nothing to do with Him being around."

Day 39: Wednesday

Day 39: Wednesday: Jesus camps at the Garden of Gethsemane – Peter talks about why he delayed telling the disciples about the death of Judas.

"This is Wednesday, day 39 of the resurrection," said Peter.

The images showed Jesus getting up from His resting place in the foothills of the Mount of Olives. He bathed in the stream flowing from the mountain and started walking toward Jerusalem. On the way He stopped at a fig tree, plucked some of the fruit and began to eat.

Eventually He arrived at the Garden of Gethsemane. He stopped at a campsite, sat down and rested His back against a large rock.

"That is the same rock we have seen before," said Jeremiah. "It still has the stains from His blood. That is where He prayed that last night, when the Temple guards came for Him."

"That is right. He will rest here all night," said Peter.

"Where are the rest of you?" asked Jeremiah.

"We have been staying in the house with Mary Magdalene and Mother Mary, and her sons that had just arrived," said Peter. "Most of us were looking for Jesus around where He told us to meet Him – at the Mount of Olives. They spread out to cover the lower slopes as well, thinking He might not be able to climb so high. When they didn't find Him, they returned to that house in the evening to spend the night. However, if you remember from the Gospel of Luke, I took a little detour on this day."

Jeremiah looked startled, and then remembered the account of Peter telling the disciples and other followers that he had found Judas dead - but that account was after the ascension. Judas had been dead at least three or four days before Peter broke the news. "Was that difficult for you, Peter, finding him that way?" Jeremiah remembered how the scene had affected him, and he had not even lived with Judas as a brother for more than two and a half years as Peter had.

"It was difficult, Jeremiah," said Peter. "My emotions were all over the place, as you might say. We had all lived together for well over two years, and had gone through such amazing times that it seemed as if we had always been together. Then when he brought the Temple guards to our campsite, everything changed. Later we understood about that being part of the heavenly Father's plan, but at the time we were hurt to our very core. It was devastating. Then Jesus rose from the dead and helped us understand what had happened. We forgave Judas, but it was forgiveness from faith in Jesus and obedience to Him, not forgiveness from our hearts. Oh, don't misunderstand me; we did forgive him, but our relationship would take a long time to heal. But we never got that time."

Jeremiah sat silent for a moment. "Is that why you were looking for Judas? Was it about healing your relationship?"

"Jesus had asked us to meet with Him, and since He kept insisting that we were going to be on our own now, we knew He was going to leave us. I wanted Judas to have the chance to be a part of that. He was still a disciple, even though he was going his own way."

"But how did you know where to look for him?" asked Jeremiah.

"I remembered talk about buying some land to establish a central point for our ministry. It would be a place where some of us would always be to welcome the sick, the demon possessed, the poor, whoever needed help. There would always be food for the hungry, and rest for the weary. Judas had been in charge of this project, and I remember him giving a report on who he had talked to and where a likely site was located. It was a place to start, at least. But then I found him."

The images showed Simon Peter talking with the landowners that Jeremiah had seen with Judas. They were guiding Simon Peter to a spot, and pointing him toward the plot of land. The landowners were shaking their heads, as if to say they had shown Judas the way a couple of days ago, but had not seen him since.

Jeremiah saw Simon Peter walking down that same slope that he had seen Judas walk, and saw his startled reaction when he saw the body. Simon Peter bowed respectfully, and then began to look more closely, as if to make sure that this poor soul was actually Judas. He had been lying there long enough for the birds and small animals to make identification difficult. When Peter saw the money bag still slung around his shoulder, he knew it was Judas. Bowing again, he turned and walked back to town.

"I didn't speak of this immediately to the other disciples for several reasons," said Peter. "First, our concern right then was Jesus – meeting with Him and taking the next step. It was not the right time to talk about the death of Judas. Second, it was just too emotional for me to talk about. We never had the chance to heal our relationship. Seeing him there on the ground like that was horrible. No one should have to die like that, and lie there alone. I contacted the landowners, asked them to bury his body, and paid for their services. I told the other followers of Jesus on that Sunday, when we were all gathered together. I think there were around a hundred and twenty of us there. But all that happened after the ascension."

Day 40: Thursday

Day 40: Thursday: The disciples, Mother Mary, Jesus' brothers, Mary Magdalene and others gather at the upper room in Jerusalem - travel to garden of Gethsemane - meet Jesus at the foothills of the Mount of Olives – final messages and blessings from Jesus – Jesus ascends into heaven in full view of the group – two men in white send everyone back to Jerusalem with a message of His coming back as He ascended – Peter and Jeremiah discuss the Kingdom of Heaven.

"This is Thursday, day 40 of the resurrection," said Peter.

"This is it! This is when Jesus ascended!" said Jeremiah. "This is what I have been waiting for!"

The images showed that house in Jerusalem that Jeremiah had seen so often. Everyone was getting up and getting ready for the day. As usual, the women rose first, to prepare the cooking fire and breakfast. They ate as they cooked, and served the men their breakfast as they rose. Jeremiah wondered how the brothers of Jesus would get along with the disciples, but there seemed to be no friction. Simon Peter was in charge of the disciples, Mother Mary was in charge of her four sons, and everyone was well behaved.

When everyone had finished their breakfast, they gathered for prayer. Simon Peter led the prayers and singing, and after a short silence, Mother Mary asked to speak. Everyone turned to listen to her.

"I know everyone went to the Mount of Olives yesterday to look for Jesus," she said, "and I have heard some of you say you would like to look elsewhere, just in case." She looked at the sons of thunder, and their faces reddened with embarrassment. "But He told us to meet Him there, and I have received a strong feeling in my heart, that today is the day that He will meet us at the appointed site."

Mary Magdalene's eyes shone with excitement, and the sons of thunder jumped up, ready for action. The brothers of Jesus looked

259

at each other, and then the oldest one spoke, his voice a little tentative.

"From what you have said, we understand that it had been Jesus who had visited us as we were preparing for this journey. We did not recognize Him then, and a couple of us are not sure we would recognize Him now." He looked at the other brothers, who nodded encouragement. "If we see someone there, how will we know we have the right person?"

Simon Peter looked at the young disciple John. "He's the one who always has the inner knowledge – when none of us recognized Him at the Sea of Tiberias, John was the first to call out, 'It is the Lord!' – if we cannot recognize the man who meets us, we will let John tell us who it is."

They split up into groups of two or three, and left the house at different times, heading to the Mount of Olives by different routes. Peter said, "We were still being careful not to be seen by the Temple or Roman guards, especially with the women that were traveling with us."

Jeremiah nodded, and watched the disciples walking toward the Mount of Olives, each group arriving from a different direction. They all gathered at the Garden of Gethsemane at their usual campsite and from there on, they traveled in one group. John was helping Mother Mary over the rough places and at the steeper spots of the slope. Mary Magdalene was with them, but she needed no man's help; she strode alongside the sons of thunder, who seemed a little in awe of her. Some of the other women who had been helping them were there, and the other disciples helped those who needed a hand at times.

As they climbed up the lower slopes of the Mount of Olives, they slowed their pace so the women could keep up. When they were half way to the top, John gave a cry and pointed to a sheltered area off the path, where a man was sitting on a rock. As He stood up, everyone was able to see He was Jesus. He leaned heavily on His staff, and they had never seen Him look so thin or so ill. Silently everyone walked closer to Him, forming a semicircle around the Lord. A cloud of mist was forming around the mountaintop, and the women stood close together, as if for support. Mother Mary's sons were comforting her, as she wept for her firstborn, and Jeremiah knew she had never seen Him looking as ill and exhausted as He did now.

Jesus spoke: "Peace be with you all for being here with Me, at the end of My final journey on earth. I will say again the things you need to hear. Remember as I told you before, for God so loved the world, that He gave His only begotten Son, that whosoever believeth in Him should not perish, but have everlasting life. Do not depart from Jerusalem, but wait for the promise of the Father, which you heard from Me. For John indeed baptized in water, but you will be baptized in the Holy Spirit not many days from now."

James said, "Lord, are you now restoring the kingdom to Israel?"

Peter said to Jeremiah, "Do you see the annoyed looks on some of our faces? That young man always thought he was headed for some earthly kingdom, even though he had been hearing Jesus talk about the kingdom of heaven for three years. Most of us knew by that time that we were not going to stage a military coup and take over Roman occupied Israel. We felt he was wasting the time we had left with our Lord. But here is the answer."

Jesus said, "It is not for you to know the times or seasons which the Father has set within His own authority. But you will receive power when the Holy Spirit has come upon you. You will be my witnesses in Jerusalem, in all Judea and Samaria, and to the uttermost parts of the earth. In My Father's house are many mansions; if it were not so, I would have told you. I go to prepare a place for you. And if I go and prepare a place for you, I will come again, and receive you unto Myself, that where I am, there you may be also. My blessing will go with you."

The mist was rising to form a cloud, covering the top of the Mount of Olives. As Jesus ended His speech, He raised His hand in a gesture of blessing, and then He began to walk toward the top of the Mount of Olives. As He reached the top, the cloud covered Him completely, hiding Him from His family, disciples, and friends below. The group waited, each breath a prayer, looking intently at the cloud where Jesus had been.

Suddenly the cloud rose above the top of mountain, and the center of the cloud broke apart in the shape of a massive star exposing the entire top of the Mount of Olives. Jeremiah could see the deep blue sky in the center. The sunrays burst through the edges of the star shaped space in the cloud, lighting the scene with multiple colors. Standing at the top of the mountain was a radiant white figure that Peter, James, and John all recognized instantly – Jesus as He looked at His transfiguration. "It is the Lord!" they cried, and they all watched as He rose up above their heads, into the heavens.

Everyone was transfixed at this figure, growing bigger and bigger and shining like a thousand suns, occupying the entire blue sky as He ascended. As Jesus ascended, they all saw a vision of a new heaven and a new earth. They all heard Jesus saying, "Behold, I shall be with you in the tabernacle within you. Myself within you shall wipe away all tears from your eyes; and there shall be no more death, neither sorrow, nor crying, neither shall there be any more pain. Behold, I make all things new and possible for believers. I am the Alpha and the Omega, the beginning and the end." The voice faded away like an echoing sound in the valley, and Jesus was gone. As they were watching, the clouds became thicker and moved to cover the top of the mountain. The heavenly light, which was still penetrating the clouds and lighting up the top of the mountain like a snow cap, slowly faded back to normal sunlight.

They were all still looking toward heaven when suddenly two men dressed in white were standing beside them. "You men of Galilee," they said, "Why do you stand looking into the sky? This Jesus, who was received up from you into the sky will come back in the same way as you saw Him go into the sky."

"We did not know who those men in white were, but I suppose we needed someone to help us through this part of the ascension," said Peter to Jeremiah. "They had to tell us what to do next; we were too mystified and confused to know what to do. They stood there until we began the walk back into town. We reached the Temple and prayed. Then we all went back to that upper room where most of us had been staying. Many of the women went to their own homes in Jerusalem. We spent the next three days in prayer and supplication, either there in that room or at the Temple."

"Even on that last meeting people were still asking Jesus about an earthly kingdom, but He was still talking about receiving power from God," said Jeremiah.

"It is easier to talk about an earthly kingdom than it is trying to keep Jesus as king in your heart," said Peter. "You will see what happened when we were baptized with the Holy Spirit – after you've come all this way with us, we wouldn't want you to miss out on that. And, actually, the kingdom of Israel did finally happen – well, not a kingdom, but at least a country, in 1948, but the important thing is the kingdom of heaven that our Lord kept talking about, not the earthly kingdom."

"The people in your day kept wanting the kingdom of heaven to be an earthly kingdom, and some people in my day talk about the kingdom of heaven as a place they are trying to get to," said Jeremiah, "I know we are in heaven now -- but Jesus says the kingdom of heaven is among you, or the kingdom of heaven is within you -- like these verses in Luke 17:20 where our Lord told us that 'The kingdom of God does not come with observation, neither will they say, 'Look here!' or 'Look there!' For the kingdom of God is within you."

"Yes," said Peter, "the kingdom of heaven is within you. It is all about letting Jesus be the king of you, with your heart as His throne. When Jesus is your king, you are living in your own kingdom of heaven on earth and do not have to fear for anything – and when you die and are received into the kingdom of heaven here, you feel at home right away!"

Jeremiah said, "So, rather than living your life hoping to get somewhere, you are living your life as if you're already there. I like that concept, but how is it possible?"

Peter's smile was gentle. "When Jesus says all things are possible through Him, then you can believe it! We only really understood what He was talking about when we were baptized with the Holy Spirit. After that, the spirit of God was really alive in us, and, as you have read in the Bible, all things were possible."

"And now I am really looking forward to Pentecost!" said Jeremiah.

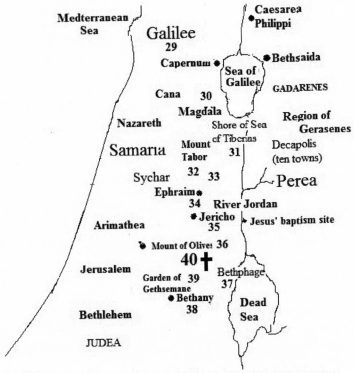

Sightings and movements of Jesus after resurrection
Days 30 - 40

Jesus' return journey from Galilee to the Mount of Olives,
the site of the ascension

Sightings and movements of Jesus from
resurrection to ascension   Days 1 - 40
Thick arrows indicate route of return journey

Day 43: Sunday

Day 43: Sunday: The disciples of Jesus meet with 120 – Simon Peter announces the death of Judas – they cast lots for the replacement for Judas – the lots fall on Matthias.

"Before we look at Pentecost," said Peter, "there is one more day you need to see."

Jeremiah looked confused. What had he missed?

"The twelfth apostle was chosen on the Sunday after the ascension," said Peter. "It is recorded by Luke in the book of Acts, but I thought you might like to see it for yourself."

"I would like to see that!" said Jeremiah.

"Remember," said Peter, "Jesus had ascended to heaven on Thursday. The disciples, Jesus' family, and the women were there to see it and to hear His final words. We went to the Temple to pray, and then to the upper room of that house. For the next few days, we alternated between praying at the temple and praying at the house. We spread the word among the other believers that we would meet on Sunday at this spot."

"Why on Sunday; why not sooner?" asked Jeremiah.

"We needed time to spread the word, and we didn't want to interfere with the Sabbath restrictions. If we had tried to meet on Friday, before the Sabbath, it would have been too soon to contact everyone. We did not want to attract the attention of the Temple guards and the Romans, so we had to be careful where we met. We decided Sunday evening would give us enough time, and honor the day of our Lord's resurrection. In addition, since this was not an emergency that would call for disobeying the Sabbath laws, we did not need to break them at Jerusalem now. No one's life was in danger, and there was no emergency that needed action on the Sabbath. Anyway, we wanted to reach as many as we could, and we needed time to do that. I'm not sure that we reached all of them, but around 120 came to the meeting."

Jeremiah said, "That phrase of Luke's 'in those days' has been interpreted in different ways. I had always thought it meant 'generally,' or 'around that time.'"

Peter nodded. "Yes, that was what Luke was trying to convey. I was actually the one who told the story to Luke – both Luke and Mark were close to Paul and myself in the early days of our ministry. They were with John, Paul, and me in Rome, and a few other places."

Jeremiah watched as the images showed Simon Peter and the other disciples standing behind a table in the upper room. They were talking quietly among themselves as the others arrived. It was crowded with so many there. They filled the room, and were packed into the stair leading up to it. There were even men perched in the windows, and there was standing room only on the back of the entryway.

When they had all gathered, Simon Peter stood and led them in prayer, praising God for the Lord Jesus, and asking for guidance during their meeting. When the prayer ended, he addressed the crowd, saying, "Brothers, it was necessary that this Scripture should be fulfilled, which the Holy Spirit spoke before by the mouth of David concerning Judas, who was guide to those who took Jesus. For he was numbered with us, and received his portion in this ministry."

The crowd of followers murmured, but no one challenged him. Simon Peter continued with new information: "Judas had bought a field, and had evidently slipped and fallen to his death. I saw his body and have made arrangements for the burial. Judas is with us no more. But there are more scriptures to fulfill: It is written in the scroll of Psalms, 'Let his habitation be made desolate. Let no one dwell therein,' which I believe is talking about the field he bought. No one will live there. There is also another one, 'May another take his office.' Therefore it is necessary to choose one of the men who have been with us the whole time the Lord Jesus went in and out among us, beginning from John's baptism to the time when Jesus was taken up from us. One of these must become a witness with us of His resurrection."

He sat down, and John rose to speak. "Brothers, who among you have been with us all this time?" Everyone started looking around, and several names were spoken, but two names were repeated the most: Matthias and Barsabbas. The two men came forward and stood near the disciples. Jeremiah remembered there had been 72 in the circle of disciples of Jesus from Judea, who helped Him in His ministry. As Simon Peter nodded, John prayed, "Lord, you know everyone's heart. Show us which of these two you have chosen to take over the apostolic ministry in the place of Judas."

Simon Peter cast the lots, although Jeremiah couldn't tell anything from how they fell. But he was the only confused one, for a shout went up: "Matthias!" they cried. There was a lot of hugging and clasping of forearms and Matthias took his place among the other eleven as the twelfth apostle.

Peter looked at Jeremiah. "Matthias was Judean, like Judas. Matthias was from the family Matthias who fought for worshipping our God hundreds of years back, instead of Greek idols, at Modein."

"I don't see his name mentioned much after that," said Jeremiah. "Was he a good choice?"

"Yes," said Peter. "He was an excellent choice. However, many of our names are not mentioned after this time. It would take too many books to record all that we did. The most important material about our Lord Jesus Christ has been recorded. The results of our actions, those of us who traveled to spread our Lord's message, are the believers who formed the first Christian churches. Those believers and churches are all the record we needed at that time. Now, you, Jeremiah, will continue the story as you write and talk about Jesus during His journey from His resurrection to His ascension.

Day 50: Sunday

Day 50: Sunday: Pentecost is an old Jewish festival, so many Jews are gathered in Jerusalem – the Holy Spirit comes in rushing wind and flames at the meeting of the followers of Jesus – speaking in different languages – outside in the street, the Jews from many foreign lands are astounded to hear God praised in their own language – Simon Peter speaks to the crowd – three thousand new followers are baptized that day

"Are we finally going to see what happened on Pentecost?" said Jeremiah. "I've always tried to imagine it."

"Yes, we are finally at the day of Pentecost," said Peter. "Many Christian traditions count this as the birth of the Christian church, where the believers went from being just a Jewish sect to being an organized group. Three thousand people were led to believe in Jesus the Messiah at once!"

"I always remind my congregation that the word Pentecost was the old name for the Jewish Harvest Festival, or Festival of Weeks, which commemorates God giving the Ten Commandments at Mount Sinai, fifty days after the Exodus. It is thought that the believers were meeting on that day to celebrate that festival."

"At that time we were following every Jewish law and tradition. We were Jews – Jews who had a Messiah! It was a little later that we became known as Christians," said Peter. "So, Jeremiah, let's think about this. Fifty days after the Exodus, Moses receives the Law. Fifty days after the Resurrection, God chose this day to pour out His Holy Spirit on the believers. What does that suggest to you?" Peter waited while Jeremiah thought about that.

"I know that Jesus is the fulfillment of the Law and the Prophets," said Jeremiah. "And since Moses and the Ten Commandments would represent the Law, perhaps the pouring out of the Holy Spirit on the day that commemorates them is another kind of fulfillment of the prophecies."

271

"That's right! Joel had prophesied about this day, many years ago, but we'll see later where I talk about that. Let's begin now."

The images showed the upper room, filled with many of those same 120 people that Jeremiah had seen earlier at the election of Matthias with maybe a few others who were not at the first meeting. It was morning, and they were gathered in prayer. Most were kneeling on the floor, but the more elderly ones sat on floor mats, benches or stood, leaning on a staff or against a wall. Suddenly, they heard what Jeremiah thought sounded like the beginning of a tornado. With a bang, all the doors and windows of the house flew open. Startled, everyone looked up and around as a sound like a blowing wind filled the house. Those kneeling jumped to their feet, and Jeremiah saw what looked like a moving fire enter the room, about seven feet off the ground.

The fire separated into tongues of flame, which flew around the room, each separate tongue of flame coming to rest over the head of each one of them. As each flame came to rest over a head, the person's look of fright and confusion was replaced with a look of awe and joy. Excitedly, they all began to talk to each other, but each one in a different language. As each one began to speak, their flame seemed to melt into their head, as water trickling from a sponge.

Jeremiah had never imagined a scene like this. He had never thought about when the flames had disappeared, although, he realized now, they must have vanished somehow before the believers went out into the crowd, since no one in the crowd had commented on it. And the noise! Jeremiah had never heard such a noise. Even in an international airport, where many different languages could be heard, he had experienced nothing like this. He had been looking forward to seeing the baptism in the Holy Spirit, with tongues of fire and speaking in other languages, but he had not expected the noise to be so overwhelming! Some of the language was beautiful, some was more guttural, and there were some clicking noises that sounded to Jeremiah like the language of some tribe in Africa.

Evidently the believers were a little overwhelmed by the noise also, as they ran downstairs and out into the street, still talking excitedly in their new languages. The people in the street were Jews who had come from many lands to celebrate the Festival of Weeks in Jerusalem. It was clear that they were both fascinated and disturbed by this group, as each person from a different country heard them speak in their own native language. One of the men said, "Aren't these men Galileans? Then how is it that each of us hears them speaking in his own native language?"

Another said, "We are Parthians, there are Medes and Elamites, I see residents of Mesopotamia, Judea and Cappadocia, Pontus and Asia. Here are Credans and Arabs – and we all hear them declaring the wonders of God in our own languages!"

They were clearly amazed and perplexed, and they kept asking each other what it could mean. "They are filled with wine!" one exclaimed. Then Simon Peter stood up above the crowd where he could be seen, and the other eleven stood with him.

"You men of Judea, and all you who dwell in Jerusalem, let this be known to you, and listen to my words. For these are not drunk, as you suppose. It is only nine in the morning! But this is what has been spoken through the prophet Joel:

'It will be in the last days, says God,
That I will pour out my Spirit on all flesh.
Your sons and daughters will prophesy.
Your young men will see visions.
Your old men will dream dreams.
Yes, and on my servants and on my handmaidens in those days,
I will pour out my Spirit, and they will prophesy.
I will show wonders in the heaven above,
and signs on the earth beneath;
blood, and fire, and billows of smoke.
The sun will be turned into darkness
and the moon to blood
before the coming of the great and glorious day of the Lord.
And everyone who calls
on the name of the Lord will be saved.

Peter turned to Jeremiah, "This means that in the days of old the Spirit of God was poured out on only those people God had chosen to be His prophets. Now, God pours out His spirit on every one of us who believes, who calls on the name of the Lord. We do not need to listen to a prophet to hear the word of God – the Spirit of God resides in us, and tells us what we need to know."

273

"I know that is what the Bible is saying, but I still see far too many people who still want to be told by some authority figure what God wants them to do," said Jeremiah. "It is good to listen to sermons and teachings, but it is also good to read the Bible and listen within your heart for the wisdom of the Lord."

"Good, Jeremiah," said Peter. "Let's see a little more before we talk again."

The images showed Simon Peter continuing his message to the crowd: "Men of Israel, hear these words: Jesus of Nazareth, a man approved by God to you by mighty works, and wonders and signs, which God did by Him in the midst of you, even as you yourselves know. Him, being delivered up by the determined counsel and foreknowledge of God, by the hand of lawless men, crucified and killed, whom God raised up, having freed Him from the pains of death, because it was not possible that He should be held by it. For David says concerning Him:

I saw the Lord always before my face,

For he is on my right hand, that I should not be moved.

Therefore my heart was glad, and my tongue rejoiced.

Moreover my flesh also shall dwell in hope.

because you will not leave my soul in hell,

neither will you allow your Holy One to see decay.

You made known to me the ways of life.

You will make me full of gladness with your presence.'"

"Jeremiah," said Peter, "What else strikes you about this speech?"

"Look at how confident you are!" cried Jeremiah. "Look at the scriptures you are quoting! Were you that eloquent before? And such courage! Before this day, you were all sneaking around Jerusalem in fear of the Temple guards, or the Roman guards, or anyone who might point you out to the authorities. But look at you now, making a speech right in the streets of Jerusalem. And especially, a speech about Jesus! You were fearless!"

"You have heard it said, 'Perfect love casts out all fear,' and being filled with the Holy Spirit was, in a way, being filled with perfect love. We knew we had nothing to fear from men because we were filled with the power of God. No matter what they could do to us, we belonged to Jesus. They could treat us just as badly as they did Jesus, but it didn't matter. We were the Lord's, and nothing else mattered. Our mission was to tell everyone about Jesus so they could share the same love and Holy Spirit that we did. Listen to what came next:"

The images showed Simon Peter saying, "Brothers, I may tell you freely of the patriarch David, that he both died and was buried, and his tomb is with us to this day. Therefore, being a prophet, and knowing that God had sworn with an oath to him that one of his descendants would sit on his throne, he, foreseeing this spoke about the resurrection of the Messiah that neither was He left in hell, or did His flesh see decay. This Jesus God raised up, to which we all are witnesses. Being therefore exalted by the right hand of God, and having received from the Father the promise of the Holy Spirit, He has poured out this, which you see and hear. For David did not ascend into the heavens, but he says himself,

'The Lord said to my Lord:
"Sit by my right hand
Until I make your enemies
a footstool for your feet."

"Let all the house of Israel therefore know certainly that God has made Him both Lord and Messiah, this Jesus whom you crucified."

The crowd's mood had changed completely during this speech. Some seemed sorrowful, some agitated, and others moved to tears. Several of them began to ask Simon Peter and the other apostles, "Brothers, what shall we do?"

Simon Peter said, "Repent and be baptized, every one of you, in the name of Jesus the Messiah for the forgiveness of your sins, and you will receive the gift of the Holy Spirit. For to you is the promise, and to your children, and to all who are far off, even as many as the Lord our God will call to Himself."

Jeremiah spoke, "Wow, Peter, you were really on fire!" and stopped, realizing that when the flame had been above Simon Peter's head, he had appeared to be on fire. They both laughed at the words Jeremiah had chosen.

"And I didn't stop there," said Peter. "Luckily you are spared reading or hearing the entire speech, but the Bible does record that I warned them and pleaded with them, with words such as, "Save yourselves from this corrupt generation." That might have been a bit over the top, a bit melodramatic, but, as you say, I was on fire. I had been baptized with fire by the Holy Spirit, and I was empowered to speak so convincingly that three thousand people accepted the message that day. We baptized those three thousand, and it was a good thing there were over a hundred of us, because otherwise it would have taken all night."

Peter continued, "That was the beginning of the church. We continued meeting together for prayer, but there were so many of us now that we began meeting in one of the Temple courts. We shared our belongings; we shared our food. It was a beautiful time. The people in the city embraced us, and we received new followers every day. It was a little like what being in heaven is, now."

Epilogue

Epilogue: Jeremiah's return journey home – he is in the hospital with his wife – he tells of his experience and his mission – Jeremiah writes the book on his experience – he presents it to the congregation on Easter Sunday.

Jeremiah watched as the final image faded. He looked at Peter. "I saw it; I saw it all - just as it happened." His eyes were shining with tears of joy.

"Yes, you did," said Peter. "You have learned what our Lord wanted to teach you, and now it is time for you to go and teach others -- not only your own congregation, but as many people as you can reach with your words." He rose, and Jeremiah followed him out into the streets of heaven. Suddenly Jeremiah realized they were walking toward the place where he had first arrived.

"I should feel such joy that I am being sent with this message," said Jeremiah, "and I do feel joy, but also sorrow that I have to leave here."

"You are not the first to feel so," said Peter. "All who come before their time and who are sent back to finish their purpose are sad. Of course! This is heaven! Who would want to leave?"

Jeremiah laughed a little at that, but he still felt torn. They had arrived at the place, and Peter turned to face him.

"Your wife Victoria is waiting for you," said Peter, and Jeremiah instantly brightened. Peter continued, "Would you like to see what your family is doing now?"

At Jeremiah's nod, Peter showed him a hospital room. From his years of hospital visits Jeremiah knew it was an intensive care unit. Even though he knew he would see himself in the hospital bed, it was still a shock to see his body lying there, with tubes and wires leading to different machines, sustaining his life. His wife was sitting close to him, reading the Bible, as he knew she had been doing all this time. The doctor from the church poked his head in the door. "Any change?" he asked, but Victoria shook her head 'no'.

"In your world, you have been in a coma for 50 days," said Peter. "It might take a few days or so for you to remember what you have seen here, but do not be anxious. You will remember, by the power given you by our Lord, and you will write a book and give teachings that will cover the earth."

Jeremiah looked again at his body. He knew the tubes were keeping his body nourished and breathing, but he looked so thin and weak. He remembered how tired he had felt on earth, and how wonderful it had felt in heaven to move around without ever feeling weary, without ever feeling the aches of old age. But he also remembered his wife, and their grandchildren. And his church, and the people who had been praying for him the whole time he had been gone.

Peter just watched him, and then said, "Are you ready?"

Jeremiah took one last look around heaven, and said, "Yes."

Immediately it seemed his spirit body was traveling down from heaven, down to the hospital, through the hospital roof to the corridors, passing through the glass doors of the intensive care unit. Jeremiah felt his spirit body hovers over his physical body a while. He watched his wife as she read, listening to the sound of her voice saying, 'we redeem our life in the name of Jesus Christ,' amid the beeping of the machines. Suddenly, without any warning, Jeremiah felt his spirit travel back through that dark tunnel and slip back into his body. His eyes were closed. His body felt warm but still weak, and he realized all those tubes and needles felt just as uncomfortable as they looked. Then he realized he also felt his wife's hand, holding his tightly. He gave her hand a squeeze, and heard her gasp.

He opened his eyes, and she was there. She looked at him intently, and then jumped up to call the doctor and nurses saying, "He is moving his hands and opening his eyes! He is alive, alive, alive! Praise the Lord for saving his life!" As they rushed in, Jeremiah moved his left hand close to his mouth, and signaled them to pull out the breathing and feeding tubes. The intensive care doctor examined him, shining a light into his eyes, and asking him to clench his hand in a handshake.

Jeremiah did all that was asked by his physician. He knew they were giving him other tests – he recognized the chest X-ray and the electrocardiogram, but he was too weak to do anything except hold his wife's hand. Jeremiah didn't know how long they waited for the results, but when the doctor came back into the room he was elated. "Jeremiah is out of danger!" he said. "Jeremiah, you have made a full recovery! We can get you off life support and move you to another room for a couple of days of observation and then send you home."

Tears of joy streamed drown the cheeks of Victoria as the nurses carefully removed all the tubes and wires. The worst part was when they cleaned his mouth, throat, and nose with those suction catheters. Jeremiah almost wished he were unconscious again, in heaven with Peter, but when he felt his wife's hand still firmly holding his, he knew whatever he was going through was worth it to be with her. They didn't let him talk much that first day – for one thing, he had an oxygen mask covering his mouth and nose, but he knew he felt grateful. Jeremiah wasn't exactly sure what he was grateful for, but he kept thanking Jesus and Peter. Victoria seemed a little confused by her husband thanking someone named Peter, but the doctor assured her that he would be more lucid the next day or two.

Sure enough, the next day Jeremiah felt much more like his old self, especially when they removed the oxygen mask. His wife and the Reverend Philip were both at his bedside most of the day. When he felt as if he could talk steadily, he told them what had happened. "My spirit was taken up to heaven," he said, "but the Apostle Peter told me it was not my time to stay there." Victoria held him close at those words. "You remember I had always been fascinated by Easter and the resurrection of Jesus – what He had been doing all that time before His ascension." He stopped for breath, and the Reverend Philip offered him some water from the tray. He sipped it gratefully, and then continued.

"I met the angel Gabriel! He told me that I had been brought there to learn something, and then he took me to the Apostle Peter. Peter said they wanted to show me what Jesus had done after He was raised from the dead, during those 35 days that are not recorded in the Bible. Peter showed me where Jesus went, the people he talked to, everything! And I am to write a book and share it with the world."

He fell back against his pillow, exhausted. Victoria and the Reverend Philip looked at each other, each wondering if what they were hearing was a divine vision or the ravings of someone with brain damage. As Jeremiah told them more and more about his heavenly visit, they began to believe him. Finally they were convinced, although Victoria looked a little concerned.

The Reverend Philip smiled. "I will take on more of your duties at church," he said. "This is a priority for you, a holy priority, and everyone at church will rally around to help." He turned to Victoria. "We won't let him do anything but write that book. I can do the sermons, we have teams in place that can visit the sick, and there are a couple of young men that I would like to see teaching on Sunday mornings and Wednesday nights."

The reverend turned back to Jeremiah and said, "We've had 50 days without you to figure out how to get things done around that church. We can just keep that going while you finish the book, while it is still fresh in your memory." He winked at Jeremiah. "After that, though, you're back in the saddle. I'll need a little time off!"

They all laughed and Victoria looked a little less worried. "We need to make sure you are completely recovered before you do anything," she said. "You can write as your strength allows you."

Jeremiah came home and was happy just to be there, in his own room instead of a hospital bed. The cardiologist had sent him home with a restricted diet, but Victoria was able to turn even those bland ingredients into meals that Jeremiah loved. His children and grandchildren, Dev, Andy, Usha with her husband Martin, Jessica, Erica, Lauren, Samuel, and Gavin came to spend time with him. One Sunday evening, the choir came and sang many of Jeremiah's favorite hymns.

As his strength allowed, he wrote everything down, just as he remembered it. As Peter had said, Jeremiah really did remember everything. The mental images kept appearing as he progressed, without any interruption. Victoria and the Reverend Philip were his best critics, always making sure they could understand what he had written. They encouraged him to write the entire story, not just what he had seen, so that the readers would have someone they could identify with in the story. Whenever anyone asked him what the title would be, he just smiled and said, "I do not have the title yet. It will be provided by our Lord Jesus Christ when the time is right."

It took much longer than Jeremiah had anticipated, but at last, the book was finished. Only Victoria and the Reverend Philip knew what the book was about. It was kept secret from the congregation – all they knew was that book was coming out on Easter Sunday, and that each person would be receiving a copy.

On that Easter Sunday, the church was even more crowded than it had been the previous year. Big boxes of the books had been stacked near the front of the church, and everyone hoped the sermon would be something from the new book. No one had seen a copy yet, but when Jeremiah slipped out of the door leading to his office during the hymn before the sermon, the excitement reached a new level.

In his office, Jeremiah picked up his copy of the book and knelt on the floor, so grateful that at first no words would come. He thanked Jesus and Peter for giving him this insight and gift of knowledge from heaven. He held up the book as an offering to God. "I have completed the first step, Peter," he said. "I have finished the book, and now I ask your blessing, to cover the earth with this message."

Jeremiah returned to his place in the service just as the hymn was ending. He strode to the pulpit and said, "My sermon today is from the book you know I have been writing this past year. You all know of my delight in the Easter season, and the Lord blessed me with the knowledge of what He had done on earth those 40 days beginning with that first Easter." He held the book up so the congregation could see the title, and as they read it to themselves, they smiled, grinned, and some even began to laugh.

"Yes," said Jeremiah, "The Lord rewarded my lifelong curiosity with what I most wanted to know. He let me see what had happened during His last days on this earth, and the Apostle Peter told me to write what I had seen, and to cover the earth with the message. I have written what I saw, and the message begins today." He opened the book and began reading his sermon to the congregation, starting with the title: **RESURRECTION JOURNEY**.

General Notes

The author has combined the gospels to present this version of the resurrection story.

The biblical quotations are either from the King James Bible or the New Heart English Bible, both in the public domain. Some passages are paraphrased by the author and the editor.

Jeremiah the Old Testament Prophet

This is not the Jeremiah in *Resurrection Journey*, although our character's mother might have named him for this prophet. The Jeremiah of the Old Testament preached the destruction of Judah, the southern kingdom of the Jews, beginning when he was just a boy, and he lived to see the destruction take place. His words describing the new covenant that God will make: 'I will put my laws in their minds and I will write them on their hearts. I will be their God and they will be my people.' (Jeremiah 31:31-33) is echoed in these words of Jesus: 'This wine is the token of God's new covenant to save you – an agreement sealed with the blood I will pour out for you.' (Luke 22:20).

Additional notes of interest are given after the **Notes on Day 50.**

Notes by Day of Resurrection

Notes on Day 1

Approximately 21 people saw Jesus on the day of His resurrection.
Below I have listed the number of people, who they were, and the gospel source.

1   Mary Magdalene   Mark 16: 9-10
1   Peter   Luke 24:34
6   other women   Matthew 28:9-10
2   followers (Cleopas and his wife) going to Emmaus Mark 16:12-13, Luke 24:13-32
11 disciples (Thomas absent) Mark 16:14, Luke 24:35-43, John 20:19-23

This list does not include the angels and other men in white talking to the women.

Angels or Men in White at the Tomb
Matthew 28:2 lists one angel of the Lord
Mark 16:5 lists one young man wearing a white robe (usually denotes an angel)
Luke 24:4 lists two men in dazzling apparel (usually denotes angels)
John 20:1-2 lists two angels in white

Garden Tomb
Even though most scholars agree that this is not the tomb of Jesus, it is still the place where many visitors visit a tomb that would have been very like the one where Jesus was laid, and we have used this for the site in *Resurrection Journey*. Jesus met all the women and Peter in the gardens around the area of the tomb, although it is possible that Jesus might have entered just inside the

walls of Jerusalem when He met the group of women. He did not travel inside the city out of concern for being detected.

Jerusalem

Jesus' ancestor King David captured the city and made it his capital, and it has been in contention ever since. In the days before Jesus alone, the conquerors (or destroyers) included Babylon, Alexander the Great, Egypt, Seleucids of Syria, the Jews, and then Rome. After Jesus, the list includes, in order: the Jews, Rome, the Jews, Rome, Muslim Arabs, the Seljuk Turks, the Crusaders, the Muslims, Turkey's Ottoman Empire, and then the British during WWI. After the war, the city was divided between the Jews and the Palestinians, and the state of Israel was formed in 1948. Finally in 1967 Israel took control of the entire city after the Six-Day War.

When Jesus walked to Jerusalem for the last Passover feast He would celebrate on earth, He said, "It wouldn't do for a prophet of God to be killed except in Jerusalem! O Jerusalem, Jerusalem, the city that kills the prophets and stones God's messengers! How often I have wanted to gather your children together as a hen protects her chicks beneath her wings, but you wouldn't let me." (Luke 13:33-34).

When the Jerusalem Jews demanded a miraculous sign to prove His authority, Jesus answered them, 'Destroy this temple, and in three days I will raise it up.' The Jews then said, 'It has taken forty-six years to build this temple, and will you raise it up in three days?' But He spoke of the temple of His body. (John 2:19-21). As predicted by Jesus, Jerusalem was completely destroyed in 70 AD and in 135 AD, and the Temple was leveled to the ground, with only the Wailing Wall as a reminder of the Temple that is gone forever.

Jesus came here to die, but He was also resurrected here, and the new church was born here (see **Pentecost** – Day 50)

Mary Magdalene

Mistaken for a prostitute for many years, Mary Magdalene is now recognized as a wealthy woman from Magdala, a fishing town not far from where Jesus based his ministry in Capernaum. She was one of the women who contributed from her resources to support

Jesus and His disciples. According to Mark 16:9, Jesus had exorcized her of seven demons.

Mary was at the crucifixion, she followed His body to the tomb, and she was the first one there on Sunday morning to finish the burial rites. Jesus chose her to be the first to see Him resurrected, and instructed her to tell the disciples, thus she is called the Apostle to the Apostles. There is a possibility that she was at the site of ascension, though her name does not appear.

Her name is mentioned 12 times in the King James Version of the New Testament. She appears in all four gospels at the cross, but after the gospels she is not spoken of by name.

Nicodemus

A Jewish leader who came to Jesus in secret to ask questions, Nicodemus proved he was a believer when he helped Joseph of Arimathea to bury Jesus in the stone tomb. He brought around 100 pounds of myrrh and aloe to prepare the body of Jesus and wrap it in linen strips before they placed Jesus in the tomb. He was the first Jewish leader from Jerusalem to recognize "we know that thou art a teacher come from God: for no man can do these miracles that thou doest, except God be with him." John 3:2

He was described by Jesus as "the teacher of Israel," (John 3:10) implying he was well trained in Old Testament law and tradition. When Temple priests and leaders were conspiring to kill Jesus, Nicodemus counseled the court of the Sanhedrin by saying, "Does our law judge a man before it hears him and knows what he is doing?" John 7:51. He might have informed Jesus of the discussion by the Temple priests and leaders: "Nor consider that it is expedient for us, that one man should die for the people, and that the whole nation perish not" John 11:50 and "Now Caiaphas was he, which gave counsel to the Jews, that it was expedient that one man should die for the people. John 18:14. It might have been upon the receipt of this information that Jesus decided to surrender to the Temple guards, so His trial, death and resurrection could take place in Jerusalem.

Emmaus

Two disciples (possibly two of the 72 mentioned in the gospels - Cleopas and probably his wife or another disciple) were walking to Emmaus from the center of the city of Jerusalem, on the first Easter Sunday after hearing about the resurrection of Jesus. They were joined by Jesus, whom they did not recognize. They discussed the death and rumors of the resurrection of Jesus, with Jesus giving them all the scriptural background needed to understand what was happening. When they arrived at Emmaus they persuaded Jesus to eat a meal with them, which is the first meal Jesus had eaten since that supper with His disciples 72 hours previous. It was at that time they recognized He was the resurrected Jesus. Jesus traveled to Emmaus, west of Jerusalem, to avoid the Temple guards and Temple spies searching for Him on that historic Sunday. Then He returned to the city in the darkness of night.

Scholars have not found the exact location of that old village, but the Crusaders placed it as the Arab village El-Qubeibeh, seven miles northwest of Jerusalem. Josephus, the first-century historian, said the village Ammaous was three and a half miles from Jerusalem, for a round-trip total of seven miles.

Jonah

Jonah was the Old Testament prophet who ran away in fear when God called him to give a prophecy to the people of Nineveh. He lived in a Galilean village of Garh-hepher, near Nazareth 700 BC. Jonah had taken a ship headed in the opposite direction, but when a storm came up, Jonah was thrown into the sea in an effort to save the ship. When a 'big fish' swallowed him, he remained alive for three days until the fish spit him out on a beach. Jesus referenced Jonah's ordeal in Matthew 12:40: "For as Jonah was in the belly of the great fish for three days and three nights, so I, the Son of Man, will be in the heart of the earth for three days and three nights."

It is likely that Jonah was not completely swallowed into the stomach. If he had, he would not have survived the maceration of skin by the strong stomach acids for three days according to distinguished basic scientist Dr. T.R. Shantha. He hypothesizes the possibility that: 1. He simply rode holding the fins and was thrown out as the fish went to the surface. 2. One of his legs or arms was stuck in the blow hole through which the whale and dolphin breathe, and he was expelled by the force of expiration, or 3. He was sitting in the throat in the upper part of the food pipe (esophagus), irritating the fish as he was trying to get fresh food and water from the sides and was expelled by the force of gas from the stomach through the throat when the fish's belly hit a sandbar. It is possible he stayed there alive for three days, breathing the air that was swallowed by the fish. Many scholars believe this story is not to be taken literally, but that it is an illustration for a particular teaching, and never actually happened.

Pilate

He was the fifth Prefect of the Roman province of Judaea, from AD 26–36. He was the judge at Jesus' trial and authorized the crucifixion of Jesus. Pilate was the final authority on all legal matters in the area, sort of a one-man Supreme Court, and only select cases came before him. He was reluctant to sentence Jesus to death (the gospels mention a dream his wife had) but the Jews insisted, threatening Pilate with the wrath of Caesar, shouting, "If you release this man, you are not a friend of Caesar." He yielded to the decision of the masses.

In all four gospel accounts, Pilate avoids responsibility for the death of Jesus. Matthew says, "When Pilate saw that he could prevail nothing, but that rather a tumult was made, he took water, and washed his hands before the multitude, saying, I am innocent of the blood of this just person: see ye to it. Then answered all the people, and said, His blood be on us, and on our children." Mark depicts Jesus as innocent of plotting against the Roman Empire and portrays Pilate as hesitant to execute Jesus. In Luke, both Pilate and Herod Antipas, the Tetrarch of Galilee, agree that Jesus did not conspire against Rome, finding nothing treasonable in Jesus' actions. In John, Pilate states "I find no guilt in Him (Jesus)" and he asks the Jews if Jesus should be released from custody – but the crowd demands the release of Barabbas.

Several years later, when Pilate ordered a bloody attack on a crowd of unarmed Samaritans, he was ordered to Rome to answer the charges and was never heard from again. He was replaced by Marcellus.

Temple Mount

This site is sacred to three important monotheism religions (belief that there is only one God, as found in Judaism, Christianity, and Islam). This Jerusalem hilltop has a huge boulder where tradition tells us Abraham almost sacrificed his son Isaac, King David built an altar, and Muhammad ascended to heaven and returned. King Solomon built the first Jewish temple there, which was later leveled by the Babylonians. The Jews rebuilt it, and then Herod the Great enlarged the temple and the size of the hilltop itself: the Western Wall (Wailing Wall) is part of the wall that acted as a retaining wall for the new construction. When that temple was destroyed in 70 AD by the Romans, the Western Wall remained (it is a retaining wall, holding back tons of dirt) and since it is all that is left of the Temple, it is considered the most sacred site of the Jewish people.

In 135 AD, Hadrian filled in about 50 feet of earth over the top of where the temple stood, enlarged the temple mount, and built a temple of Jupiter. In 325 AD Constantine tore down the Temple of Jupiter and assumed Hadrian built the temple of Jupiter on top of the spot where the temple of Solomon once stood. Constantine then built an octagonal church on the site. In 691 AD the Muslims found the foundations of Constantine's octagonal church and built the dome of the Rock on the same place.

Today visitors can approach the Wailing Wall and enter the Dome of the Rock. Since the Dome of the Rock was built over where the Temple once stood, this can also be considered the spot where Jesus stood, was interrogated, was sentenced to death and was then led to the Pretoria for the death sentence to be carried out by crucifixion.

Messiah

Messiah is a designation or title that for the Jews means 'anointed' or 'consecrated.' The Hebrew word is *mashiah* and the Greek word is *Christos*, which in English is translated Christ. Kings, priests, and prophets were all anointed, but the Messiah is regarded as the perfect union of all three, chosen by God to lead His people as prophesied. In the Christian religion, this person is our Lord Jesus Christ.

Notes on Day 2

Appearance of angels

Angels appear 81 times in the New Testament, and 13 times in Old Testament. The angel Gabriel is mentioned four times in the Bible. The first time the word angel appears in the Old Testament is Genesis 19: 1 where two angels appear at Sodom, and visit Lot, the only righteous man there. At the end of the Bible in Revelation 21:11, 12 angels appear with the names of the 12 tribes of Israel written on them, standing at the gates of the high wall which had 12 foundations with the names of the 12 apostles of the Lamb (meaning Jesus).

An angel appears to shepherds in the fields and announces the birth of Jesus, and other angels appear and praise God, then they disappear: Luke 2:8-15.

Angels in the Life of Jesus

Jesus was talking to Nathaniel and other disciples. "And He saith unto him, Verily, verily, I say unto you, hereafter ye shall see heaven open, and the angels of God ascending and descending upon the Son of Man." John 1:46-51 In *Resurrection Journey*, angels born as women descended to care for Him and His ministry. The following is a list of some of the angels in the life of Jesus:

1. Angel Gabriel announces the birth of John the Baptist, and names him (Luke I: 11-17)
2. Angel Gabriel appears and foretells to Mary the birth of Jesus (Luke 1:26-37)
3. An angel foretells to Joseph the birth of Jesus and names Him (Matthew 1:20-21).
4. An angel announces to shepherds the birth of Jesus (see Appearance of Angels above)
5. Three separate times the angels direct Joseph: first for the Holy Family's flight to Egypt, second for their return to Israel, and the third to reside in Nazareth (Matthew 2: 13, 20)

6. Angels ministers to Jesus at His Temptation (Matthew 4: 11)
7. An angel ministers to Jesus in Gethsemane (Luke 22:43)

Spear in the chest

It was typical for the Romans to put a spear in the chest of an enemy soldier to be sure the enemy is dead and not merely feigning death. It was also usual during a crucifixion for the Romans to put a spear in the chest of the one crucified. The spearing was the last act done to Jesus to make sure He was dead. This was done before the centurion reported that Jesus was dead, so that Pilate could consent to give the body to Joseph of Arimathea for burial. The act of spearing also fulfilled the scripture that said, 'they shall look on him whom they pierced' and 'a bone of him shall not be broken to hasten his death.' (John 19:37; Zechariah 12:10; Psalm 22:16)

Angels care for Jesus after the Temptation

The amount of time for someone to recover from fasting for 40 days is two weeks, so the women from Galilee who followed Him, who had been angels, cared for Jesus the two weeks that it took for Him to recover and begin His ministry.

Isaiah

Isaiah is the Jerusalem prophet who wrote many of the prophecies of Jesus, including the name Immanuel (Isaiah 7:14), shoot of stump of David's family . . . defend the poor and exploited (Isaiah 11:1 – 4), wounded and crushed for our sins . . . led as a lamb to the slaughter . . . put in a rich man's grave (Isaiah 53:5, 7-9). His task was to preach doom to Israel, the northern kingdom of the Jews – the destruction of the cities and their people, but his words also contain the hope of restoration.

Notes on Day 3

Bethlehem

Bethlehem is located on a ridge in the Judean hills, six miles south of Jerusalem. It is called the City of David because it was David's birthplace and boyhood home (1 Sam 17:12). It was here that the prophet Samuel anointed David as King (1 Sam16:4-13). The prophet Micah had predicted that Bethlehem would be the birthplace of the Messiah (Micah 5:2).

Caesar Augustus, who had defeated Anthony and Cleopatra, ordered a census to be taken which required everyone to be registered in the place of their ancestors. This required Joseph and the pregnant Mary to leave Nazareth and register at the birthplace of Joseph's ancestor David. What would usually be a three-day trip might have turned into a five or six day trip when you consider Mary's condition and the crowded roads due to the high amount of traveling for the census. Later John the Baptist preached in this region (Matt.3:1; Luke 3:3).

It was here that Jesus was born, as predicted by Micah. The oldest church in the world, the Church of the Nativity, is built over a cave where, tradition says, Jesus was born. Visitors begin their pilgrimage under the front altar, where stairs lead to a series of candlelit caves. The first one is the grotto of the Nativity, which has a silver star embedded in the floor to remind us of the Star of Bethlehem.

The little town of Bethlehem was very active in the Old Testament. Rachel, the wife of Jacob, was buried there. Ruth and Boaz lived in Bethlehem.

Journey to Egypt
Joseph, Mary, and Jesus traveled 330 miles from Bethlehem to reach Egypt and another 411 miles back to Nazareth via Bethlehem and Jerusalem. It is likely that the family joined one of the many caravans on the trade route that went to Egypt, to avoid being robbed on the way by bandits that plagued individual travelers. They had to travel by a route that afforded them enough water for both themselves and the donkey that Mary was probably riding. Sometimes the toddler was carried by Mary, and sometimes Joseph carried the young Jesus on his shoulders. There is a possibility that Joseph, Mary, and Jesus rode on some of the camels of the caravan they had joined, but of course we will never know for sure.

The author estimates a traveling rate of 15 to 21 miles per day, based on the group traveling mostly in the mornings and evenings. They rested in the heat of midday, pitching a tent for shade from the

293

sun's heat. On the way there, traveling with a toddler, the journey took around 21 days. On the way back to Nazareth, the journey took around 27 days.

Herods and Jesus
Three different rulers named Herod touched the life of Jesus.
1. **Herod the Great** ruled the Jews at the time of Jesus' birth
2. **Herod Archelaus** ruled in Judea when Jesus returned from Egypt
3. **Herod Antipas** ruled in Galilee when Jesus was on trial.

Herod the Great
Herod was the King of the Jews, but he was an outsider, from the neighboring nation of Edom, or Idumea. This was the Herod who tried to kill the baby Jesus in Bethlehem. From a warning in a dream, Joseph took the baby and Mary to Egypt. Herod had asked the Wise Men, who had approached him asking about the arrival of a future king, to come back and tell him where the child was. When they were warned in a dream not to tell Herod, they did not tell the king, but took another road home after visiting Jesus.

When the king realized they were not returning, he found where the promised child would be born, and ordered the slaughter of boys born in Bethlehem and the surrounding area aged two years and younger.

During his reign, Herod the Great executed several members of his own family, including his wife Mariamne. Local leaders who disagreed with his plans were also executed. For this reason, The Roman Emperor Augustus said about Herod: "I would rather be Herod's pig than Herod's son." It is easy to imagine such a man ordering the massacre of all male infants in Bethlehem for no better reason than a rumor that one had been born "King of the Jews." His ambition also took other forms – he was known for his colossal building projects, including the expansion of the Second Temple in Jerusalem (Herod's Temple) and the port at Caesarea Maritima.

Herod Archelaus
Herod Archelaus was the ruler in Judea when Jesus and His parents returned from Egypt. Mary and Joseph were afraid of this

ruler, and in response to a message from an angel in Joseph's dream, went to Galilee to live, settling in Nazareth, which is why Jesus is called a Nazarene. (Matthew 2:21-23)

Notes on Day 4

Shepherds' Field
At the eastern edge of Bethlehem is the only level field in that area. Tradition tells us it was here on the night of Jesus' birth that angels appeared to shepherds guarding their flocks, to announce the birth of Jesus. Since this was the only level field, it is likely that it was here that David, tending his family's sheep, was anointed King by the prophet Samuel.

Kerioth
Kerioth was a village in the south of Judah which was probably the home of Judas Iscariot. It is assumed to be his village because of the name Iscariot (meaning man from Kerioth) that is always placed with the name Judas as an identifier to separate him from another Judas in the gospels. It is possible that Judas was born in Kerioth. It is plausible that many decades back, his ancestors moved to this location to escape the constant unrest and wars surrounding Modein and Jerusalem.

The village with that name no longer exists, but it has been identified with the ruins of el-Kureitein.

Calvary, Golgotha, and Place of the Skull
This is the site where it is believed Jesus was crucified. The name Calvary is from the Latin name of the site; the name Golgotha is the Greek translation of the Aramaic title which means 'place of the skull.' Early writings describe it as a hill looking like a skull, near a gate into Jerusalem. The traditional placement of the site comes from Helena, the mother of Constantine I. She also identified the location of the Tomb of Jesus, and her son Constantine I built the church of the Holy Sepulcher around the entire site.

Notes on Day 5

Bethany

Bethany is located to the east of Jerusalem, on the far side of the Mount of Olives. Today this is an Arab village named Al-Azariyah (meaning 'the place of Lazarus' in Arabic) in the Palestinian West Bank. The alleged tomb of Lazarus (scholars are not certain that this is actually his tomb) is a local tourist attraction, and Christians built a church near it in the fourth century AD, soon after Christianity was declared legal in Rome. See **Martha**.

Bethphage

Bethphage is located close to Bethany on the slopes of the Mount of Olives. It was at Bethphage that the disciples found the foal of a donkey for Jesus to ride into Jerusalem on the day Christians commemorate as Palm Sunday.

Mary the sister of Martha and Lazarus

The three siblings lived together in Bethany, on the other side of the Mount of Olives. Mary is remembered for sitting at the feet of Jesus while Martha bustled about in the preparation of food. Mary is also remembered for anointing Jesus with expensive perfume during a meal which she and her sister prepared to thank Him for raising Lazarus. Their father Simon was said to have been cured of leprosy by Jesus.

Martha

The sister of Mary and Lazarus, she was the one who was busy preparing a big meal for Jesus while Mary sat at His feet. Remembered mainly for her preference for action over attentive listening, she also had a more spiritual side. At the tomb of Lazarus, she said yes when Jesus asked her if she believed that He was the source of eternal life. She also said that though her brother was dead, she believed God would give Jesus whatever He asked. Jesus stayed five days in their house before His arrest and crucifixion.

Their father Simon was said to have been cured of leprosy by Jesus. At this time of their lives, none of these siblings were married, possibly due to the stigma of leprosy.

Abraham and the Twelve Tribes of Israel

Born around 2100 BC, Abraham was originally named Abram (honored father), and he was born and lived with his family in Ur, an important city in the Sumer empire. Abram's father decided to move to Canaan (Genesis 11:31) and so their entire family left their town on the west bank of the Euphrates River and followed a caravan route that would eventually take them to Canaan. They stopped before they got there, and settled in the town of Haran.

This was where Abram was told by God to leave his country and his father's house. He was to go to the land that God would show him, and God would cause Abram to be the father of a great nation. Abram was around 75 years old at the time, but he did as God asked, and was rewarded with a covenant that gave him a new name, Abraham (father of many).

Abraham had two sons. The first was Ishmael, who was considered the father of the Arab people. The second was Isaac, who was the father of the Jews. God ordered Abraham to sacrifice Isaac, and Abraham was obedient, and about to do this (at a large rock now enshrined at the Dome of the Rock), when God stopped him and allowed Isaac to live. Isaac's son Jacob, later named Israel, fathered 12 sons, who founded the Twelve Tribes of Israel: Reuben, Levi, Dan, Gad, Issachar, Joseph, Benjamin, Simeon, Judah, Naphtali, Asher, and Zebulun. Abraham, Isaac and Jacob are called the Patriarchs of Judaism.

Notes on Day 6

Salome the daughter of Herodias

Her dancing so pleased her stepfather that he granted her anything she wanted. After conferring with her mother, she asked for the head of John the Baptist on a platter. See **Herodias** for more details.

297

Salome the supporter of Jesus

She was a follower of Jesus who was there at the crucifixion. James and John, her sons, are the ones Jesus called the 'sons of thunder.' There is a possibility that she participated in nursing the resurrected Jesus in Jerusalem.

Gethsemane

Just across the narrow Kidron valley, on the lower slope of the Mount of Olives, was the grove of olive trees called the Garden of Gethsemane where Jesus and His disciples often went to pray and rest. The original olive trees were cut down by the Romans in the siege of Jerusalem in 70 AD, but visitors now can see a small grove of olive trees in the courtyard of the Church of All Nations. This was the site of Jesus' arrest on Thursday night.

Non-violence

When Simon Peter cut off the ear of Malchus, Jesus says, "Put up again thy sword into his place: for all they that take the sword shall perish with the sword." It is the opinion of this author that this is a message to all rulers, kings, and armies not to use force, but to solve problems peacefully, and non-violently.

Notes on Day 7

Pool of Siloam

This pool was actually a reservoir inside the city gates, which was fed with water from the Gihon Spring, flowing nearly 600 yards in a tunnel cut through solid rock. This arrangement by King Hezekiah, meant that the people of Jerusalem would have all the water they needed if they were besieged behind the city walls.

It was at this pool that Jesus sent a blind man to wash his eyes from the mixture of spit and dirt that Jesus had placed on the blind man's eyes to heal him. The man went and washed, and came back seeing with fully restored vision. (John 9:7).

Pool of Bethesda

This is the pool that is associated with the man who was unable to get to the 'healing waters' and who was healed by Jesus. The healing took place on a Sabbath day and shows that healing is not dependant on some location or special water, but on faith.

It is near the Sheep Gate, and is surrounded by five covered colonnades, or porches.

Notes on Day 8

Mount of Olives

The Mount of Olives is actually a series of hills, two miles long, with three peaks. The highest peak is about 2900 feet above sea level, and may be the site of Jesus' ascension. On the hillside facing Jerusalem was 'an olive grove called **Gethsemane**' (Matthew 26:36), where Jesus often went to pray and rest. It was less than a 30 minute walk down the east slope of Jerusalem and across the **Kidron valley** to the Garden of Gethsemane. It is to this place Judas led the temple guards to arrest Jesus.

The original olive trees were cut down by the Romans in 70 AD for the siege of Jerusalem. Today the Chapel of the Ascension commemorates the probable site of the ascension.

Galilee

Galilee is a northern region of Israel. It is bounded in the east by the banks of the Jordan River and the Sea of Galilee, and stretches west 30 miles toward the Mediterranean Sea. It measures approximately 50 miles in a north/south direction. Galilee is an area of fertile land and rolling hills, supporting farmers who grow grapes, olives, and barley. Fishermen make good use of the Sea of Galilee. Josephus (the Jewish historian of Jesus' day) says there were around 240 small villages in the area. With no major towns, the region kept its rural character for many years.

In *Resurrection Journey*, the last two meetings of Jesus with His disciples took place in Galilee: the first one on Day 22 on the shores of the Sea of Tiberias, and the second one on Day 29, a mile from Capernaum in the hills where He named the Twelve Disciples, and near where He possibly gave the some of the Sermon on the Mount and Sermon on the Plains. Jesus told His disciples three times to meet Him in Galilee, which was the place of His last meeting where He told them to baptize in the name of the Father, the Son, and the Holy Spirit.

Notes on Day 9

Medical incidents at the Garden of Gethsemane on the Thursday night of the Arrest

Many medically related incidents happened at the Garden of Gethsemane in about a three-hour period. They are:

1. Jesus agonizing over the stress of sorrow – His soul is sorrowful, contemplating His upcoming death. He knew in advance what He was going to face
2. Jesus falling as He walked to pray at a rock projection, sustaining injury to His face
3. Bloody sweat dripping from the face as He prayed leaning against the rock
4. Drop in body temperature of Jesus as He agonized
5. Sleep state of the disciples in spite of Jesus waking them up three times between His prayers of agony
6. Peter cutting off the right ear of Malchus, the Temple leaders' servant, and Jesus healing the ear
7. Jesus' tending and befriending reaction after Peter cut off the ear of Malchus and surrenders to temple guards voluntarily
8. Temple guards had Startle Reaction or Response with some of them falling on their back, when Jesus comes forward voluntarily to surrender to them
9. Disciples exhibited the "Fight or Flight" Reaction as Jesus was arrested. "Forsook and fled" is akin to running amuck or running away from the situation.

These are explained in detail in a forthcoming book.

Notes on Day 10

Joseph of Arimathea

Joseph was a member of the Sanhedrin, the highest Jewish governing body in Israel. The Sanhedrin had orchestrated the death of Jesus, and Joseph was a secret disciple (perhaps one of the 72) of Jesus who feared the Jewish leaders. (John 19:38) When Joseph went to Pilate and asked for the body of Jesus (Mark 15:43) he was in effect announcing his relationship with the crucified Jesus. The act of taking the body not only endangered his career with the Sanhedrin, but it also made him ritually unclean (touching a dead body) and thus not able to participate in Passover, the Jewish holiday that Jews from the surrounding countryside had come to Jerusalem to celebrate.

Bible scholars agree that no one else was ever buried in that tomb in which he laid the body of Jesus. The present author suggests Joseph might have been buried in the cemetery on the slopes of the Mount of Olives, which is one of the preferred sacred burial places of the ancient Jews – on the Eastern side of Jerusalem, with the notion that they will be the first to witness the Messiah coming from the East.

Arimathea

Arimathea is the Greek name for the Hebrew village of Joseph, who gave his newly cut tomb to receive the body of Jesus. Since the Greek is an approximation of the Hebrew pronunciation of the actual village, scholars are not sure where the location of Arimathea was, but three of the possibilities are Ramallah (eight miles north of Jerusalem), er-Ram (five miles north of Jerusalem), and Rentis (fifteen miles east of Tel Aviv.

Notes on Day 12

Ephraim

Ephraim is a city, but there is also a forest and mountain range that are known by that name. The city is also associated with Ophrah at present day et-Taribeh, about 14 miles northeast of

Jerusalem. The forest is in the hill country west of the Jordan River, and it was there that Absalom's soldiers were defeated by David's army. The mountain range of Ephraim is west of the Jordan River.

The Old Testament hero Joshua gave this area its name when he gave this territory to the tribe of Ephraim. It was from this area that Joshua challenged the crowd: "Choose today whom you will serve," and "But as for me and my family, we will serve the Lord." (Joshua 24:15) His challenge was accepted, and the people chose the Lord over the idols. Joshua died at Ephraim at the age of 110.

After raising Lazarus from the dead, Jesus retreated to the hilly forest of Ephraim, possibly staying there for one to three weeks. By that time He had probably heard the rumors of the plot to kill Him. Nicodemus, a secret disciple and member of the Sanhedrin, might have told Jesus or informed Him through intermediaries that the Temple priests and leaders were plotting to kill Him without a trial. (John 7:50-52) When Nicodemus asked the Sanhedrin "Does our law condemn anyone without first hearing him to find out what he is doing?" they replied, "Are you from Galilee, too? Look into it, and you will find that a prophet does not come out of Galilee."

Nicodemus probably attended the meeting of Temple priests and leaders at which they said: "Ye know nothing at all, nor consider that it is expedient for us, that one man should die for the people, and that the whole nation perish not." John 11:50 After hearing these, John 11:54 says that Jesus therefore walked no more openly among the Jews; but went thence into a country near to the wilderness, into a city called Ephraim, and there continued with His disciples. It is this author's belief that it was in this area, at this time that He decided it was best to surrender to the Temple priests and leaders during the Passover festival instead of being killed in a remote area. This is the last time Jesus camped with His disciples before going back to Bethany, and then on to Jerusalem to surrender to the Temple leaders at the Garden of Gethsemane.

Timeline of Last Days of Jesus

From Ephraim He journeyed to Bethany on a Saturday, and was anointed by Mary. Jesus entered into Jerusalem on the foal of a donkey on Sunday, disrupted the Temple services on Monday and Tuesday, and rested on Wednesday. On Thursday He had the Last

Supper with His disciples, and surrendered late on Thursday night. Jesus knew what Judas had planned with His consent, and that is why Jesus told him 'to do in a hurry what you have to do.' Jesus knew that to accomplish what the Father had set out for Him to do He had to surrender to the authorities at that time. The Temple priests possibly would have preferred to kill Him in a remote place, but Jesus did not give them that chance.

Trial of Jesus a secret

It is the opinion of this author that the people who called for the release of Barabbas were the cronies of the Temple leaders who wanted Jesus to die. The Sanhedrin kept the trial a secret. Those who waved palm branches to welcome Him into the city did not know a trial was taking place when the Temple leaders and their friends called for the release of Barabbas on the steps of the Pretoria.

Notes on Day 13

Jericho

The Jericho of Jesus' day is known as one of the oldest settlements on earth, an oasis in the area, with many springs supplying water for citrus fruit, vegetables, and dates. It was not far from a ford across the Jordan River, so it was of strategic importance as well as having natural wealth. It was here that the tax collector Zacchaeus climbed a tree to see Jesus and had a life changing experience. This was also where blind Bartimeus cried out to Jesus that he wanted to see, again with life changing results.

Jordan River

The Jordan River flows from the Sea of Galilee to the Dead Sea, but it has its beginnings north of there, getting most of its water from four streams that merge north of the Sea of Galilee to form what many call the Upper Jordan. This river is the most important one in Israel, and is the site of Jesus' baptism.

"In those days came John the Baptist, preaching in the wilderness of Judaea, He was saying, Repent ye: for the kingdom of heaven is at hand. For this is he that was spoken of by the prophet

Esaias, saying, The voice of one crying in the wilderness, Prepare ye the way of the Lord, make his paths straight." (Matt 3:1-3)

John the Baptist

His birth had been foretold to his father by the angel Gabriel, who gave his name and also instructions on his upbringing. John's mission was to prepare the way for the Messiah, and he did this by calling for the Jews to repent of their sins and return to God, baptizing them in the Jordan River when they did so. When Jesus appeared to be baptized, John protested, but Jesus insisted on observing the forms. When Jesus was baptized, the heavens opened and the Holy Spirit descended like unto the form of a dove, with a voice from heaven saying, "you are my Son, whom I love; with you I am well pleased." John had completed his mission, and many of his disciples left to follow Jesus.

John the Baptist was the cousin of Jesus. When Mary was three months pregnant with Jesus, she visited Elizabeth, who was six months pregnant with John. So, the cousins met twice – once before their births, and the second time during the baptism of Jesus.

John was beheaded at the order of **Herod Antipas** – see his entry and that of **Herodias** below for the details.

Herod Antipas

This son of Herod the Great ruled the northern region of his father's kingdom, which included Galilee. He is most famous for ordering John the Baptist beheaded (at the request of Salome, speaking for her mother) and for mocking Jesus the morning of His crucifixion. Herod was in Jerusalem for the Passover celebration, and Pilate sent Jesus to Herod, since Jesus was from Galilee. Herod hoped to see Jesus perform a miracle, but when He just stood there, Herod put a royal robe on Him and sent Him back to Pilate, wearing a royal robe to mock His claims as king.

Herodias

She is best known for advising her daughter Salome to ask King **Herod Antipas** for the head of John the Baptist. Herodias had been married to her half uncle, Herod Philip, and Salome was their daughter. When Herodias divorced Herod Philip and married his brother Herod Antipas, John the Baptist spoke out against that marriage, calling it incest under Jewish law. When her daughter's dancing pleased the king, Herodias was able to get her revenge – the head of death of John the Baptist on a platter.

Notes on Day 16

Sychar

Jesus has a conversation about living water with a Samaritan woman at Jacob's well at this village. Scholars do not know the exact location of the village, but it is thought to be near Shechem in central Israel. There is a modern village in the area that has a similar sounding name (Askar) near an old well about 100 feet deep.

Notes on Day 18

Nain

Nain is ten miles north of Nazareth. It was here that Jesus raised the son of a widow from the dead. (Luke 7:14) Elijah, who ministered from about 865 to 850 BC, had performed that same miracle. (1 Kings 17:17-24) Visitors today can see a ruined church that had been built in 300 AD.

Notes on Day 19

Nazareth

The word Nazareth means a branch or shoot, which may remind Christians of the prophecy in Isaiah 11:1 'Then a shoot will come out of the stump of Jesse, and a branch from its roots will bear fruit.' Nazareth is located about 20 miles southwest from Capernaum In Jesus' day, fellow villagers from Nazareth did not think much of the idea of one of their own becoming a miracle worker; according to Luke, they mobbed Him and took Him to the edge of the hill, intending to push Him over, but He slipped away through the crowd. (Luke 4:29-30) After that He moved His ministry to Capernaum due to their disbelief and attempt to harm Him.

Matthew does not mention violence, but talks about their skepticism and disbelief, to which Jesus said, "A prophet is not without honor, save in his own country, and in his own house." Matt 13:54-58

At that time, there were probably a few hundred people who lived in Nazareth, but today it is the largest Arab city in Israel. Visitors can visit the well where the young Jesus might have drawn water, called Mary's well. Though the well is enshrined within a church, there are water fountains placed outside that let visitors drink from the spring that fed the old well. Nearby is the Church of the Annunciation, a Catholic church built over what tradition says was Mary's home, where the angel Gabriel appeared to her and announced the coming birth of Jesus.

Notes on Day 21

Cana

Scholars are unsure where this village, famous for a wedding where Jesus turned water into wine, was located. Two sites are considered possible: Kafr Kanna, located five miles from Nazareth, where 'wine from Cana' is sold, and Khirber Qana, an uninhabited mound eight miles from Nazareth. The word Cana means 'reed' and many schools favor Khirber Quana, whose mound is in a valley where reeds grow.

It was at this first recorded miracle of Jesus where He addresses His mother as 'woman,' marking the beginning of the transition from His family of birth to His family of believers. The other miracle at Cana was a long-distance one. A nobleman's son was sick at Capernaum, and no one could help him – not even their local rabbi's prayers at their synagogue. The nobleman had heard that Jesus had come to Galilee, and found Him in Cana. Jesus told him to go, that his son will live, and the man found out later that the boy had recovered that same hour when Jesus said your son will live.

Mary the mother of Jesus

Called Mother Mary in *Resurrection Journey* to differentiate her from the many other Marys, she is an obedient young woman who says yes to the angel and becomes the mother of the Messiah. She is a scolding mother when 12 year old Jesus stays at the Jerusalem temple instead of returning with His family. She is an impatient mother at Cana when she tells her son to take care of the lack of wine. Initially Jesus refuses, but she tells the servants to do whatever He tells them.

Jesus separates Himself from His family of birth when He calls her 'woman' (twice - one time at Cana, another time from the cross) and when He says whoever does the will of My Father is My mother, brother, and sister. This does not represent a lack of caring – Jesus loved His mother – but rather addresses the distinction between Jesus the son and Jesus the savior. She is there at His crucifixion, burial, and ascension. When He was on the cross, Jesus directed one of His disciples, probably John, to care for her, at which time He addressed her as Mother. Jesus was her first born; she also had four other sons and at least two daughters.

Notes on Day 22

Sea of Galilee

The Sea of Galilee is actually a freshwater lake, thirteen miles long and seven miles across at its widest point. Its location 700 feet below the Mediterranean Sea, and the configuration of hills around it bring the fierce and sometimes deadly storms for which it is known. Some call it the Sea of Tiberias, named for a city that used to be on its western shore. Others call it Harp Sea, or the Sea of Kinnereth (Hebrew for harp) as this sea is shaped like an old Hebrew harp. The Jordan River flows southward through this sea to the Dead Sea.

In Jesus' day there were fishing villages along the northern shores, and it was from these that He called most of His disciples. It was here that Jesus walked on water, calmed the storm, and showed the disciples where to cast the net to catch a bounty of fish. He met the 12 disciples for the third time after His resurrection on the shore of this sea, cooking and serving fish and bread to the disciples.

Tiberias
Founded by Herod Antipas in 20 AD as a new capital of Galilee, its location on the western shore of the Sea of Galilee seemed ideal, until it was found by the builders of the city that the site had been a cemetery. To Jews who observed the law, this made Tiberias ritually unclean – any Jew going there would have to perform cleansing rituals before worshipping. The Gospel of John mentions people from Tiberias arriving by boats to hear Jesus. (John 6:23) It was on the shores of the sea somewhere near that old city of Tiberias that Jesus saw His disciples for the third time and shared a meal with them after His resurrection.

Conversation of Judas
Part of the conversation Judas had with Jesus is from the Gospel of Judas, page 23.

Herod Agrippa I
Reigned AD 37-44; best known for killing the Apostle James, who was the first of the disciples to be killed. (Acts 12:2-3) Herod died at age 54, after getting deathly ill after a crowd in Caesarea cheered him as a god. "An angel of the Lord struck Herod with a sickness, because he accepted the people's worship instead of giving the glory to God. So he was consumed with worms and died." (Acts 12:23)

Notes on Day 23

Magdala
Magdala is a fishing village on the west shore of the Sea of Galilee, a few miles south from Capernaum. **Mary Magdalene** was very likely from this village, with the name Mary of Magdala or Mary the Magdalene shortened to Mary Magdalene.

Notes on Day 24

Capernaum

Capernaum is located about 20 miles northeast of Nazareth, along the north shore of the Sea of Galilee. In the days of Jesus it was both a center of trading and a fishing village, with synagogues and a Roman garrison. Some of the villagers were farmers, and some processed olive oil. Capernaum became the center of Jesus' early ministry – many of His disciples lived there already: Peter, Andrew, James, John, and Matthew. The village was on a branch of the trade route known as the Way of the Sea, which linked Egypt and Arabia in the south with the countries north of Israel.

Peter's house was believed to be where Jesus and His disciples lived and where their ministry was based in Capernaum. Jesus had moved here from Nazareth due to the unbelief of the people in His hometown. He was able to do many miracles and healings in and around Capernaum, including the raising of Jairus' daughter from the dead. Later in His ministry, Jesus abandoned the town and predicted its death, which occurred in the AD 600s by Arab invaders.

In 1968 archaeologists began 18 years of excavations on what they believe was Peter's house and a first-century synagogue. The ruins of Capernaum are owned by the Franciscans, who have a monastery next to the site of Peter's house.

Notes on Day 26

Bethsaida

Bethsaida was a fishing village along the northeast shore of the Sea of Galilee. Three of Jesus' disciples (Peter, Andrew, and Philip) were from there. No village by that name exists today, but three different sets of ruins have been suggested. Two, el-Araj and el-Misadiyye, are directly on the shore, and are so close together that they might have been one large city. The third is et Tell, a mile and a half inland, which archaeologists favor, explaining that this site was on the shore until an earthquake and landslide changed the area.

Notes on Day 27

Mount of Beatitudes – Sermon on the Mount – Sermon on the Plains

Matthew records these teachings as taking place on a mountain or hillside, and Luke has a similar teaching on a plain. The oral tradition of the times suggests that these words were spoken at different times at different places by Jesus, probably often repeated for the sake of memory, and thus could have been recited both on a mountain and on a plain, as well as other sites. Both hillsides and plains are found in many places along the Sea of Galilee about one mile west of Capernaum. In the place known today as the Mount of Beatitudes, a small chapel commemorates the Sermon on the Mount. The Plain of Gennesaret, a likely place for some of the Sermon on the Plains, is nearby.

The author has included the Sermon on the Mount (the first part of which is referred to as the Beatitudes) and the Sermon on the Plains from the King James Version of the Bible. The word Beatitudes is from the Latin 'beati' meaning 'blessed be' which begins the first sentences of the teaching.

The Sermon on the Mount
Matthew 5

3 Blessed are the poor in spirit: for theirs is the kingdom of heaven.

4 Blessed are they that mourn: for they shall be comforted.

5 Blessed are the meek: for they shall inherit the earth.

6 Blessed are they which do hunger and thirst after righteousness: for they shall be filled.

7 Blessed are the merciful: for they shall obtain mercy.

8 Blessed are the pure in heart: for they shall see God.

9 Blessed are the peacemakers: for they shall be called the children of God.

10 Blessed are they which are persecuted for righteousness' sake: for theirs is the kingdom of heaven.

11 Blessed are ye, when men shall revile you, and persecute you, and shall say all manner of evil against you falsely, for my sake.

12 Rejoice, and be exceedingly glad: for great is your reward in heaven: for so persecuted they the prophets which were before you.

13 Ye are the salt of the earth: but if the salt have lost his savor, wherewith shall it be salted? It is thenceforth good for nothing, but to be cast out, and to be trodden under foot of men.

14 Ye are the light of the world. A city that is set on a hill cannot be hid.

15 Neither do men light a candle, and put it under a bushel, but on a candlestick; and it giveth light unto all that are in the house.

16 Let your light so shine before men, that they may see your good works, and glorify your Father which is in heaven.

17 Think not that I am come to destroy the law, or the prophets: I am not come to destroy, but to fulfill.

18 For verily I say unto you, Till heaven and earth pass, one jot or one title shall in no wise pass from the law, till all be fulfilled.

19 Whosoever therefore shall break one of these least commandments, and shall teach men so, he shall be called the least in the kingdom of heaven: but whosoever shall do and teach them, the same shall be called great in the kingdom of heaven.

20 For I say unto you, That except your righteousness shall exceed the righteousness of the scribes and Pharisees, ye shall in no case enter into the kingdom of heaven.

21 Ye have heard that it was said by them of old time, Thou shalt not kill; and whosoever shall kill shall be in danger of the judgment:

22 But I say unto you, That whosoever is angry with his brother without a cause shall be in danger of the judgment: and whosoever shall say to his brother, Raca, shall be in danger of the council: but whosoever shall say, Thou fool, shall be in danger of hell fire.

23 Therefore if thou bring thy gift to the altar, and there rememberest that thy brother hath ought against thee;

24 Leave there thy gift before the altar, and go thy way; first be reconciled to thy brother, and then come and offer thy gift.

25 Agree with thine adversary quickly, whiles thou art in the way with him; lest at any time the adversary deliver thee to the judge, and the judge deliver thee to the officer, and thou be cast into prison.

26 Verily I say unto thee, Thou shalt by no means come out thence, till thou hast paid the uttermost farthing.

27 Ye have heard that it was said by them of old time, Thou shalt not commit adultery:

28 But I say unto you, That whosoever looketh on a woman to lust after her hath committed adultery with her already in his heart.

29 And if thy right eye offend thee, pluck it out, and cast it from thee: for it is profitable for thee that one of thy members should perish, and not that thy whole body should be cast into hell.

30 And if thy right hand offend thee, cut it off, and cast it from thee: for it is profitable for thee that one of thy members should perish, and not that thy whole body should be cast into hell.

31 It hath been said, Whosoever shall put away his wife, let him give her a writing of divorcement:

32 But I say unto you, That whosoever shall put away his wife, saving for the cause of fornication, causeth her to commit adultery: and whosoever shall marry her that is divorced committeth adultery.

33 Again, ye have heard that it hath been said by them of old time, Thou shalt not forswear thyself, but shalt perform unto the Lord thine oaths:

34 But I say unto you, Swear not at all; neither by heaven; for it is God's throne:

35 Nor by the earth; for it is his footstool: neither by Jerusalem; for it is the city of the great King.

36 Neither shalt thou swear by thy head, because thou canst not make one hair white or black.

37 But let your communication be, Yea, yea; Nay, nay: for whatsoever is more than these cometh of evil.

38 Ye have heard that it hath been said, An eye for an eye, and a tooth for a tooth:

39 But I say unto you, That ye resist not evil: but whosoever shall smite thee on thy right cheek, turn to him the other also.

40 And if any man will sue thee at the law, and take away thy coat, let him have thy cloak also.

41 And whosoever shall compel thee to go a mile, go with him twain.

42 Give to him that asketh thee, and from him that would borrow of thee turn not thou away.

43 Ye have heard that it hath been said, Thou shalt love thy neighbour, and hate thine enemy.

44 But I say unto you, Love your enemies, bless them that curse you, do good to them that hate you, and pray for them which despitefully use you, and persecute you;

45 That ye may be the children of your Father which is in heaven: for he maketh his sun to rise on the evil and on the good, and sendeth rain on the just and on the unjust.

46 For if ye love them which love you, what reward have ye? do not even the publicans the same?

47 And if ye salute your brethren only, what do ye more than others? do not even the publicans so?

48 Be ye therefore perfect, even as your Father which is in heaven is perfect.

Matthew 6

1 Take heed that ye do not your alms before men, to be seen of them: otherwise ye have no reward of your Father which is in heaven.

2 Therefore when thou doest thine alms, do not sound a trumpet before thee, as the hypocrites do in the synagogues and in the streets, that they may have glory of men. Verily I say unto you, They have their reward.

3 But when thou doest alms, let not thy left hand know what thy right hand doeth:

4 That thine alms may be in secret: and thy Father which seeth in secret himself shall reward thee openly.

5 And when thou prayest, thou shalt not be as the hypocrites are: for they love to pray standing in the synagogues and in the corners of the streets, that they may be seen of men. Verily I say unto you, They have their reward.

6 But thou, when thou prayest, enter into thy closet, and when thou hast shut thy door, pray to thy Father which is in secret; and thy Father which seeth in secret shall reward thee openly.

7 But when ye pray, use not vain repetitions, as the heathen do: for they think that they shall be heard for their much speaking.

8 Be not ye therefore like unto them: for your Father knoweth what things ye have need of, before ye ask him.

9 After this manner therefore pray ye: Our Father which art in heaven, Hallowed be thy name.

10 Thy kingdom come. Thy will be done in earth, as it is in heaven.

11 Give us this day our daily bread.

12 And forgive us our debts, as we forgive our debtors.

13 And lead us not into temptation, but deliver us from evil: For thine is the kingdom, and the power, and the glory, forever. Amen.

14 For if ye forgive men their trespasses, your heavenly Father will also forgive you:

15 But if ye forgive not men their trespasses, neither will your Father forgive your trespasses.

16 Moreover when ye fast, be not, as the hypocrites, of a sad countenance: for they disfigure their faces, that they may appear unto men to fast. Verily I say unto you, They have their reward.

17 But thou, when thou fastest, anoint thine head, and wash thy face;

18 That thou appear not unto men to fast, but unto thy Father which is in secret: and thy Father, which seeth in secret, shall reward thee openly.

19 Lay not up for yourselves treasures upon earth, where moth and rust doth corrupt, and where thieves break through and steal:

20 But lay up for yourselves treasures in heaven, where neither moth nor rust doth corrupt, and where thieves do not break through nor steal:

21 For where your treasure is, there will your heart be also.

22 The light of the body is the eye: if therefore thine eye be single, thy whole body shall be full of light.

23 But if thine eye be evil, thy whole body shall be full of darkness. If therefore the light that is in thee be darkness, how great is that darkness!

24 No man can serve two masters: for either he will hate the one, and love the other; or else he will hold to the one, and despise the other. Ye cannot serve God and mammon.

25 Therefore I say unto you, Take no thought for your life, what ye shall eat, or what ye shall drink; nor yet for your body, what ye shall put on. Is not the life more than meat, and the body than raiment?

26 Behold the fowls of the air: for they sow not, neither do they reap, nor gather into barns; yet your heavenly Father feedeth them. Are ye not much better than they?

27 Which of you by taking thought can add one cubit unto his stature?

28 And why take ye thought for raiment? Consider the lilies of the field, how they grow; they toil not, neither do they spin:

29 And yet I say unto you, That even Solomon in all his glory was not arrayed like one of these.

30 Wherefore, if God so clothe the grass of the field, which today is, and tomorrow is cast into the oven, shall he not much more clothe you, O ye of little faith?

31 Therefore take no thought, saying, What shall we eat? or, What shall we drink? or, Wherewithal shall we be clothed?

32 (For after all these things do the Gentiles seek:) for your heavenly Father knoweth that ye have need of all these things.

33 But seek ye first the kingdom of God, and his righteousness; and all these things shall be added unto you.

34 Take therefore no thought for the morrow: for the morrow shall take thought for the things of itself. Sufficient unto the day is the evil thereof.

Matthew 7

1 Judge not, that ye be not judged.

2 For with what judgment ye judge, ye shall be judged: and with what measure ye mete, it shall be measured to you again.

3 And why beholdest thou the mote that is in thy brother's eye, but considerest not the beam that is in thine own eye?

4 Or how wilt thou say to thy brother, Let me pull out the mote out of thine eye; and, behold, a beam is in thine own eye?

5 Thou hypocrite, first cast out the beam out of thine own eye; and then shalt thou see clearly to cast out the mote out of thy brother's eye.

6 Give not that which is holy unto the dogs, neither cast ye your pearls before swine, lest they trample them under their feet, and turn again and rend you.

7 Ask, and it shall be given you; seek, and ye shall find; knock, and it shall be opened unto you:

8 For every one that asketh receiveth; and he that seeketh findeth; and to him that knocketh it shall be opened.

9 Or what man is there of you, whom if his son ask bread, will he give him a stone?

10 Or if he ask a fish, will he give him a serpent?

11 If ye then, being evil, know how to give good gifts unto your children, how much more shall your Father which is in heaven give good things to them that ask him?

12 Therefore all things whatsoever ye would that men should do to you, do ye even so to them: for this is the law and the prophets.

13 Enter ye in at the strait gate: for wide is the gate, and broad is the way, that leadeth to destruction, and many there be which go in thereat:

14 Because strait is the gate, and narrow is the way, which leadeth unto life, and few there be that find it.

15 Beware of false prophets, which come to you in sheep's clothing, but inwardly they are ravening wolves.

16 Ye shall know them by their fruits. Do men gather grapes of thorns, or figs of thistles?

17 Even so every good tree bringeth forth good fruit; but a corrupt tree bringeth forth evil fruit.

18 A good tree cannot bring forth evil fruit, neither can a corrupt tree bring forth good fruit.

19 Every tree that bringeth not forth good fruit is hewn down, and cast into the fire.

20 Wherefore by their fruits ye shall know them.

21 Not everyone that saith unto me, Lord, Lord, shall enter into the kingdom of heaven; but he that doeth the will of my Father which is in heaven.

22 Many will say to me in that day, Lord, Lord, have we not prophesied in thy name? and in thy name have cast out devils? and in thy name done many wonderful works?

23 And then will I profess unto them, I never knew you: depart from me, ye that work iniquity.

24 Therefore whosoever heareth these sayings of mine, and doeth them, I will liken him unto a wise man, which built his house upon a rock:

25 And the rain descended, and the floods came, and the winds blew, and beat upon that house; and it fell not: for it was founded upon a rock.

26 And every one that heareth these sayings of mine, and doeth them not, shall be likened unto a foolish man, which built his house upon the sand:

27 And the rain descended, and the floods came, and the winds blew, and beat upon that house; and it fell: and great was the fall of it.

The Sermon on the Plains
Luke 6

20 And he lifted up his eyes on his disciples, and said, Blessed be ye poor: for yours is the kingdom of God.

21 Blessed are ye that hunger now: for ye shall be filled. Blessed are ye that weep now: for ye shall laugh.

22 Blessed are ye, when men shall hate you, and when they shall separate you from their company, and shall reproach you, and cast out your name as evil, for the Son of man's sake.

23 Rejoice ye in that day, and leap for joy: for, behold, your reward is great in heaven: for in the like manner did their fathers unto the prophets.

24 But woe unto you that are rich! for ye have received your consolation.

25 Woe unto you that are full! for ye shall hunger. Woe unto you that laugh now! for ye shall mourn and weep.

26 Woe unto you, when all men shall speak well of you! for so did their fathers to the false prophets.

27 But I say unto you which hear, Love your enemies, do good to them which hate you,

28 Bless them that curse you, and pray for them which despitefully use you.

29 And unto him that smiteth thee on the one cheek offer also the other; and him that taketh away thy cloak forbid not to take thy coat also.

30 Give to every man that asketh of thee; and of him that taketh away thy goods ask them not again.

31 And as ye would that men should do to you, do ye also to them likewise.

32 For if ye love them which love you, what thank have ye? for sinners also love those that love them.

33 And if ye do good to them which do good to you, what thank have ye? for sinners also do even the same.

34 And if ye lend to them of whom ye hope to receive, what thank have ye? for sinners also lend to sinners, to receive as much again.

35 But love ye your enemies, and do good, and lend, hoping for nothing again; and your reward shall be great, and ye shall be the children of the Highest: for he is kind unto the unthankful and to the evil.

36 Be ye therefore merciful, as your Father also is merciful.

37 Judge not, and ye shall not be judged: condemn not, and ye shall not be condemned: forgive, and ye shall be forgiven:

38 Give, and it shall be given unto you; good measure, pressed down, and shaken together, and running over, shall men give into your bosom. For with the same measure that ye mete withal it shall be measured to you again.

39 And he spake a parable unto them, Can the blind lead the blind? shall they not both fall into the ditch?

40 The disciple is not above his master: but every one that is perfect shall be as his master.

41 And why beholdest thou the mote that is in thy brother's eye, but perceivest not the beam that is in thine own eye?

42 Either how canst thou say to thy brother, Brother, let me pull out the mote that is in thine eye, when thou thyself beholdest not the beam that is in thine own eye? Thou hypocrite, cast out first the beam out of thine own eye, and then shalt thou see clearly to pull out the mote that is in thy brother's eye.

43 For a good tree bringeth not forth corrupt fruit; neither doth a corrupt tree bring forth good fruit.

44 For every tree is known by his own fruit. For of thorns men do not gather figs, nor of a bramble bush gather they grapes.

45 A good man out of the good treasure of his heart bringeth forth that which is good; and an evil man out of the evil treasure of

his heart bringeth forth that which is evil: for of the abundance of the heart his mouth speaketh.

46 And why call ye me, Lord, Lord, and do not the things which I say?

47 Whosoever cometh to me, and heareth my sayings, and doeth them, I will shew you to whom he is like:

48 He is like a man which built an house, and digged deep, and laid the foundation on a rock: and when the flood arose, the stream beat vehemently upon that house, and could not shake it: for it was founded upon a rock.

49 But he that heareth, and doeth not, is like a man that without a foundation built an house upon the earth; against which the stream did beat vehemently, and immediately it fell; and the ruin of that house was great.

Notes on Day 31

Mount Tabor

Located approximately six miles southeast from Nazareth, this mountain was believed to be the one on which the Transfiguration of Jesus occurred. Jesus had taken His disciples Peter, James, and John to the mountain to pray. **Moses** and **Elijah** arrived also, in glowing robes, and the face of Jesus shone like the sun, and His clothes became as bright as light. Peter, after seeing this celestial vision, wanted to build three shrines (tabernacles) there, one for Jesus, one for Moses, and one for Elijah, but Jesus said no. Many buildings were built and destroyed in the centuries that followed, and now visitors can see churches, a monastery, the wall that surrounds the mountaintop, and some ruins.

Moses

Because he received the **Ten Commandments** from God for the Israelites, Moses is known as 'Moses the Law-giver.' At the Transfiguration on Mount Tabor, with Jesus and Elijah, Moses represents the Law that Jesus both fulfills and replaces. Moses is said to be the author of the first five books of the Bible (Genesis, Exodus, Leviticus, Numbers and Deuteronomy - the Torah) though many scholars dispute such a claim.

319

Moses was born when the Israelites, who were slaves in Egypt, were growing in number and the Pharaoh was concerned that in a conflict they would side with the enemies of Egypt. When the Pharaoh ordered all newborn Israelite boys to be killed, Moses' mother hid him and he was adopted as a foundling by the Egyptian royal family. He was considered as part of the royal Egyptian family, but when he was grown, he killed an Egyptian slave master, and fled across the Red Sea to Midian. He stayed 40 years, at which time he found God in the form of a burning bush.

God sent Moses to request the release of the Israelites, but the Pharaoh was reluctant to part with this large workforce. It took ten plagues to convince him to let the Israelites go. It took 40 years walking in the desert to reach the land that God had promised He would give them, and along the way God gave Moses the Ten Commandments for the Israelite People. Moses himself did not enter the Promised Land – he had disobeyed God by striking a rock with his staff to cause water to flow, claiming the miracle as his own, when God had said for him to speak to the rock and water would flow. Moses was able to see the Promised Land from Mount Nebo, and died at the age of 120 and was buried in the valley.

References to 40 Days

The number forty is used many times in the Bible as a time of dedication and as a period of trial. Here are some of the references to 40 days in the Bible:

1. For 40 days, Jesus fasted in the wilderness after His baptism (Matt 4:2; Mark 1:13; Luke 4:2)
2. Jesus met with His disciples as a group five times during the 40 days between His resurrection and His ascension on 40th day (Acts 1:3)
3. Moses fasted and prayed 40 days on the mountain (Exodus 24:18)
4. 40 days, the Children of Israel were tested while Moses was on the mountain (Exodus 32:1)
5. Moses was on the mountain 40 days after seeing the golden calf (Exodus 34:28)
6. 40 days after birth, male children of Israel were dedicated to God at the Sanctuary, according to the Sinai Covenant

(Lev 12:1-4). According to Luke 2:22-23, Joseph and Mother Mary presented Jesus at the Temple in Jerusalem.

7. 40 days Israelite spies reconnoitered (explored) the land of Canaan (Num 13:25)
8. 40 days, Ezekiel lay on his right side to symbolize the 40 years of Judah's transgressions (Ez 4:6)
9. For 40 days, Jonah was in the Assyrian city of Nineveh (Jonah 3:4)

Elijah

The prophecy in Malachi 4:5 claimed that before 'the great and dreadful day of the Lord arrives,' the prophet Elijah would return and prepare the way for the Messiah. When the angel Gabriel announced the birth of John the Baptist, he said, 'He will be a man with the spirit and power of Elijah, the prophet of old. He will precede the coming of the Lord, preparing the people for His arrival." (Luke 1:17) In Matthew 17:11-13, Jesus said that John fulfilled the prophecy of Malachi.

The original Elijah was one of the most powerful prophets in the Old Testament. He called down fire from heaven, raised a widow's son from the dead at Nain (using a method that resembled modern CPR - cardio pulmonary resuscitation), and was taken up to heaven on a whirlwind behind a fiery chariot. God had sent this prophet to win back the hearts of the Jewish nation, and indeed, John the Baptist's mission was very similar – to win back the hearts of the people so that they would accept Jesus their Messiah.

Elisha is the Old Testament prophet who was mentored by Elijah. When Jesus wanted to justify healing Gentles, He used the example of Elisha healing the Syrian soldier who had leprosy.

Ten Commandments (Exodus 20:2-17)

Moses gave these commandments which he received from God on the top of **Mount Sinai**.

I am the LORD your God, who brought you out of the land of Egypt, out of the house of bondage:

1. You shall have no other gods before Me.
2. You shall not make for yourself a carved image — any likeness of anything that is in heaven above, or that is in the

earth beneath, or that is in the water under the earth; you shall not bow down to them nor serve them. For I, the LORD your God, am a jealous God, visiting the iniquity of the fathers upon the children to the third and fourth generations of those who hate Me, but showing mercy to thousands, to those who love Me and keep My commandments.

3. You shall not take the name of the LORD your God in vain, for the LORD will not hold him guiltless who takes His name in vain.

4. Remember the Sabbath day, to keep it holy. Six days you shall labor and do all your work, but the seventh day is the Sabbath of the LORD your God. In it you shall do no work: you, nor your son, nor your daughter, nor your male servant, nor your female servant, nor your cattle, nor your stranger who is within your gates. For in six days the LORD made the heavens and the earth, the sea, and all that is in them, and rested the seventh day. Therefore the LORD blessed the Sabbath day and hallowed it.

5. Honor your father and your mother, that your days may be long upon the land which the LORD your God is giving you.

6. You shall not murder.

7. You shall not commit adultery.

8. You shall not steal.

9. You shall not bear false witness against your neighbor.

10. You shall not covet your neighbor's house; you shall not covet your neighbor's wife, nor his male servant, nor his female servant, nor his ox, nor his donkey, nor anything that is your neighbor's.

Mount Sinai

This is both the place where Moses encountered God in a burning bush, and where he received the **Ten Commandments**, along with other laws for the young Jewish nation. The Israelites camped at the foot of this mountain about a year (last 22 chapters of Exodus, Leviticus, Numbers chapters 1-11) after being liberated from their bondage in Egypt.

The mountain is located between the Gulf of Suez and the Gulf of Aqaba. The Monastery of Saint Catherine is at the foot of the mountain, built in the AD 500s. One of the oldest surviving copies of the Bible, the Codex Sinaiticus, was discovered in 1844 on a trash heap in that monastery.

The Great Commandments of Jesus

When asked which is the great commandment in the Law, Jesus answered, "Thou shalt love the Lord thy God with all thy heart, and with all thy soul, and with all thy mind. This is the first and great commandment. And the second is like unto it, Thou shalt love thy neighbor as thyself. On these two commandments hang all the law and the prophets. (Matt 22:34-40). These commandments are considered to sum up and/or supersede the **Ten Commandments** of Moses.

Jesus is the way to salvation

According to our Lord Jesus Christ, even though true love is the core of how we should treat others, it is NOT what gets us into heaven. It doesn't matter how much good work we do, or how much we say we love God and our neighbor: none of this can take away our sins and get us into heaven. Only Jesus can do that, and our only way to receive forgiveness and salvation from sin is to believe in Him. Our only way to salvation is to believe in Jesus who is the Son of God, who died on the cross, shed His blood on the cross for our sins, and rose from the dead, resurrected, to provide evidence for His message.

In support of these concepts, Jesus Himself said, "He that believeth on Him is not condemned; but He that believeth not is condemned already." (John 3:18) Salvation does not come from obeying the Ten Commandments – our good works do not save us, but by God's grace we are saved. (Acts 15:11, Ephesians 2:8-9) Salvation cannot be earned; it is a free gift from God (Ephesians 2:7, 1 John 5:11) if only we will accept it. (Mark 16:16, John 3:16, John 3:18) Sin causes spiritual death (Romans 6:23) which is eternal everlasting separation from God.

Once we accept Jesus as our savior, the Spirit of God will come to us, and will change us as described by Peter and Paul. The Spirit has been available to everyone with one condition, identified by Peter on the day of Pentecost: "Each of you must turn from your sins and turn to God, and be baptized in the name of Jesus Christ for the forgiveness of your sins. Then you will receive the gift of the Holy Spirit. This promise is to you and to your children, and even to the Gentiles - all who have been called by the Lord our God" (Acts 2:38-39). Three thousand people that day followed Peter's advice, and the Christian church was born 50 days after Jesus' resurrection, 10 days after His ascension.

Several years later, Paul taught what it meant to be filled with the Holy Spirit. When the Holy Spirit (Holy Spirit and Holy Ghost are synonymous) enters our lives, He will produce this kind of fruit in us: "love, joy, peace, patience, kindness, goodness, faithfulness, gentleness, and self-control" (Galatians 5:22-23) Love and good works are not the way to salvation, but are the result of salvation.

Sabbath Day work as opposed to the Laws of Moses

God's law said the Sabbath is a day of rest (Exodus 20:10-11) but the religious leaders added many rules to that law, creating an environment where to 'heal' on the Sabbath is to 'work' on the Sabbath. Jesus healed seven times on the Sabbath, angering the religious leaders. Here is a list of the people who were healed or released of demons on the Sabbath:

1. Man with a demon (Mark 1:21-28)
2. Peter's mother-in-law (Mark 1:29-31)
3. Lame man by the Pool of Bethesda (John 5:1-18)
4. Man with a deformed hand (Mark 3:1-6)
5. Crippled woman (Luke 13:10-17)
6. Man with dropsy (Luke 14:1-6)
7. Man born blind (John 9:1-16)

The way in which food was prepared was strictly controlled on the Sabbath, so when Jesus and His disciples ate grain from a field, that was considered 'work' and they were rebuked.

Why Jewish religious leaders opposed Jesus

Jesus constantly broke the rules and regulations that had taken over the religion of the people. He opposed the outward forms that

324

masked an empty belief. He knew that sacrifices did not cleanse the soul of sin. He knew that external prayer and fasting was many times done only to impress, not from actual piety. He said the Sabbath was made for man, not man for the Sabbath. He taught that God is spirit, and seeks those who worship Him in spirit, not necessarily in a Temple.

Notes on Day 34

Judas Iscariot

Probably from the town of Kerioth in southern Israel close to Jerusalem and Bethlehem, Judas is best known as the disciple who brought the temple guards to Jesus in the Garden of Gethsemane late in the night after they had shared what Christians call the Last Supper. It was at that time when Jesus said to him "That thou doest, do quickly" indicating Jesus knew of His coming arrest in the garden of Gethsemane, hence His agony with blood stained sweat. (John 13:27) "And being in anguish, he prayed more earnestly, and his sweat was like drops of blood falling to the ground." Luke 22:44

Judas: Birth, Mission, and Death is the subject of a forthcoming book by this author. There is a possibility that Judas knew more about Jewish history and Messiah than the other 11 disciples. He was a Judean zealot.

Akeldama (Field of Blood)

Acts 1:19 states this is the place of Judas Iscariot's death, and the name Akeldama is the Greek translation of Field of Blood. This tells us that Judas did not die immediately after the Sanhedrin pronounced the death sentence on Jesus.

Judea

The Romans divided the Jewish homeland into regions, and Judea was part of the southern area. The word Jew is from the Latin word Judaeus, which means a person from Judea. Of the twelve disciples, only Judas was a Judean, the rest are Galileans.

Notes on Day 37

Death of Judas
Judas died 40 days after he led the Temple guards to the Garden of Gethsemane.

Notes on Day 39

Chronology of the ages of Mary, Joseph, Jesus, and the other 6 children

Jesus had four brothers, all of whom are named in the gospels. He had at least two sisters, but the exact number of sisters and their names are not given. The following is a list of the approximate ages of the family at the most important events, from the birth of Jesus to His death. The assumptions made to produce this list are given at the end.

1. **Birth of Jesus:** Mary is 16, Joseph is 26. See Day 3 for a visit to the birth of Jesus.
2. **Stay at Bethlehem:** Mary is 16-18, Joseph is 26-28, and Jesus is less than 2 years old. Wise Men visit Jesus at Bethlehem.
3. **Journey to Egypt:** Mary is 18, Joseph is 28, and Jesus is less than 2 years old. The family travels to Egypt, 330 miles southwest of Bethlehem.
4. **Return to Nazareth:** Mary is 21, Joseph is 31, and Jesus is around 5 years old. No one knows how long the family stayed in Egypt. The family travels from Egypt 411 miles to reach Nazareth.
5. **Birth of James, second son of Joseph and Mary:** Mary is 22, Joseph is 32, and Jesus is 6.
6. **Birth of Joses, third son of Joseph and Mary:** Mary is 24, Joseph is 34, Jesus is 8, and James is 2.
7. **Birth of Judas, fourth son of Joseph and Mary:** Mary is 26, Joseph is 36, Jesus is 10, James is 4, and Joses is 2.
8. **Joseph and Mary Journey to Jerusalem:** Mary is 28, Joseph is 38, Jesus is 12, James is 6, Joses is 4, and Judas is 2.
9. **Birth of Simon, fifth son of Joseph and Mary:** Mary is 30, Joseph is 40, Jesus is 14, James is 8, Joses is 6, and Judas is 4.

10. **Birth of the first sister of Jesus:** Mary is 32, Joseph is 42, Jesus is 16, James is 10, Joses is 8, Judas is 6, and Simon is 2.

11. **Birth of the second sister of Jesus:** Mary is 34, Joseph is 44, Jesus is 18, James is 12, Joses is 10, Judas is 6, Simon is 4, and the first sister is 2.

12. **Death of Joseph:** Mary is 45, Joseph is 55, Jesus is 29, James is 23, Joses is 21, Judas is 19, Simon is 15, the first sister is 13, and the second sister is 11.

13. **Jesus begins His ministry:** Mary is 46, Jesus is around 30, James is 24, Joses is 22, Judas is 20, Simon is 16, the first sister is 14, and the second sister is 12. Miracle at Cana.

14. **Jesus is crucified:** Mary is 49, Jesus is around 33, James is 27, Joses is 25, Judas is 23, Simon is 19, the first sister is 17, and the second sister is 15

The assumptions made are based on the natural contraceptive properties of breast-feeding, which would give the children a natural spacing of 1 ½ years to 2 years apart. Their births and ages are approximate; for convenience, we have used a 2-year cycle.

Other factors include the stress of travel and relocation to Egypt, so that Mary did not get pregnant while she was in Egypt with Joseph and Jesus. The high infant mortality rate at that time called for families to have as many children as possible, so as soon as they were settled in Nazareth, Mary became pregnant and resumed the normal life of a mother, giving birth to at least six children.

Mary had four other sons, named James, Joses, Judas, and Simon. She had at least two daughters, and the author has named them Hannah and Abigail. The children of Mary are mentioned in the following passages: Matt. 12:46; 13:55; Mark 6:3; John 2:12; 7:3, 5, 10; Acts 1:14; 1 Cor. 9:5; Gal 1:19.

One of the more controversial teachings of the Catholic Church deals with the perpetual virginity of Mary. This doctrine maintains that Mary remained a virgin after the birth of Jesus and that biblical references suggesting Jesus had siblings are really references to cousins (Catechism of the Catholic Church, paragraph 510). The Catholic doctrine of the eternal virginity of Mary is not supported by scripture as referenced above.

Not listed above, but related to the events, is John the Baptist, who was beheaded at the age of 30, after baptizing Jesus at the beginning of His ministry. Jesus and John the Baptist are of the same age, with only three months difference in age according to the gospels.

Notes on Day 40

Kidron Valley

This steep valley 2 ¾ miles long is more of a ravine between the hilltop city of Jerusalem to the west and the ridge of hills called the Mount of Olives to the east. The valley is known as the Valley of Jehoshaphat on the eastern side of Jerusalem, between the city and the Mount of Olives. Jesus passed through this valley many times before and after His last supper. Temple guards went through this valley to arrest Jesus in the Garden of Gethsemane.

In the time of Josiah, this valley was the common cemetery of the city (2 Kings 23:6; Jer. 26:23) hence the greatest desire of the Jews is to be buried there, from the idea that the Kidron is the "valley of Jehoshaphat" mentioned in Joel 3:2. There is a possibility that Joseph of Arimathea requested to be buried here after giving his tomb for the burial of Jesus. He believed that he was not worthy to occupy the tomb that had seen the resurrection of his master, Jesus the Messiah.

Did 500 people witness Jesus' ascension?

Paul's account of those who saw Jesus after His resurrection: "that He was buried, that He was raised on the third day according to the Scriptures, and that He appeared to Cephas, then to the twelve. Then He appeared to over five hundred brothers at once, most of whom remain until now, but some have also fallen asleep. Then He appeared to James, then to all the apostles, and last of all, as to the child born at the wrong time, He appeared to me also."
(1 Corinthians 15:4-8)

None of the gospels talks about such an event (the sighting of Jesus by 500 people at one time in one place), and an event of such magnitude would have easily alerted Temple leaders, Temple spies, and the Romans. Can you imagine what could have happened if all these groups had been alerted? It is the belief of this author that 500 people whom Paul describes are people Jesus encountered or visited during His 150 plus mile journey from Jerusalem to Galilee and back to the Mount of Olives, during the 40 day time between His resurrection and His ascension.

It is important to note that He appeared as the resurrected Jesus as recorded in the gospels to 21 people on Sunday, plus one more (Thomas) eight days later at Jerusalem, for a total of 22 people. The remaining number He saw during His 150 mile journey for 40 days. We want to remind the reader that there was no meeting with 120 gathered immediately after the ascension. This meeting took place three days later on Sunday in Jerusalem.

The verses from the New Testament: Acts 1:3-4, Acts 10:40-41, Acts 13:31 and 1 Corinthians 15:4-8, as discussed in the introduction, list the recorded isolated or group visits by our Lord. There are indications that some of them accompanied Him for some distances as He travelled.

We believe that He also revealed that He is the resurrected Jesus to a group of Samaritans on His journey. That group alone can amount to hundreds. The other contacts during His ministry had no clue that He was the resurrected Jesus visiting and talking to them. Not even His four brothers and two sisters knew the rabbi who visited them was their brother. Even His disciples could not identify Him at first sight when He appeared to them.

Jesus seeing the 500 people "at once" means one time individually during His journey, not in a mass gathering. That means Jesus saw an average of 12-14 people each day of His resurrected life during His 40 day journey. Some days He might have seen 20-50 and other days none. This is specially so when He was returning from Galilee on the 29th day journeying toward the Mount of Olives.

There are two people in the Old Testament who are said to have ascended to heaven alive, besides Jesus. They are Elijah and Enoch. Even then, there is speculation whether it really happened as they state, or whether they just disappeared into oblivion, which was interpreted as haven been taken up by God alive. On the other hand, Jesus' ascension was witnessed by many.

Notes on Day 50

Pentecost

Originally known as the Jewish Festival of Weeks, this ancient Jewish pilgrimage festival commemorates the giving of the Law on Mount Sinai by Moses. It occurs 50 days after Passover, so the Greek Jews gave it the name Pentecost, meaning Fiftieth Day.

Christians consider this day as the birthday of the Church, since it was on that day, 10 days after the Ascension and 50 days after the Resurrection, that the Holy Spirit was given to the disciples and followers of Jesus, who had followed His instructions to wait in Jerusalem until they received the gift of His Father. The Holy Spirit baptized the followers with fire, and they promptly went out into the streets of Jerusalem and demonstrated the faith and power of Jesus so convincingly that 3,000 Jews became believers and were baptized that day, perhaps receiving the Holy Spirit (although this is not specifically noted). Acts 2:1- 13

Additional Notes of Interest

Healing miracles of Jesus

Jesus combined His healing ministry with the teaching of forgiveness and the kingdom of heaven. No other prophet performed as many healing miracles as Jesus did, but He did more than just heal the sick – He forgave their sins and gave them a new life in the process. The following is a list of the healing miracles of Jesus:

1. Healed the official's dying son (John 4:43-54)
2. Drove the demon out of the madman in the synagogue (Mark 1:21-28; Luke 4:31-37)
3. Healed Peter's mother-in-law from her high fever (Matthew 8:14-17; Mark 1:29-34; Luke 4:38-41)
4. Healed the lepers (Matthew 8:1-4; Mark 1:40-45; Luke 5:12-16)
5. Healed the paralyzed man (Matthew 9:1-8; Mark 2:1-2; Luke 5:17-26)
6. Healed the invalid at the Pool of Bethesda (John 5:1-15)
7. Restored the shriveled hand of a man (Matthew 12:9-14; Mark 3:1-6; Luke 6:6-11)
8. Cured the illness of the Roman centurion's servant (Matthew 8:5-13; Luke 7:1-10)
9. Raised the son of a widow from the dead at Nain Luke 7:11-17)
10. Made the dumb and blind man to speak and see (Matthew 12:22-23; Luke 11:14)
11. Sent evil spirits from the madmen to the pigs at the region of Gadarene (Matthew 8:28-34; Mark 5:1-20; Luke 8:26-39)
12. Healed a woman of an 18 year flow of blood (Matthew 9:18-26; Mark 5:21-43; Luke 8:40-56)
13. Raised the daughter of Jairus from the dead at Capernaum (Matthew 9:18-26; Mark 5:21-43; Luke 8:40-56)
14. Healed two blind men and the dumb man (Matthew 9:27-34)

331

15. Healed the sick at Gennesaret (Matthew 14:34-36; Mark 6:53-56)
16. Healed the daughter of the Syrophenician woman (Matthew 15:21-19; Mark 7:24-30)
17. Healed the deaf and dumb man in Decapolis (Mark 7:31-37
18. Healed the blind man of Bethsaida (Mark 8:22-26)
19. Healed the Epileptic boy (Matthew 17:14-21; Mark 9:14-29; Luke 9:37-43a; 17:5-6)
20. Healed ten lepers at once (Luke 17:11-19)
21. Healed the man born blind (John 9:1-41)
22. Healed the crippled woman (Luke 13:10-17)
23. Cured the man with dropsy (Luke 14:1-6)
24. Raised Lazarus from the dead – on the fourth day (John 11:1-44)
25. Gave vision to the blind man or men near Jericho (Matthew 20:29-34; Mark 10: 46-52; Luke 18:35-43)
26. Restored the ear of the high priest's servant Malchus, cut off by Peter (Luke 22:49-51
27. Healed many other unnamed people (Matthew 12:15-21; Luke 6:17-19)

In addition to the above reported healings, He also healed hundreds when He taught among the people. Some were healed by touching His garment, or by holding His hand, or just by a look from Jesus. His healings were also accomplished over long distances, such as the centurion's slave.

Miracles of Jesus that are related to Nature
1. Converted water into wine at the wedding at Cana (John 2:1-11)
2. Helped the disciples to catch fish (Luke 5:4-10)
3. Calmed the storm on the Sea of Galilee (Matthew 8:23-27; Mark 4:35-41; Luke 8:22-25)
4. Fed the 5,000 with a few loaves of bread and two fish (Matthew 14:13-21; Mark 6:30-44; Luke 9:10-17; John 6:1-15)
5. Walked on the water (Matthew 14:22-33; Mark 6:45-52; John 6:16-24)

6. Fed the 4,000 with a few pieces of fish and bread (Matthew 15:29-39; Mark 8:1-10)
7. Told Peter to get a coin out of the mouth of a fish to pay the temple tax (Matthew 17:24-27)
8. Cursed the fig tree so that it withered – it did not have fruit when He was hungry (Matthew 21:18-22; Mark 11:12-14, 20-26)
9. Told disciples where to catch fish, after the resurrection (Second miracle of a catch of fish) (John 21:1-11)

People raised from the dead

A total of nine people were raised from the dead in the Bible. Here is the list:

Old Testament: Three raised by prophets
1. Elijah raised the son of the Zarephath widow (1 Kings 17:17-22)
2. Elisha raised the son of the Shunammite woman (2 Kings 4:30-37)
3. Elisha's bones raised up a dead man (2 Kings 13:21)

New Testament: Three raised by Jesus
1. Jesus raised Lazarus, close to Bethany and Ephraim, after 4 days (John 11:38-44)
2. Jesus raised the widow's son at Nain (Luke 7:11-17)
3. Jesus raised the daughter of Jairus at Capernaum (Matthew 8:28-43, Mark 5:1-20, Luke 8:26-39)

New Testament: In the name of Jesus
1. Jesus raised Himself; He was resurrected without the intervention of another. (Matthew 28:5-8, Mark 16:1-8, Luke 24:1-11, John 20:1-10)
2. Peter raised Dorcas (Acts 9:36-42)
3. Paul raised Eutychus who fell from the window (Acts 20:7-12)

All of these except Jesus experienced a second death. Jesus did not die and His spirit ascended in full view of His disciples, mother, brothers, other women, and two men in white. Further, Jesus needed no intermediary to raise Himself from the dead, as the Old Testament prophets or His followers did.

In the forthcoming book, **"How Jesus Died: The Truth"** this author will examine His death and resurrection in more detail, explaining why He could not have lived on earth more than the 40 days that He did.

According to Matthew 27:52, many came out of the tombs. We do not consider this to be a raising from the dead experience. It was their spirits, which had been trapped for years waiting for the Messiah, which were released and were now free to rise to the heavens and appear in the presence of our Lord Jesus Christ.

No religious leader or god incarnate has ever achieved the numbers of healings, natural miracles, and insightful teachings about eternal life – and in a span of three years! Jesus was truly the Son of God and the Messiah, who took our sins on the cross, redeemed us from sin, and paved the way for our eternal life.

Old Testament prophecies about Christ quoted in the gospels

Jesus knew well the prophecies foretelling the Messiah. The four gospels quote many Old Testament prophecies as Jesus is fulfilling them, but there are many more that are fulfilled, but not quoted as such.

The following is a list of prophecies that were fulfilled by Jesus, referenced in both the Old Testament and in the New Testament Gospels.

Jesus origins, birth, and early life:
1. Jesus descended from Abraham (Genesis 12:3; Matthew 1:1), Isaac (Genesis 17:19 Luke 3:34), and Jacob (Numbers 24:17; Matthew 1:2)
2. From the tribe of Judah (Genesis 49:10; Luke 3:33)
3. A descendant of Jesse. (Isaiah 11:10; Romans 15:12)
4. Of the family of David (2 Samuel 7:12–16; Psalms 89:3-4; 110:1; 132:11; Isaiah 9:6–7; 11:1; Matthew 22:44; Mark 12:36; Luke 1:69-70; 20:42-44; John 7:42)
5. Heir to the throne of David (Isaiah 9:7; Luke 1:32-33)

6. Born to a woman, under the law (Genesis 3:15, Galatians 4:4).
7. Elijah would announce His coming (Isaiah 40:3–5; Malachi 3:1; 4:5; Matthew 3:3; 11:10–14; Mark 1:2–3; Luke 3:4–6; 7:27; John 1:23)
8. Born of a virgin. (Matthew 1:23; Luke 1:26-27, 30-31; Isaiah 7:14)
9. Time of birth (Daniel 9:25; Luke 2:1-2)
10. Born in Bethlehem (Micah 5: 2; Matthew 2:6; Luke 2:4-5, 7; John 7:42)
11. Worshipped by shepherds (Psalms 72:9; Luke 2:8-15)
12. Honored by great kings (Psalms 72:10, 15; Isaiah 60:3; Matthew 2:1-11)
13. Murder of children of Bethlehem by Herod (Genesis 35:19-20; 48:7; Jeremiah 31:15; Matthew 2:16-18)
14. Travel and stayed in Egypt for a time (Hosea 11:1; Matthew 2 15)
15. Lived in Galilee (Isaiah 9:1-2; Matthew 4:15)
16. Lived in Nazareth (Isaiah 11:1; Matthew 2:23)

Ministry:
1. Priest after the order of Melchizedek (Psalms 110:4; Hebrews 5:5-6)
2. The good shepherd to His people (Ezekiel 37:24; Matthew 2:6)
3. Proclaim a jubilee to the world (Isaiah 58:6; 61:1; Luke 4:18-19)
4. Ministry of healing (Isaiah 53:4; Matthew 8:17).
5. Teach by means of parables (Isaiah 6:9-10; Psalm 78:2; Matthew 13:14-15, 35)
6. Gives rest to our souls (Isaiah 61:1-2; 63:14; Jeremiah 6:16; Matthew 11:29-30; Luke 4:18-19)
7. Adored by children (Psalms 8:2; Matthew 21:15-16)
8. Triumphal entry into Jerusalem (Isaiah 62:11; Zechariah 9:9; Psalm 118:26; Matthew 21:5; Mark 11:7, 9, 11; John 12:13-15)
9. Authority in the Temple (Malachi 3:1; Matthew 21:12)

10. Gentiles will seek Him as the Messiah and minister to Gentiles (Isaiah 9:2; 11:10; 65:1; Matthew 4:16, Romans 11:25)

Journey to the Cross:
1. Disbelieved and rejected by the rulers (Psalms 69:4; 118:22; Isaiah 6:10; 8:14; 29:13; 53:1-3; Matthew 15:8-9; 21:42; Mark 7:6-7; 12:10-11; Luke 20:17; John 12:38-40; 15:25)
2. Rejected by the Jews (Isaiah 8:14; 28:16; 53:3; Luke 23:18; Acts 4:11; 1 Peter 2:6-8)
3. Not believed (Isaiah 53:1; John 12:37-38)
4. Like a shepherd who is struck down (Zechariah 13:7; Matthew 26:31; Mark 14: 27)
5. Betrayed by a friend for 30 pieces of silver (Zechariah 11:12-13; Psalm 41:9; 55:12-13; Deut 27:25; Matthew 27:9-10; Matthew 26:14-15; John 13:18; Luke 22:47-48)
6. Betrayal money used to buy the potter's field (Zechariah 11:13; Matthew 27:6-7)
7. Silent to accusations (Isaiah 53:7; Mark 15:4-5)
8. Sneered at and mocked (Psalms 22:7-8; Luke 23:35)
9. People shook their heads at Jesus (Psalms 109:25; Matthew 27:39)
10. Insulted (Psalms 69:9; Romans 15:3).
11. Accused by false witnesses (Psalms 35:11; Mark 14:57-58)
12. Spit on and struck (Isaiah 50:6 Matthew 26:67; 27:30)
13. Scourged (Isaiah 53:5 Matthew 27:26)
14. Hated without reason (Psalms 35:19; John 15:24-25)
15. Sacrificed for others (Isaiah 53:5; Romans 5:6, 8; Matt 26:61)
16. Cast lots for clothing (Psalm 22:17-18; Matthew 27:35-36; John 19: 24)
17. Pierced (Zechariah 12:10; Psalms 22:16; John 20:25-27)
18. Jesus would be given vinegar and gall (Psalm 69:21; Matthew 27: 34; John 19:29)
19. Pray for enemies (Psalms 109:4; Isaiah 53:12; Luke 23:34)
20. Dying words foretold (Psalms 22:1; 31:5; Matthew 27:46; Mark 15:34; Luke 23:46)

21. Not one of His bones would be broken (Exodus 12: 46; Numbers 9:12; Psalm 34:20; John 19:36)
22. Crucified with sinners (Isaiah 53:12; Mark 15:27-28)
23. Die with criminals (Isaiah 53: 9, 12; Luke 22: 32)
24. His side would be pierced (Zechariah 12:10; Psalms 22:16; John 19:37)
25. Commits His spirit to God (Psalms 31:5; Luke 23:46)
26. Buried in a rich man's tomb (Isaiah 53: 9 Matthew 27: 57-60)

Resurrection, ascension, and sending the Holy Spirit:
1. Rise from the dead on the third day (Psalm 16:10-11; Hosea 6:2; Matthew 12:40; Luke 24:46)
2. Ascended to God's right hand (Psalm 110:1; Matthew 23:44-46; Mark 12:36; Luke 20:42; Acts 2:34-36; Heb 1:13; Corinthians 15:4, Ephesians 4:8)
3. Jesus sent the Holy Spirit (Isaiah 44:3; Joel 2:28; John 20:22; Acts 2:16-17)
4. New covenant (Isaiah 55:3-4; Jeremiah 31:31; Luke 22:20; Hebrews 8:6-10)
5. Anointed and eternal. (Psalms 45:6-7; 102:25-27; Hebrews 1:8-12)
6. Prophet (Deuteronomy 18:15; Acts 3:20, 22)

Index

343

344

Explanation of Table of the Chronology of Jesus' Family

Jesus had four brothers, all of whom are named in the gospels. He had at least two sisters, but the exact number of sisters and their names are not given. The table on the inside back cover lists the approximate ages of the family at the most important events, from the birth of Jesus to His death. This table is based on several assumptions, given below.

The assumptions made are based on the natural contraceptive properties of breast-feeding, which would give the children a natural spacing of 1 ½ years to 2 years apart. Their births and ages are approximate; for convenience, we have used a 2-year cycle.

Other factors include the stress of travel and relocation to Egypt, so that Mary did not get pregnant while she was in Egypt with Joseph and Jesus. The high infant mortality rate at that time called for families to have as many children as possible, so as soon as they were settled in Nazareth, Mary became pregnant and resumed the normal life of a mother, giving birth to at least six children.

Mary had four other sons, named James, Joses, Judas, and Simon. She had at least two daughters, and the author has named them Hannah and Abigail. The children of Mary are mentioned in the following passages: Matt. 12:46; 13:55; Mark 6:3; John 2:12; 7:3, 5, 10; Acts 1:14; 1 Cor. 9:5; Gal 1:19.

One of the more controversial teachings of the Catholic Church deals with the perpetual virginity of Mary. This doctrine maintains that Mary remained a virgin after the birth of Jesus and that biblical references suggesting Jesus had siblings are really references to cousins (Catechism of the Catholic Church, paragraph 510). The Catholic doctrine of the eternal virginity of Mary is not supported by scripture as referenced above.

350